Women and the Law

Women
and the Law

Susan Atkins and Brenda Hoggett

BASIL BLACKWELL

First published in 1984 by Basil Blackwell Ltd,
108 Cowley Road, Oxford OX4 1JF.

Basil Blackwell Inc.
432 Park Avenue South,
Suite 1505
New York, NY10016, USA

British Library Cataloguing in Publication Data

Atkins, Susan
   1. Women—Legal status, laws, etc.—
England
   I. Title   II. Hoggett, Brenda M.
   344.202'878   KD4058.W6

   ISBN 0-85520-181-9
   ISBN 0-85520-180-0 Pbk

Also included in the Library of
Congress Cataloging in Publication lists.

Typeset by System 4 Associates, Gerrards Cross, Buckinghamshire
Printed and bound in Great Britain
by Billing & Sons Limited, Worcester.

Contents

Preface

In this book we set out to examine the law's treatment of women, not from the point of view of the law itself, but from that of the women whose lives it governs. Our traditional legal education has been, in many ways, a hindrance to our understanding of the issues. We owe a great deal to the re-education provided by our students on women's studies courses and by our colleagues in the women law teachers' groups. Special thanks are due to Diana Kloss, who helped to set the project up, and to Andrew Ashworth, Irene Cox, Linda Luckhouse and Judith Mayhew, for comments, suggestions and practical help. They are not, of course, to be blamed for any errors or omissions, or for the views expressed, which are entirely our own.

Alison Lampard has been an enormous help in typing parts of the manuscript and enabling us to meet the deadline. Elizabeth Bland has done wonders in turning our unwieldy typescript into a finished text for publication. Blackwells have shown extraordinary patience in waiting for the text and extraordinary efficiency in completing their own part of the process. We are most grateful to them all.

Best thanks of all go to Steve Atkins and John Hoggett for their constant encouragement, co-operation and advice.

The text was completed before one of us became a Law Commissioner. It goes without saying that the views expressed here are not those of the Law Commission. Nor will our views necessarily remain unchanged should the Law Commission come to consider, or reconsider, reform of the law on any of the topics we discuss. But our analysis is not deprived of its validity by the recognition of the practical politics of law reform. There is room for both, and if the one contributes to the other, so much the better.

Susan Atkins
Brenda Hoggett
July 1984

Introduction

This is not a legal textbook. There are already many admirable accounts of the legal rules governing most of the subject matter with which we deal. These accounts have obvious limitations. In order to give a complete and accurate statement of the law, it is necessary to adopt the same habits of thought, the same definition of the issues and the same approach to solving them as were adopted by those who produced the rules in the first place or by those who can be expected to apply them. Our purpose is quite different. We seek to understand how the law has perceived women and responded to their lives. Our object is not to give a biased account of the law but to uncover the extent to which the law itself is biased towards a particular view of life. Even today that view can readily be recognized as one reflected in male rather than female eyes.

We do not suggest that this is the result of any conscious male conspiracy — far from it. Any conspiracy theory would have to confront the problem posed by the real and important advances made in the legal status of women over the past 150 years, though men still predominate at the centres of power and influence. If there has been a conspiracy, it has been singularly ineffective in recent times. In any event, a conspiracy requires the recognition of common objectives and agreement upon the means to be used to achieve them. The history of the legal status of women tends in the opposite direction. Once a source of inferiority has been identified and analysed, there has been considerable pressure for change. Often that pressure has been resisted for long periods. Often change has come about because of other pressures which have had little to do with improving the the status of women as such. But still it has come about. Retrograde steps — and there have certainly been many of these — have tended, rather, to be associated with the disappearance of women's issues from the agenda.

Nor is this a work of history or sociology. We do not seek to explain the social situation of women today or how it came about, but we shall be making extensive use of the work of scholars in those disciplines who have described and analysed it. If we may state the obvious for a moment, the experience of being a woman is not the same as the experience of being a man. It is necessary to make this simple point time and again because of the tendency of law and law-makers to ignore it. Assumptions and judgments which spring from the experience of being a man will look very different when viewed from that of being a woman.

Of course, a crucial task of feminists in the fields of history, sociology and psychology has been to expose the extent to which the differences in that experience are socially constructed rather than biologically determined. We do not have to believe that the existing gender order is inevitable in order to recognize that it exists. The law can obviously be part of that process of social construction. We shall meet many examples of this in the accounts which follow. The law has done as much as any other social institution to define and promote the separate spheres of activity appropriate to men and women. Equally, however, the law can be part of the process of breaking that construction down. It can liberate women from their separate sphere. It can abandon all the rules which presuppose that one sex will enter one sphere and the other will enter another. It can even seek to break down the divisions which exist between the separate spheres themselves. Sometimes the law lags well behind changes in the actual experience of the women and men involved; sometimes it assumes changes which have not yet taken place; and sometimes it does both at once. We would be the last to suggest that the law is consistent in its approach to women.

For that reason, among others, we have our doubts about how far the law itself can be said to constrain women's behaviour. It is certainly plausible to suggest that it does so at the level of ideology. Hilary Land, for example, has argued that social policies (which cannot be separated from legal policies) play an important part in maintaining an ideology of the family and of the particular roles which men and women are expected to play within it: 'social policies are a very important means by which these values, and hence the major inequalities between the sexes, are maintained.'[1] Clare Ungerson, however, has suggested that 'this conclusion has the status of a hypothesis; the range of response to consistent state intervention, increasingly contradictory and contorted as it is, lies between submission on the one hand and rebellion on the other.'[2] We do not have the empirical data upon which to found a conclusion.

It is certainly not necessary for us to reach one. As we consider the impact of the law on key aspects of women's lives, we shall find several themes which crop up time and again. One is a change in the type of mechanism which may be used as a means of control. At first criminal or quasi-criminal sanctions may attempt to ensure that they conform to the way of life expected of them. Later on these may be replaced with administrative structures which, though less overtly coercive, may apparently attempt to produce the same result. In dealing with prostitution, for example, the law has swung from one to the other and back again and looks now to be reverting to administrative controls once more. But it is unlikely that this has had any effect in determining whether or not women become prostitutes.

A second theme will be the persisting view that women are less responsible than men. This is not simply the view that, if given the right to exercise responsibility by the law, women will choose not to exercise it but that they will actually welcome laws which deprive them of the right to choose. This justification was particularly popular at the nadir of female rights and can be found earlier in the work of Blackstone, who considered that the married woman was 'so great a favourite' of the English law because the disabilities which it imposed upon her were for her own protection and benefit.[3] A later editor of Blackstone's *Commentaries* was highly critical of this view, but this was because he thought that the law gave the married woman too little protection rather than too much, in particular for her sexual reputation, which was then her greatest asset.[4] There is, however, little reason to believe that most of the laws designed to protect women from the harsh realities of life had any such effect. It is just as likely that excluding her from the market place where she wished to be, for example, or refusing to interfere between husband and wife, were themselves among those harsh realities which she had to face, live with or circumvent. Yet we still find the idea that women are less responsible than men in several areas of law. For example, they are not permitted to know better than others whether they should seek the law's redress against an aggressor within the home. They have last gained parity with men in the upbringing of their marital children, yet at the same time the autonomy of parents has been deprived of most of its meaning, and the state (through government and judiciary) has taken over from the family as arbiter of what is best for a child. Women have also gained the right to complain of some of the more glaring inequalities they face in the market place, but ways have been found of deflecting many of those grievances elsewhere. There is a persuasive case that the rights which the modern law has extended to women are not rights at all.

A third theme will be a time scale in the law's objectives, which is common to a surprising number of disparate areas of law. We have identified three phases in the formulation and promulgation of law in this country. There was a traditional phase, which lasted more or less intact until around 1830, during which the gender order was simply not a problem. However individual men and woman may have ordered their lives, the inferior legal status of women was clear. They were largely, although not entirely, excluded from public life and from the benefits and responsibilities of citizenship. Those who wished or had to work outside the home were excluded from most of the professions and segregated into employments in which they could be accorded inferior treatment. Those who worked inside the home would usually be working for the benefit of its male owner.

This is not to suggest that the legal status of women had remained identical over the centuries, still less that it ever achieved the degradation associated with classic peasant societies elsewhere in the world. Indeed, a large part of Macfarlane's argument that England was never a classic peasant society is founded upon the legal status of single women.[5] In civil laws they enjoyed the same status as men, although their rights of inheritance might not be identical. They could certainly own property and carry on a business and might even enjoy the public law rights associated with these, at least for a while. Not only did single women enjoy relatively high status, but also it seems from the evidence about rates and age of marriage that there were quite large numbers of them. English society may never have treated its women quite as badly as did others.

That did not stop it from also perceiving those surplus women as a problem in themselves, particularly when they had neither property nor business to support them. We find a transitional phase which lasted from around 1830 until the 1960s and 1970s, during which there was tension between two conflicting pressures. On the one hand lay the individualism which was already embedded in the thought of English men and an increasing number of those surplus single women (and even some of those who got married). On the other hand lay the social and economic pressures which produced the modern phenomenon of housewife marriage and the concept that the separate spheres of men and women were the inevitable, natural and functional consequences of industrial capitalism. The result was the progressive removal of women's disabilities in both private and public law: married women were given much the same rights as single, and both were given many of the same rights as men. But behind this thin veneer of formal equality lay the structural inequality produced by the relegation of most married women to their separate sphere. The independent status of married women could be subordinated to the prior demands of their families — those not only of their children but also of their husbands or disabled or elderly relatives. The independent status of single women could also be subordinated to the expectation that they would eventually marry.

Since 1970 we have seen radical changes in the laws affecting the separate spheres of men and women. In this modern period family laws have ceased to discriminate on grounds of sex, so that they are theoretically capable of reflecting role reversal, role sharing and other diverse forms of intimate relationship. Employment laws have sought to prevent discrimination on grounds of sex, marital status or pregnancy. Even welfare laws and taxation are coming to abandon their presumption that men and single women occupy one sphere, while married and cohabiting women occupy the other. But the process is far from complete. Nor do we find that the values underlying modern legislation are inevitably translated into action by the courts and other agencies.

Even now, however, we find that the removal of discrimination is always perceived in male terms. Every social development in the lives of women has tended to force into the open the deficiencies of the law in responding to that development. But the deficiencies have almost always been those perceived by men from the point of view of a male-ordered world. Women's problems have become defined as problems because men have realized that if the law treated them in the same way as it treats women, men would consider it unjust. Thus laws which seek to force women and men into separate spheres are now increasingly thought to be wrong, as are laws which put the stability of the home and family above the ordinary legal rights of the people within it. But there has been little enthusiasm for laws which seek to adjust the relationship between the separate spheres, to redefine what each entails. If anything, the attempt to redress the balance between breadwinner and homemaker has been under attack in recent years. Sometimes the attack has been launched in the name of feminism itself. Yet this is only another exercise in seeking to make the experience of women conform to that of men. We need a deeper understanding of the inadequacies of such methods of analysis before we can go forward.

We intend not to precribe the way forward but to contribute as best we can to the process called for by Deem:

> A non-sexist education is part of a much more complex struggle for the liberation of women; but it is a part of that struggle which must have a high priority, for action without knowledge is no better than knowledge without action. And women must not only educate and persuade other women to fight for changes, whether these are legislative, organizational or attitudinal, they must also educate and persuade men that changes are necessary, not just in education but in the whole organization of society. The arguments in favour of a non-sexist system of education are a good point at which to commence this persuasion; there is no other way in which the full creative and flexible potential of human beings, so essential to the liberation of *people*, will begin to be realized.[6]

Only when women are aware of the extent of the discrimination against them, of how it operates and of how to use the law and to influence law reform to their own ends will further progress be made.

Women in Society

1

The Historical Legacy

It is often assumed that men have always been the breadwinners and that women have been occupied almost exclusively in unpaid domestic duties at home. Indeed, such a division of labour is commonly held to be 'natural', to be justified by reference to biology. Such views are not limited to popular conception. As Scott and Tilley point out of academic writers, 'most general works on women and the family assume that the history of women's employment, like the history of women's legal and political rights, can be understood as a gradual evolution from a traditional place at home to a modern position in the world of work.'[1]

However, close scrutiny of history shows such perceptions of women to be false. First, both single and married women have always been engaged in paid work, although their numbers and the types of work have varied. Second, the present patterns and hallmarks of female employment have not always existed. Many have developed only recently. For many years, however, the law in relation to women has been distinguished by the perception of them as potential mothers. It is this biological difference between the sexes that has governed women's opportunities for education and paid employment and continues to tax the minds of legislators and judiciary today.

Legal Regulation in the Early Years

The early Anglo-Saxon legal codes, recorded since the reign of Aethelbert (AD 570—616), give an indication of how women were perceived in pre-feudal England. Anglo-Saxon society was essentially tribal, the legal system based on kinship and family groupings. Women were as essential to the family group as were the men, not simply because their procreative function ensured the continuation of that social group but also because they contributed to production. An Estate Book written in about 1000, entitled 'The Rights and Duties of All Persons', laid down the wage rates for country women, which varied not only by status, whether free or unfree, but also according to specialized skills.[2] However, women's economic value was not limited to their productive value. Anglo-Saxon laws also laid down precise but distinct economic values of child-bearing and child-rearing; separation and widowhood settlements were similar to those reintroduced only in the twentieth century. There seems to have been no presumption that a wife always took care of the children. If on separation she did, she had a larger settlement than if they had stayed with the father. These records show that women, even in marriage, were accorded an independent status and were not dependent solely upon the male members of their families. There appear to have been no legal restrictions on job opportunities for women and no societal notions of the inferiority of women generally.[3]

The change from tribal law to state law under feudalism was a gradual process, but by the thirteenth century feudalism was firmly established, with its hierarchy of land holding and personal loyalties based on military service. With the break-up of the family as the basic social, economic and political unit of society, women's position changed dramatically. Because men's power stemmed from land-holding and inheritance, women were important only for the provision of legitimate heirs. Even single women, who retained some legal rights, were important only as prospective wives and mothers. The writings of lawyers of the time note the complete subjugation of married women (Gratian, 1139—42) and thus the inferiority of women generally (Bracton, *c.*1300).[4] At the same time as women's procreative work was relegated to a secondary and subservient position, most of the productive work undertaken by women was downgraded. But the causal connection between family status and employment status was neither simple nor universal.

In the fourteenth century shortage of labour put the whole feudal system under threat. The Black Death of 1348, which, it is estimated, wiped out half the total population, exacerbated an already acute labour shortage and considerably increased wage rates for those free labourers who were able to demand them. National legislation was passed to negate the threats to cheap labour on which the feudal system depended. The Statutes of Labourers 1349, 1351 and 1360 pegged the agricultural wage rates, rendered void any covenants of craft apprenticeships in relation to boys and girls who were previously agricultural workers, and enforced the bondage of anyone who was found to be without means of support. The Statute of Labourers 1388, which set national agricultural wages, established a woman's rate regardless of occupation or degree of skill. The male rates, all higher, varied with skill. Although limited to agricultural work, this Act established the principle which affected all female wages thereafter.[5] Thus it seems that women's inferior personal status under feudal law was not directly responsible for their low wages, but it rendered them susceptible to the harshest treatment in a national attempt to control wages.

At times of economic depression, when the consequent reduction in wage rates and availability of work reduced female employment, single women suffered most. Agricultural wages were set irrespective of marital status. Single men and women lived on the farms where they worked. Married men were expected to augment their incomes with their wives' earnings from either home industry or work on the family smallholding. Although their work contracted at times of depression, married women were able to supplement the family income in a way that would not have provided subsistence for a single woman.

As with patterns for the availability of work, there appear to have been distinct trends in the ways in which the law dealt with the problem of indigent single women. One way was to force them into domestic service; the other way was to compel them to marry. The methods by which the law sought to dispose of surplus labour in these ways varied with the centuries. In the fifteenth century (as later) women without work or women in manufacturing work on extremely low wages turned to prostitution. In an order of 1492 the City of London attempted to solve the problem in a way which became a precedent for law-makers in the following centuries: 'no single women, being of good health and mighty body able to labour from the age of 12 years [may] take nor keep from henceforth house of chambers by themselves. . . but [must] go to service till they be married.' Administrators of the Poor Laws in the seventeenth and eighteenth centuries dealt with single women in the same way. In some areas this policy was pursued to such an extent that employers would take servants only from the parish, thus reducing women's job opportunities and their rates of pay even further.[6]

For some, children provided the only means of escape. Pinchbeck quotes evidence put to the Poor Law Commissioners in 1832 that under the Poor Law 'pre-marital pregnancy was the single woman's only means of escape from the inadequate dole supplied by the parish. Following this, the parish either provided her with a husband or gave her an increased allowance for her child. In either case she was better off financially.'[7] For although no allowances were made directly to married women either, the unemployment benefit received by married men covered the subsistence of the whole family. Additionally, in districts which operated the so-called 'Speenhamland' system married men in employment had their wages made up to subsistence level on a family needs basis, an early type of family income supplement.

Where marriage gave some women a means of support, it gave many women an opportunity to practise their crafts. In the early years there appear to have been no restrictions on the entry of women to craft occupations. As Lewenhak points out: 'There is scarcely a gild-occupation in the later Middle Ages whose regulations do not make clear that somewhere women as well as men were members of the craft or mistery.'[8] It is unclear exactly when or how lower wages for women were established — whether women themselves were prepared to work for less or had lower wages imposed on them by outside forces. The wages of skilled non-agricultural workers were set locally, either by the market or by the Justice of the Peace. What is clear, however, is that the greater segregation of women in semi-skilled, lower-status jobs within the craft industries from the sixteenth century onwards was a direct result of women's undercutting their male competitors. In many guilds only the wives and daughters of guild members were allowed to practise the craft. Other women were relegated to subsidiary tasks at the lowest wage rates.[9]

The restriction of job opportunities in this way bestowed some benefits on those women who were fortunate enough to be born into, or to marry into, such families. When merchant capital succeeded land as the means of support for an increasing middle class, trade took the place of the dower. Indeed, the majority of business-women in trade on their own account were widows. Some guilds, such as the Stationers' Guild, allowed widows to retain membership on remarriage, which certainly enhanced their marriage prospects. Others allowed widows to continue to trade only on remarriage to members of the same guild.

The practice of widows taking over the man's job was not exclusive to craft work. The concept of the family work unit, within or outside the home, was still operative at the beginning of the nineteenth century in a variety of occupations — mining, for example. In many ways it represented the transference of the old work unit under the feudal agricultural system to a non-agricultural system based on wage labour. But the fact that many women never saw their wages, and could not put an exact figure to their contribution to the family income, had its effect on the wage rate of women when they began to work independently of the family unit in the nineteenth century. It also undoubtedly contributed to the distinction between women's work outside the home, which attracted an economic value, and work inside the home which did not.

Legal Regulation in the Transitional Phase

All the hallmarks of female employment established in the traditional period continued into the nineteenth century and beyond. What increased significantly from the 1840s was legal intervention in women's employment. At the beginning of the nineteenth century local government was restructured and modernized, primarily in response to the social problems caused by an escalation in urbaniza-tion. With more local government intervention in industry for public health reasons, the wages and working conditions of employees ceased to be a private matter or the province of lax local administration. The conditions of women workers came to be perceived as a subject of public importance and legal concern at a time when the greater democratization of Parliament enabled a philanthropic middle class to gain readier access to parliamentary committees and Commissions of Inquiry. The Mines and Collieries Act 1842, which excluded all women and children from underground mining, and the Factory Act 1844, which for the first time regulated the hours of women's work in factories, mark the beginning of the transitional period. These Acts are important not simply because they indicate the change to governmental intervention in adult employment but also, more particularly, because they were based on the notions of womanhood which permeated all law in this period. As the Report of the Commisioners on Mines and the parliamentary debates on both the Mines and Factory Acts show, it was not the gruelling hard work which outraged Victorian society but the immorality of women engaged in such work. In the case of young women horror was expressed at the close proximity of men and women in both mines and factories, the perceived consequent high rate of illegitimacy and the near nakedness of both men and women workers. Perhaps even more concern was expressed at the greater immorality of married women who, it was alleged, left their homes and families, neglected their domestic duties and forced their menfolk to seek the comforts of public houses, thus subjecting the next generation to 'all the evils of a disorderly and ill-regulated family'.[11]

As in the family law of this period, so in employment law women were given prime responsibility for the welfare of all family members. Because of their procreative function, women were deemed weaker and in need of protection. Yet protection was only very slowly extended to traditionally female areas of work and those where women predominated. It seems as though the 'family type' conditions which existed — for instance, for domestic servants and living-in shop workers — were felt to be protection enough. Yet women in these occupations appear to have been more at risk from sexual harassment and subsequent loss of livelihood. The law's reluctance to extend the Truck Acts, which prohibited payment in kind and financial penalties, meant that many suffered extremely harsh working conditions. In both shop work and domestic service the amount of wage received in cash was very small, the rest being credited as board and lodging. There is evidence not only of exorbitant charges for these in shops but also a well established system of fines for misconduct.[12] Action to improve the situation of women through the courts failed. (In *Lane* v. *Bull* [1900] (unreported) the court held that in a claim for wages in lieu of notice a shop worker, like a domestic servant, was entitled only to the wages contracted for, not an amount of money equivalent to board and lodging which would have been provided.)

Rather than work through the legislation chronologically or occupation by occupation, this section will trace the development of the law as the protective interventionist policy on which it was based met the immense social, cultural and technological changes of the 130 years to 1970.

Women's 'Natural' Inferiority

Considering the widespread and, it would seem, customary practice of women undertaking heavy work in areas and times of shortages of male labour, it is perhaps not surprising that the 'natural' physical weakness of women was not used to justify the laws which controlled women workers. The physical inferiority of women seems to have been put forward by male workers at a local level, but only when they wished to exclude women from certain processes or from the use of particular machinery for which they wished to preserve higher wage rates. Even in such circumstances the definition of unsuitability focused more often than not on the notions of morality and femininity already mentioned. The factory legislation legalized this demarcation to a certain extent. Women were excluded from underground mining, from working on moving railway waggons, from brass casting and some white lead processes. They were restricted in maintaining and working between moving machinery. But the main thrust of concern for women related to the hours of their employment, reducing their working week and prohibiting night work. This legal intervention appears not to have affected work opportunities.[13] Restriction on hours simply lowered women's pay rates and

introduced the higher rates for men on which many equal pay cases later had
to be fought. The more powerful effect of the law was related to its definition
of women workers as different, with greater sensibilities. Men, through their
organized labour, simply took advantage of these sentiments to counter the threat
of undercutting by segregating work on the criterion of physical strength.

In professional life men proved as unwilling as their working-class brothers
to let women in their midst. Even in occupations such as medicine, which had
formerly been practised by women, male domination was jealously guarded. The
justification for excluding women was not their physical weakness, which would
have been inappropriate to these middle-class jobs, but the new sciences through
which men had wrested control in the first place. What is most interesting is
that in the cases brought by middle-class women attempting to breach the male
monopoly barriers the judges demonstrate the shift in public opinion from concern
for women's moral sensibility to acceptance of their scientifically established
intellectual weakness that took place in the late nineteenth century.[14] Such
biological determinism persisted through the discovery of the new sciences of
psychology and sociology. As Myrdal and Klein pointed out in 1956, middle-
class women pioneers in all employment fields faced a continual scientific battle
to disprove theories of comparative differences.[15]

The educational achievements of girls today have dispelled all doubts about
their intellectual abilities. In terms of examination passes and school-leaving
qualifications, girls do at least as well as boys at every stage and at every level,
with the exception of those girls who gain two or more A-levels in grammar schools
and independent schools. The statistics suggest that at these schools a higher
percentage of girls get five or more O-levels than is the case for boys but fewer
go on to take A-levels or, if they do, more girls limit themselves to just one.[16]
The problem is not that the examination system is failing girls but that the schools
are not directing or advising girls in the same way as boys who achieve similar
examination success.[17]

The reason is not hard to find. Since 1833, when central government took
control of the education of the working class (giving financial aid to voluntary
schools and regulating the curriculum), the emphasis until recent years has been
on fitting girls for domesticity. The Education Act of 1870, which set up School
Boards and instituted a proper national system of education, extended this control
and provided extra money for examination successes. Deem reports that by 1876
domestic economy had become one of the subjects that earned grants for schools.[18]
Cookery was added in 1882 and laundry in 1890. In 1902 these subjects became
compulsory, not only in state elementary schools but also in those secondary
schools that benefited from grants from the Board of Education. Thus domestic
skills were also foisted upon the private sector, and particularly upon
establishments set up by the early feminists with the aim of giving girls exactly
the same academic education as that enjoyed by boys.

The origins of these single-sex secondary schools influenced the destination
of their pupils in the labour market. They enabled women to enter the formerly

all-male professions, particularly after the Sex Disqualification (Removal) Act of 1919. But many more girls used their education to enter the new medical and paramedical professions, the Civil Service, local government and other white-collar work that was developing in the early years of the twentieth century. In 1923 the Hadow Report, *Differentiation of the Curricula between the Sexes in Secondary Schools*, stated that all children needed to be educated to earn their own living and to become useful citizens. Girls need not be taught with boys, however, nor need they be taught the same things or at the same pace, although their education should be along similar lines: 'girls have also to be prepared to be makers of homes...we consider that some definite preparation should be given during school time. This is particularly necessary at the present day, because the requisite training tends to be given less and less in the home.'[19] Such sentiments were repeated in subsequent government reports into the 1960s.[20]

The Newsom Report, when discussing girls of average and below-average ability, remarked that since marriage was the 'most important vocational concern' for many if not all girls, schooling should be provided that related to the 'wider aspects of home-making and family life and the care and upbringing of children'.[21] The Crowther Report dealt with the education of 16- to 18-year-olds, and thus with academically more able pupils, yet it too stressed the need for a 'curriculum which respects the different roles they play'.[22] In 1963 the Robbins Report on higher education noted that girls made up only a quarter of university students but two-thirds of those at teacher-training colleges, despite school-leaving qualifications that were comparable with those of boys. The report also noted the concentration of girls in a few professions and their absence from many others.

This was attributed to a lack of scientific qualifications among girls, but some courses at university level (notably medicine) were rationed by quota until the 1975 Sex Discrimination Act. The predominance of women in the second-tier professions is not due to any natural cause but is the result of a long-established education policy. In England, as elsewhere, marriage and particularly motherhood have been used to control the female workforce and to ensure the quality of future labour forces.

Maternity

The dangers to young babies of mothers working outside the home were first mentioned by Fielden in his introduction in the House of Commons of the Factory Bill 1847.[23] Having been raised in relation to female operatives in textile towns, the statistical and philanthropic societies that flourished there ensured that infant mortality became a grave public concern. However, even though the connection between women's work and infant mortality was officially accepted by 1851,[24] legislative action was resisted until 1891. There were attempts to make registration of all child-minders compulsory in the Infant Life Protection Bill 1871 and to restrict work for a period around confinement in the Factory Amendment Bill 1873. Despite evidence of similar laws abroad, both proposals were rejected on the grounds that they violated the liberty of the individual. Even when the Factory and Workshops Act 1891 made it an offence for employers knowingly to employ a woman within four weeks of confinement, feminists raised three main objections: that it was for a woman to decide if she was ready to return to work; that male trade unionists would use the Act to exclude women; and that women could simply not afford to lose wages for that length of time.[25] Campaigners who sought to protect babies by excluding their mothers from work had paid little attention to the fact that many women were forced to work by financial necessity. The Chief Lady Factory Inspectoress, in her annual report of 1906, commented on the extent of deliberate evasion of the law caused by financial hardship and called for insurance to cover the maternity period.[26] This was finally introduced in the National Insurance Act 1911.

From a concern for women workers who were mothers developed a particular way of looking at all women workers as potential mothers that was to influence the law in the following years.[27] As with notions of intellectual inferiority, the notion that woman's natural and primary role was her maternal one was widely and genuinely held, even by some of those women who were campaigning on behalf of women workers. The 1918 Report of the Women's Employment Committee of the Ministry of Reconstruction made very strong proposals for the extension of Trade Boards to establish minimum wages and the reduction of hours in factories and shops, most of which were eventually translated into legislation in the 1920s and 1930s. Nevertheless, it recommended that every inducement be given to return married women to their homes:

> as a general principle we would suggest that the only differentiation between men and women which can be justified is such as has its basis in the need of preserving women's powers unimpeded for those primary activities which are connected with the family and the home. The fact that a large proportion of adult women now possess full rights of citizenship will enable them to express themselves directly on the subject of such differentiation and to help in embodying in reformed factory legislation the results of their personal experience.[28]

The committee consisted of twelve men and twelve women, including women trade unionists, and its sentiments were later echoed by two women in the 1944 Markham Report, which noted the need for domestic servants in order to release educated housewives to participate fully in civic affairs.[29]

It is understandable that Governments should be concerned with renewing the population after periods of war. That the women who had proved their capabilities and value as workers doing essential 'men's jobs' should be rewarded as citizens, not as workers, is perhaps more surprising (but see pp. 20, 187). The way in which the law developed in relation to women workers during this period is, however, explained by the influence of these two ideas. The Sex Disqualification (Removal) Act 1919, provided that no one should be disqualified by sex or marriage from holding any public office, from entering any profession or from graduating from universities. Yet despite its broad wording the courts held that the introduction of a marriage bar did not contravene the Act's provisions; nor had any individual who was refused a job any right of litigation under it. The Act merely required the professions to lift their restrictions against women. A particular employer was still at liberty to restrict a particular job to one sex or to unmarried workers. In *Price* v. *Rhondda Urban Council* [1923] 2 Ch. 372, Mr Justive Eve rejected the argument that a marriage bar was in restraint of marriage and therefore contrary to public policy: 'It would in any opinion be pressing public policy to intolerable lengths to hold that it was outraged by this Authority expressing a preference for unmarried women over married women.'

The marriage bar operated in most public service jobs until the Second World War. It was lifted only where the demand for qualified staff exceeded supply, as in the London County Council in 1935, when it was lifted for teachers and medical staff only.[30] In some industries marriage bars were introduced as a response to the recession. (Far from protecting mothers and their babies, such action in the textile industry led to women lying about their marital status, concealing their pregnancies and returning to work immediately after confinement. In these areas of high unemployment infant and maternal mortality reached double the national average.)[31]

In the occupations where such marriage bars existed single professional women resented and feared the special treatment given to married women workers.

> They did not want to raise additional obstacles to their employment, nor their claims for equal pay, when many women as well as men, including the intellectual Beatrice Webb, believed women generally were less inherently competent than men. They still saw in these proposals . . . a threat by men trade unionists to put them out of jobs, by piling up extra complications and regulations for the employment of women, burdensome to employers. They felt that proof of equality as workers lay in emphasizing similarity in the performance of jobs and to do this, all biological differences had to be ignored.[32]

So influential was this view that the International Labour Organization reversed the stance it had taken at the 1918 Washington Convention on the restriction of shiftwork for women. The 1933 Montevideo Convention agreed that restrictions on shift work were a reason for continued sex discrimination (a point which still causes disagreement within the feminist movement).[33] The law's attitude towards married women workers, and particularly the monetary and practical assistance that were introduced, isolated the unmarried educated women who were most likely to have campaigned for equal rights for women workers generally. Single women did not seem to appreciate that a justification for their unequal treatment was the assumption that all women would get married and leave work. Rather, they concentrated on two matters: the professionalization of women's work, with legislation to raise the standards of nurses and midwives and campaigns for the professionalization of domestic servants; and equal pay. When married women were brought back into the workforce by law in 1941 (see below), their subsidiary position was firmly entrenched. An understanding of the structure of the modern law introduced in 1975 is therefore helped by an investigation of these two distinct phenomena; the accommodation of married women workers and the campaign for equal pay.

Married Women Workers

While the proportion of women to men in the paid workforce has not changed very dramatically over the last hundred years, there has been a drastic change in the percentage of married women workers. The first Census of 1861 showed that the 3 million women then in paid employment formed 34.1 per cent of the workforce. The corresponding figures for 1981 were nearly 10 million women, constituting 40 per cent of the workforce. Census figures in the twentieth century show that until the Second World War the proportion of *married* women who worked remained fairly constant at around 10 per cent, with regional variations.

There seem to be three major reasons why this was so. The first is that the changes in society which dramatically increased work opportunities for women created mainly white-collar jobs where a marriage bar operated. The Civil Service was revolutionized during this period, the Ministries of War, of Pensions, of Labour, of Food and of Shipping and the Air Board being established during the First World War, Ministries such as that of Transport soon after. Women workers in the Civil Service and local authorities increased between 1,000 and 2,000 per cent in the years 1914—18 and in finance and banking over 600 per cent. In commerce in general women formed 53 per cent of the workforce in 1918, compared with only 29 per cent in 1914.[34] As well as extending the role of central and local government, changes in the organization of shops and banks meant that these new jobs were permanent, unlike the industrial jobs in which women had been substituted for men. The second reason why married women formed so small a percentage of the labour force related to the Depression and to government policy. In 1922 married women were disqualified from drawing unemployment benefit, even if they were in occupation for which it was payable. With an ever-decreasing number of jobs available, there was a general concentration on securing an adequate wage for the family man. The third reason, of course, was the number of single women who were forced to provide for themselves after the First World War.

Although no Census was taken in 1941 because of the exigencies of war, the change in the numbers of married women working do seem to stem from that date. The National Service (No. 2) Act 1941, which conscripted to the services or to essential war work single women aged 19—30, did not apply to married women or to mothers with children under 14 living with them. But the

Registration for Employment Order 1941 required all women between 18½ and 45 to register for work, and all but mothers of young children had to go to Employment Exchanges for direction to war work suitable to them. Of all women registered under this order 63 per cent were married, the majority having household responsibilities which took them outside the compulsory scheme.[35] In order to maximize the labour supply, the Government introduced a series of measures designed to enable married women with children to work. Part-time work was established in government-controlled and private occupations, the latter induced by various exemptions from legislation.[36] Nearly 1 million women were working part-time (under thirty hours a week) by 1945, a figure which dipped only slightly after the war and had doubled by 1961. Factory welfare, already improved by the Factory Act 1937, was extended to canteens, medical services on site and better cloakroom facilities. Local authorities provided 70,000 nursery places and 125,000 places for children under 5 in elementary schools, and the Ministry of Labour subsidized 35,000 places in nursery classes or schools. A further 9,000 daily guardians were registered with the child welfare authorities, and 460 play centres provided 30,000 school-age children with after-school care.[37] In 1951, 40,000 of the maintained nursery places were still available, although the private sector had fallen to a quarter its wartime size.[38] The years since 1951 have seen further cuts in nursery provision, and women have increasingly used unregistered child-minders rather than those registered under the Nurseries and Child Minders Regulation Act 1948.[39] Although the provision of nursery places has been a matter of local authority discretion, central government policy has been clear. A decade ago the Department of Health and Social Security advised social services committees that nurseries were 'principally for children with only one parent who has no option but to go out to work' and that 'early and prolonged separation from the mother is detrimental to the child.'[40]

Despite the withdrawal of government support for married women workers (see also chapter 9), married women continued to work outside the home after the war. Female part-time workers increased from 784,000 in 1951, to 3,152,000 in 1971, to 3,543,000 in 1981. Across the whole range of employment the female work pattern today is clear. Women work full-time until the birth of their first child. The majority work only part-time whilst their children are under 10, but just under half of all married women return to full-time employment in their mid-thirties or early forties, until retirement at 60.[41] In 1981 only 6 per cent of women with children under 5 worked full-time, compared with 19 per cent who worked part-time; 57 per cent of women with children over 5 worked (mostly part-time), rising to 71 per cent with children over 10.[42] One of the major reasons why women have been offered part-time work is, of course, because it is so cheap.

In contrast to the 1920s and 1930s, when there was much parliamentary discussion on the topic of women workers, the years after the Second World War were notable for the lack of parliamentary concern about women at work. Apart from *Equal Pay in the Civil Service* and one non-parliamentary report on women in teaching, women workers did not figure as a topic for debate until 1968, even though the 1950s and 1960s were not short of academic literature on the new phenomenon. No real debate on the position of married women workers took place until the Expenditure Committee noted in its report of 1972 that the lack of child-care facilities had reduced employment opportunities for women. The Government's response stressed the need for mothers to stay at home with their children (see p. 19). Yet in 1972 the House of Lords had set up an Anti-Discrimination Committee to investigate sex discrimination, and the Equal Pay Act had been passed two years earlier. A brief history of that legislation will explain why an acceptance of equal pay was not accompanied by an acceptance of working mothers and part-time workers.

Equal Pay

The issue of equal pay arose during the two world wars as a result of the pledges Governments gave unions to counter the erosion of rates of pay for men's jobs and the usurpation of men by women workers in peacetime. Although women continued to campaign for equal pay between the wars, they won the support only of male colleagues in mixed occupations where men feared female competition.[43] The fear that women workers might undercut men and restrict men's opportunities is mentioned in nearly every government report on women workers from 1918 to 1944. The response of Governments has been to placate male workers rather than to treat women fairly. The 1915 War Pledges on maintaining levels of pay covered only men's work. The Trade Boards (forerunners of the Wages Council) were established mainly in mixed occupations, albeit those with a high concentration of female employees. The Atkin Committee on equal pay was established only as part of an agreement to stop a strike of transport workers (mainly female in 1918) for the same war bonuses as men and equal treatment. The women received the 12 per cent bonus, but the establishment of the Atkin Committee and its subsequent report meant that the issue of equal pay was conveniently shelved. It has been suggested that the introduction of equal pay into the Civil Service from 1955 to 1963 owed more to the competition of higher wages for white-collar staff in the private sector than to concern for female workers.[44]

At an international level equal pay was a central tenet of the competitive philosophy of the European Economic Community (EEC); Article 119 of the Treaty of Rome 1957 provided for equal pay for equal work. The European Law was later extended to embrace the 1955 International Labour Organization (ILO) convention on equal pay for work of equal value. The translation of equal pay into legislation in Europe and in the USA (Equal Pay Act 1963) gave fresh support to trade unionists campaigning for equal pay in the UK. Equal pay gained support throughout the 1960s for a variety of reasons. More widespread use of job-evaluation studies demonstrated to women that they were being paid much less than men for equivalent work. The Labour Government's imposition of a 3 per cent pay policy worsened their position instead of giving them the rate for the job on which the party had campaigned. As a result, women workers became more militant, and the equal pay strike at Ford in 1968 focused attention on the issue. The Trades Union Congress (TUC) retracted its support for the ILO's proposal for equal pay for work of equal value. Instead it pledged support for the rate for the job for both men and women (it returned to the ILO model in 1970). Backbench MPs reacted by proposing Equal Pay Bills in 1967 and 1969 and an Anti-Discrimination Bill with a wider ambit in 1968. The new Secretary of State for Employment set up an equal pay working party in 1968 and in 1970 put forward a Government Equal Pay Bill.

In the Equal Pay Act 1970 can be seen all the hallmarks of the trade union campaign for pay protection for men. In providing equal pay for like work, not work of equal value (section 1(4)) and in the abolition of male and female rates only for the same job (section 3) the Act incorporated the notion of the 'rate for the job'. Equal pay for work of equal value was limited to jobs which had been evaluated by the employers, leaving the initiative for introducing job-evaluation studies firmly in their hands. The Act's provisions on collective agreements, which were likely to have the widest application, did nothing to erase the existing demarcation of jobs and merely raised the woman's rate (regardless of skill) to the level of the lowest unskilled male rate (section 3(4)). Since by this means employers could minimize wage increases (a concern constantly expressed in relation to equal pay),[45] the segregation of male and female workers was positively encouraged. Terms in a contract that complied with protective legislation or special treatment accorded to women in connection with pregnancy and childbirth were specifically exempted (section 6(1)). This appeared to preserve all the old ideas of higher wages for men because of their wider utility, although tribunals have restricted such interpretation in practice, as we shall see in chapter 2. Also exempted were different provisions in relation to death and retirement (section 6(1)(c)). In the Act as originally passed in 1970 different provisions in relation to marriage were also specifically exempted. The Act was amended by the Sex Discrimination Act 1975 before it came into force, and 'marriage' was removed. However, the notion that married women were not to be treated equally lingered on in the lower wages paid to part-timers, the majority of whom are married women, until a European Court decision in 1981. The delay in the implementation of the Equal Pay Act (29 December 1975) gave the employers nearly six years to adjust their workforce patterns in order to minimize their obligations under it. The Government was well aware that this would happen and was happening. It was warned *before the event* by the TUC (which wanted a two-year implementation period) and by a Department of Employment report on the Act's implementation published in 1972.

The Equal Pay Act 1970 thus marks the end of the transitional period when women were increasingly used as workers but were demoted to second-class status by reason of their child-bearing potential. As in the private area of family law, the law, legislation and court decisions recognized women's independence from men but emphasized their biological difference and sought to protect them because

of it. One cannot deny the very real improvement in working conditions brought
about by legislation. But women made progress as workers almost in spite of
the law, which was used more to men's advantage than their own.

The Modern Law

Despite its name and the fact that it at last met one of the longest held tenets
of the women's movement, the Equal Pay Act did nothing to quieten demands
for law reform. The 1970s were marked by tremendous legislative activity
concerning women's rights, both in the public and in the private sphere. Wider
anti-discrimination legislation was introduced by William Hamilton, MP, in the
House of Commons in 1971 and by Baroness Seear in the House of Lords in
1972. The Government responded by setting up a Select Committee. Creighton
points out that this move not only enabled a very thorough investigation to be
made of the problem and of possible legal action but 'had the additional merit
of buying time for the Government when there was clearly a great deal of support
for some kind of legislation in both Houses'.[46] The delay proved to be most
fortunate. The Lords Select Committee, and the one set up in the Commons
on the reintroduction of Mr Hamilton's Bill later that year, amassed a considerable
amount of evidence, not least of the experience of the American legislation which
had been introduced in the mid-1960s. By the time the Sex Discrimination Bill
was introduced in March 1975 it was becoming clear that the existing race relations
legislation was inadequate and that a more powerful and effective approach was
needed. As in America ten years earlier, women benefited from the commitment
to a uniform approach and from measures designed to tackle the politically more
sensitive racial discrimination.

By 1975, however, it was also clear that equality of opportunity for women
was a demand that could not be ignored. The EEC, which the United Kingdom
had joined in 1972, was preparing two new Directives on the subject. The
processes of discrimination against women were also better understood. The Equal
Pay Act was amended to remove the marriage exemption; the Employment
Protection Act 1975 extended the rights of pregnant workers; the Sex Discrimination Act outlawed discrimination in employment on the ground of marriage; and
social security legislation made some changes to wives' second-class status in the
National Insurance Scheme (see p. 167). Influenced by evidence of the American
law given to the Anti-Discrimination Select Committee (1972) and gained personally in the United States by the then Home Secretary, the Sex Discrimination
Act sought to go beyond individual instances of prejudiced behaviour to tackling
the structural causes of inequality faced by women.

In the employment field the Sex Discrimination Act and the Employment
Protection Act were the first legislative measures to accept women's equal right
to jobs and job opportunities, regardless of their sex, married status and child-
bearing function. The Sex Discrimination Act propounded a strong principle:

that to treat a woman differently from a man just because she was a woman or because she was married was unlawful. The Act provided that with respect to hiring, firing, promoting, training and providing non-contractual conditions of work employers had to treat men and women who had the same qualifications in the same way. Women (and men) who felt that they had been treated differently from a similarly qualified member of the opposite sex were given the right to challenge an employer at an industrial tribunal and to receive compensation.

The Employment Protection Act marked legislative acceptance of a woman's right to combine motherhood with paid employment. It extended to pregnant employees the legal protection against unfair dismissal that had been introduced by the Industrial Relations Act 1971 and established a scheme for pay and leave with a job-protection guarantee. [47]

Since 1975 two conflicting trends can be discerned. The first is a growing understanding of the ways in which discrimination operates against girls before they start work. In the area of education attention is being drawn to the important hidden curriculum which transmits lower expectations as effectively as did the official curriculum of former years. [48] There is also some recognition of the fact that without a fundamental reorganization of the work at present undertaken by women, providing them with training in skills formerly reserved for men will not result in equality. The education system has shifted its emphasis towards the supposedly economically useful skills required by the new technologies. Indeed, apart from the work of the Equal Opportunities Commission, official acknowledgement of discrimination against girls has been limited in recent years to the areas of mathematics, the sciences and technical subjects. [49] The likely result, however, will be not the preparation of all children equally for a world of paid and unpaid work but the demotion of the arts, languages and domestic skills, which already carry a lesser value because they are associated predominantly with women and which will be further devalued if they become the province of the academically less able.

Discrimination against women once they have emerged from school and have started to work is even better understood. The Sex Discrimination Act made it unlawful to deny women the same opportunities as those enjoyed by men on the stereotyped assumption that women's primary function and concern is a domestic one. However, there is no compulsion to employ women who are suitable and able to do the job but who fail to meet the established, 'male', standards. The Employment Protection Act sought to outlaw the dismissal of pregnant women and to give a chance to combine work and motherhood to those women who had shown themselves serious about their work by their length of service. At work, however, working mothers are expected to conform to the same standards as working fathers. Only if an individual can prove that a condition or requirement imposed by an employer disadvantages women *and is unreasonable* does the law at present provide an opportunity for change. But it is now generally recognized that the way in which employment opportunities are structured discriminate against women. Equality of opportunity for men and women is increasingly perceived to include the opportunity for both sexes to combine paid work and domestic commitments. The new programme of legislation currently being discussed at the European level (see p. 60) seeks to redefine the model of equality on these lines.

There is no equivalent legislative proposal in the United Kingdom. Instead the years since 1975 have been marked by government policy which has undermined the rights recognized by that year's legislation. For example, the Employment Act 1980 reduced the protection against unfair dismissal (section 8), made the procedures for claiming maternity rights more bureaucratic (section 11) and weakened the rights themselves (section 12 — see pp. 45-46). Public expenditure cuts have fallen disproportionately on areas of education traditionally associated with women [50] and have resulted in the withdrawal of facilities which enabled many women to combine paid work and family commitments — school meals, nurseries, provision for the elderly. At a time of economic recession the concern of government, employers and trade unions alike has shifted from the issue of increased job opportunities to the question of how to save the jobs of those already in work.

It can be argued that the 1975 legislation has been successful in securing formal acceptance of the notion of equality for women generally. But in looking at how the law has worked in practice it is necessary to see how effective it has been in tackling the patterns of entrenched inequality which, as we have shown, have been built up over a long period and in countering the conflicting effects of the present recession.

2

Equality at Work

The Sex Discrimination Act widened the legal definition of discrimination and should have made it easier to prove instances of unequal treatment than was the case under the Equal Pay Act. No longer is equality guaranteed only for those women who have overcome sex discrimination and are actually doing the same jobs as men. The new Act seeks to tackle the discrimination which prevents women from getting those jobs. Wherever women are denied access to jobs, promotion or training or are treated less favourably in other ways, it is sufficient to show that they would have been treated differently had they been men — that is, that their sex has been a significant factor (section 1(1)(a)). Additionally and, as we shall see, more important, the Act allows women to challenge the rules that govern the way in which employment opportunities are structured. The new concept recognizes that a woman can be prevented from having an equal chance to a job or other benefit not because of any prejudice on the part of the employer but because of the predominating male patterns of work (section 1(1)(b)). For example, to include physics or chemistry at O-level as proof of a good standard of education for entrance to a non-scientific post might be discriminatory on the ground that statistically fewer girls are entered for such examinations and acquire those qualifications.

But since all matters covered by a woman's contract of employment are left to be decided under the modified Equal Pay Act (see p. 34), the new Act can be used only by women in precarious positions: those attempting to break into new opportunities or those out of work claiming that they have been unfairly sacked. In both cases evidence of discrimination is harder to find than in cases involving contractual benefits. Moreover, the Sex Discrimination Act specifically excludes from its scope instances when a woman is offered a job on less pay than would be offered to a man (section 6(5)). This is potentially the easiest type of discriminatory job offer to prove, but a woman has a remedy only if the Equal Pay Act applies (see p. 34).

Thus the practical limitations of the legislation are obvious. Added to the lack of legal aid for tribunal cases, they go a long way towards explaining the small number of cases brought each year (see pp. 28, 37). Moreover, the limitations imposed by the words of the statutes have exacerbated the situation. The Equal Pay Act can be used only where a woman is engaged in work broadly similar to that of a man working for the same employer (section 1(2)(a)) or where her work has been rated equivalent under a job-evaluation scheme already undertaken by the employer (section 1(2)(b)).[1] In *Macarthys Ltd* v. *Wendy Smith* Ms Smith took over a job from a man but at a lower wage.[2] She was unable to claim his higher rate under the Equal Pay Act because they had never been employed in the same job at the same time. Many cases have been brought to establish what is and is not 'broadly similar work' under the Act.[3] The guidelines which have been established do recognize the danger of artificial differences, particularly those erected on sexual stereotypes.[4] But wherever there is a *real* difference in job content the Act cannot apply. In *Maidment and Hardacre Ltd* v. *Cooper*[5] a man and a woman were engaged in exactly the same tasks for 80 per cent of their time but on different jobs for the remainder. She was unable to claim the rate of pay he earned for the 80 per cent of her work that was the same as his. The Equal Pay Act provides an all-or-nothing remedy.

Even when a woman surmounts this first hurdle and proves that she is doing work equal to that of a man under the Act, her claim may well founder on the personal differences between them (section 1(3)).[6] Such differences may include age, length of service, skill, capacity, experience, qualifications or productivity. Over the years industrial tribunals and courts have become more aware of the discrimination underlying many of the reasons which appear at face value to be totally unconnected with sexual differences. The long debate about the link between protective legislation and sex discrimination (see p. 17) made tribunal members drawn from both sides of industry aware of the double discrimination implicit in paying higher rates of pay for night work as well as night-shift bonuses.[7] The Court of Appeal has similarly rejected market-value arguments, ('He would not have come for less')[8] and stereotyped assumptions about strength.[9] A Sex Discrimination Act case pointed out the potential indirect discrimination implicit in the criterion of length of service.[10] This has led to more scrutiny of this justification of unequal pay and the linked practice of 'red circling' (relocating usually older men in less demanding jobs on their old salaries).[11]

But where an employer can succeed in showing a personal difference between the male and female workers, a claim for equal pay must fail. In *Capper Pass Ltd* v. *Allen*[12] the Tribunal accepted that the more senior male comparator did have more responsibility. However, the presentation of the employer's case demonstrated that women workers were quite deliberately restricted to an inferior position and were not allowed the same responsibility. Had the Sex Discrimination Act applied to pay, it would have been open to Ms Allen to show that she would have been allowed more responsibility had she been a man. As the law stands, the Act was of no use to her unless and until she applied for one of the more senior positions.

Recent research into the extent of occupational segregation[13] and the deliberate evasion tactics used before 1975[14] shows that the vast majority of women workers will not be able to use the existing law to tackle inequalities in their terms and conditions of work, for the following reasons. First, cases have been won which appeared to settle the questions of principle (for example, that paying part-timers a lower rate than full timers *simply* because they are part-time is discrimination).[15] But the effect of each case is limited to the particular claimant and a maximum of two years' back pay as damages under the Equal Pay Act 1970. An obdurate employer can choose to fight each case on the individual characteristics of each worker. *Electrolux Ltd* v. *Hutchinson*[16] was one of 123 cases brought against the same employer, all by women doing the same work as Mrs Hutchinson. If the indirect discrimination provisions of the Sex Discrimination Act applied to pay, just one case could be brought to force the employer to restructure the distribution of work and remuneration in a non-discriminatory way (see p. 30).

The Electrolux cases demonstrate a number of other points that will be examined in the rest of this chapter. The women who brought equal pay cases did so without the financial support of their union and in the face of union opposition. They are not unique. Some cases have been brought against unions themselves or have joined unions as respondents with the employers,[17] and research shows that collusion between employers and unions, usually at a local level, is not unusual.[18] Second, the sheer number of cases at Electrolux (an additional 105 were in the pipeline) focused attention on the wage structure generally rather than on the characteristics of the individuals concerned. As we shall see (p. 57), the more a case can be presented as a matter of collective concern, whether under the Equal Pay Act or under the Sex Discrimination Act, the more likely it is to succeed. Finally, the case demonstrates the importance of having on tribunals representatives of industry unused to settling matters of dispute at an individual level through the courts. From the start the tribunals have shown themselves to be concerned about the need for clear guidelines within which *industry* can work (though this may not necessarily benefit women workers — see p. 28). The Equal Pay Act explicitly precludes the determination of cases solely on job content. It also fails to insist on job evaluation, which is a very effective way of raising women's pay.[19] As a result, the tribunals have manipulated matters of procedure in an attempt to minimize the importance of individualities.[20] The conflict between this pragmatic approach and the more traditional notions of justice operating in the higher courts forms a central part of our analysis in this chapter.

The Right of Individual Action before a Tribunal

The Sex Discrimination Act marked a new phase in anti-discrimination legislation in this country. Rather than having to pursue a complaint of discrimination through a conciliatory body, as under the Race Relations Act 1968,[21] an individual can now take her complaint direct to a court or an industrial tribunal. The latter were chosen for equal pay cases in 1970 because they provided a 'means of redress which is speedy, informal and accessible' and because 'the tribunals are experienced in dealing with employment matters, they include representatives of workers and they sit at various centres scattered throughout the country.'[22] It appeared logical to extend their use in employment matters under the Sex Discrimination Act. However, what the Government failed to realize was, first, that accessibility and speed are not enough; that a woman worker bringing a case against her employer without legal aid and often without union support (either because of the lower unionization of female workers or because of union hostility) is in a very vulnerable position. Second, if the legal forum is made up of representatives of employers and unions whose interests and practices often perpetuate discrimination against women, the informality of the tribunals and the experience of its members may work to deny the very remedy that the law seeks to ensure. Third, the Act requires ACAS, the conciliation service for all industrial complaints, to intervene when requested to by either side or when ACAS considers there is a 'reasonable prospect of success' (section 64). Thus the conciliation stage is also undertaken by officers steeped in industrial relations, with a 'duty to try to promote the settlement of a complaint without its being determined by a tribunal',[23] rather than by the Equal Opportunities Commission (EOC), which has a duty 'to promote equality of opportunity between men and women generally' (section 53(1)(b) SDA). One of the functions of ACAS is to act as a sifting mechanism to ensure the speedy dispensation of justice claimed for the tribunals. Statistics show that since 1976 between 50 and 70 per cent of equal pay and sex discrimination cases have not reached a tribunal due to the intervention of ACAS.[24] This does not mean that complainants are necessarily turned away without any satisfaction. Indeed, statistically, complainants seem to stand a better chance of receiving monetary compensation at the conciliation stage than if they pursue their claim before a tribunal. (The Commission for Racial Equality (CRE) is conducting research into the operation and effects of ACAS on discrimination cases. It may be possible to assess the role of ACAS in more detail when its findings are published.) However, the number of cases which are brought under these Acts is extremely small and decreases every year. There were only thirty-nine equal pay cases in 1982 (compared with 1,742 in 1976) and 150 sex discrimination cases (compared with 243 in 1976). The withdrawal of the majority of cases limits the familiarization of tribunal members with the complex aspects of discrimination. It also precludes the use of the potentially more useful remedies of declaration and action recommendation, which can be made only by tribunals (section 65, and see pp. 30-31, 35).

It would seem that one reason for the withdrawal of so many discrimination cases relates to the difficulties of proving a case under the Sex Discrimination Act. Women bringing such cases are disadvantaged by the scope of the Act, the rules of procedure and the nature of the complaint. The Act covers mostly those occasions where an employer makes a choice: appointment, selection for training, promotion or dismissal (section 6). In cases of direct discrimination a complainant must prove that she would have been treated differently had she been a man (section 1(1)(a)) or single (section 3(1)(a)). The strongest evidence is male applicants or male employees who have, in fact, been treated differently, either at the time of the complaint or at some time in the past. However, even then the employee must show that her sex has been the deciding factor. Since any decision is likely to involve a variety of considerations, and since discrimination is unlikely to be openly stated,[25] the employer will probably be able to adduce other plausible reasons why the complainant has not been chosen. An individual employee is greatly disadvantaged by her inaccessibility to all the relevant material.[26] This is also true of complainants of unequal treatment in relation to non-contractual benefits, which is the other employment area covered by the Act (section 6(2)(a) and (b)). Since they are not contractual, it may be hard to prove their exact terms or their scope of operation. Research has found that many women employees are totally in the dark about the terms and conditions of employment of their colleagues.[27] Without concrete evidence to show that sex or marital status has been the cause of differential treatment, the case may become simply a question of whom the tribunal believes, the employee or the employer.

A woman may find it extraordinarily difficult to prove her case. The courts have not imposed upon employers a duty to make all necessary evidence available to a complainant. Indeed, they do not seem to have appreciated the gross inequalities between the parties in this respect. By failing to redress the imbalance they have appeared to give more weight to the interests of employers than to the tackling of discrimination. The Court of Appeal in *SRC* v. *Nasse* [1979] Q.B. 144 held that 'industrial tribunals should not order or permit the disclosure of reports or references that have been given and received in confidence except in the very rare cases where after inspection of a particular document the chairman decides that it is essential in the interests of justice that the confidences should be overridden.'[28] Yet, as Anthony Lester, QC, pointed out in argument before the House of Lords in that case, comparison is essential in proving less favourable treatment on grounds of sex and race.[29] Without evidence of the relative characteristics of others who have applied for a job or promotion or who have been dismissed, it may be very difficult, if not impossible, to prove discrimination. The House of Lords decided that where a request for evidence was resisted by an employer, the chairperson of an industrial tribunal should check the documents at the start of the case. While this appears at first sight to be a fair solution, it is open to criticism. First, the test to be applied is not whether the documents are necessary for a fair hearing but whether they are necessary for a *speedy* determination of the case (the normal civil law test). Second, the decision will be taken before the complainant outlines her case. Bias stemming from the influence of traditional concepts may be unchecked or uncheckable. The House of Lords suggested that tribunals should check the required material and that where they allow its production, arrangements should be made for names, etc., to be covered up. But the House of Lords could have required employers automatically to present all material relevant in such a way as to overcome difficulties of confidentiality. Research points to the likely effect that such a ruling would have had on management: 'many of the voluntary initiatives in the United States undoubtedly took place because of fears of legal intervention...Some employers told us that they had expected initially to have to do more than they did.'[30]

The difficulty of obtaining evidence partly explains the high proportion of discrimination cases which concern dismissal — nearly 50 per cent in 1982.[31] Unlike other selection procedures, when the important information on other candidates is often contained only in confidential documents, or the distribution of non-contractual benefits, most employees will know the relevant facts about their colleagues. The process of dismissal and the reasoning behind it will usually also be more public. The same may be true of discrimination cases involving 'access to training' and 'access to other benefits, facilities and services' under section 6. But it is not as easy for an individual to bring a case while she is still working for her employer. Also the loss of a job is more tangible, and courts have found damages easier to quantify than the loss of other opportunities or access to non-contractual benefits.

Cases involving indirect discrimination avoid many of these difficulties. For a start, the complaint does not focus on the employer's behaviour in relation to one individual. Section 1(1)(b) defines indirect discrimination as a requirement or condition which applies equally to a man but is such that the proportion of women who can comply with it is considerably smaller than the proportion of men who can do so. In order to bring a case a woman must actually be disadvantaged by the practice. So long as she can show that it does have a disproportionate impact against women and that she has suffered herself, she will win her case unless the employer can justify the practice on non-discriminatory grounds. Cases of indirect discrimination do not depend upon proving that the employer's intention was to discriminate. The focus of attention is not the attitudes and behaviour of the individuals concerned; rather, cases concern the structures that determine opportunities — for example, appointment procedures or redundancy schemes and the reasons behind them. The case is conducted at one remove from personalities. Indeed, it is not necessary to show that the employer is aware of discrimination. Indirect discrimination was included in the Act because it was recognized that certain practices may have been adopted in the past, when fewer women worked in a particular industry or there was no expectation that women would apply for particular positions, that now acted as barriers to women wanting to participate fully in paid employment.[32] Sometimes employers are aware that the continuation of past practices restricts the opportunities of present female employees. In *Steel* v. *UPOW*[33] Mrs Steel complained that despite her longer employment, past rules associated with seniority rating making postwomen ineligible for priority for good 'walks' still operated to discriminate against her. Mr Justice Phillips said, 'It is probably fair to suppose that the reason the union shared the Post Office's view on equality but not yet is not unconnected with the fact that so many of its members are men who would suffer a loss in seniority if women were to gain.' If there is evidence to show that the employer realized that women were being treated less favourably, damages will be awarded unless the employer can prove that there was no intention to discriminate (section 66(3)). However, indirect discrimination cases are brought primarily not to compensate an individual for a lost opportunity but to open up opportunities. Therefore in a successful case a complainant would seek a declaration that the employer has discriminated against the employee (section 65(a)(a)) and an order recommending that the employer change the policy (section 65(1)(c)).

Cases of indirect discrimination are not without their problems. Attention has been drawn to the difficulties faced by an employee bringing a race or sex discrimination case and attempting to obtain 'statistical information of the type which would be required. Unlike the United States where employers are required to collect statistics of the racial composition of their workforce there is no such requirement in Britain. Without such a requirement, such statistics are unlikely to be available.'[34] Even in successful cases there has been much argument as to the choice of relevant statistics. Courts and tribunals do seem to be aware of the complainant's weak position, but for the most part the courts in particular have shied away from the implications of acknowledging an individual's difficulties in this respect. They have decried the American type of discrimination case, in which full statistical information is used to prove inequalities and differential treatment,[35] but they have not discussed the fact that most American employers are required by law to prepare statistics for discrimination cases (p. 52) or that all American cases are processed through the Equal Employment Opportunity Commission and most are brought to court with its expert assistance. Instead they have stressed the informality of tribunal proceedings. This loses sight of the fact that the concept of indirect discrimination challenges conventional industrial relations thinking, which predominates at that level. In the case of *Clarke v. Eley (IMI) Kynoch Ltd*[36] evidence that all part-time workers at the factory were women and that 80 per cent of part-time workers nationally were women was vital to the decision that to choose part-timers first for redundancy was 'grossly discriminatory'. The fact that the Employment Appeal Tribunal (EAT) did *not* refer to similarly precise figures on the relative lengths of service of men and women seems significant in the light of the decision that 'last in, first out' had only a 'limited discriminatory effect'. While recognizing that 'by reason of child-bearing and other domestic commitments, fewer women than men might have long service and therefore the criterion "last in, first out" might be unlawfully discriminatory' the EAT said:

> In our view, bearing in mind that Parliament has encouraged the making of redundancy agreements between employers and unions and *that 'last in, first out' has for very many years been far the most commonly agreed criterion for selection*, it would be right for an industrial tribunal to hold that the adoption of 'last in, first out' was a necessary means (*viewed in a reasonable and common-sense way*) of achieving a necessary objective, i.e. an agreed criterion for selection. (Emphasis added)

This lack of awareness by the higher courts of the purpose of indirect discrimination has heightened the second problem faced by women seeking to use it. Once a complainant has shown that an employer's practice or condition has a disproportionate effect on women generally, and that she herself is disadvantaged by it, the employer has then to justify the practice on non-discriminatory grounds. The higher courts have lowered the stringent standard of proof imposed on employers by the EAT.[37] In a race relations case the House of Lords rejected the test of 'necessity' and implicitly gave more weight to traditional business concerns than to society's interest in combating discrimination.[38] Indeed, it went so far as to suggest that cost could justify the imposition of a rule with which ethnic minorities could not comply on religious or conscientious grounds. More recently the Court of Appeal has held that an employer will have justified a proven discriminatory condition if there are *adequate* grounds for it.[39] Lord Justice Eveleigh defined 'adequate grounds' (a definition of 'justifiable' which the Court of Appeal found in a dictionary) as reasons which 'would be acceptable to right-thinking people as sound and tolerable'.[40] In previous discrimination cases the discriminatory attitudes of others (for example, trade unions, the rest of the workforce or clients) had not been accepted as justifying discrimination,[41] but the Court of Appeal in the Ojutiku case unanimously decided that the discriminatory attitudes of employers justified the MSC's refusal to sponsor the applicants on an employment training course. Lord Justice Eveleigh demonstrated most clearly why 'right-thinking people' are unlikely to appreciate the concept of indirect discrimination or to recognize it in normal business practices: 'Many people are without the necessary qualifications for certain pursuits . . . Some lack them through their own fault, some through misfortune or lack of opportunity, but that is life.' Lustgarten's remarks apply equally to women. 'An attitude that allowed employers wide latitude to do what they think is reasonable is precisely what the legislation is trying to challenge: entrenched unthinking practices keep blacks on the outside looking in.'[42] All the evidence suggests that employers are going to find it much easier to satisfy the Court of Appeal's new test. This will make it much harder for women to win discrimination cases in future.

Despite these difficulties, the cases show that the anti-discrimination legislation can be used by women to break through and challenge the unions' and management's almost total control of their chances and conditions of employment, particularly where a large number of women bring cases or where one case has broad implications. In some instances women have acted after the completion of union negotiations to their detriment;[42] in others a case has interrupted negotiations which subsequently have been superseded or redirected by a determination of the legal position.[44] Elsewhere a union has been drawn in at the end of the case to negotiate a satisfactory pay settlement or conditions of employment.[45] In such instances recourse to a tribunal has proved a powerful way of making a union act in women's interests.

The use of legal action in this way is quite different from that envisaged when the Sex Discrimination Act was passed. It cuts across the ethos of industrial tribunals, which equates the interests of unions and workers. It is also totally alien to the civil law traditions of the higher courts. The rest of this chapter looks at how the attempts of the legal system to assimilate the new law have affected its development and its usefulness to women in their working lives.

The Right of Individual Action in the Appeal Courts

The higher courts appear to have been unaware of the importance of legal action taken by women as a means of exercising control over their own working lives when discriminated against through traditional practices or by both sides of industry. Instead of taking the lead in developing a clear and distinct jurisprudence which would aid such attempts, the Court of Appeal has decried what the EAT has tried to do in that direction. The statement of Lord Justice Lawton that 'the Courts should I think lean in favour of a simplicity of meaning which will safeguard informality in procedure'[46] loses sight of the fact that the informality of the tribunal system was designed for the employee's benefit. It serves as a counter-weight to the lack of legal aid in situations where an employer will almost certainly be legally represented, increasing the inequality of parties in the presentation of the case.

The reversal of the EAT on matters of interpretation and procedure appears to have stemmed largely from a different way of looking at cases. Although some judges have shown themselves to be out of sympathy with the legislation,[47] these courts seem to have been influenced not by personal prejudice but by their perception of cases as matters of individual justice. While the tribunals use their experience of industrial life to attempt to understand the evidence and interpret the issues in a way that is consistent with the purpose of the legislation, the higher courts have similarly tried to make sense of the cases in their terms and according to their conceptual framework. For example, in overturning the heavy burden of proof that the EAT had imposed on employers in equal pay cases Lord Denning, in the Court of Appeal, said:

> We have been shown a series of judgments of the EAT where many phrases have been used which come near to the burden of proof to prove a serious crime: 'It must be clear and convincing', 'not fanciful' and such like . . . As we said long ago, the burden of proof required depends on the nature and gravity of the subject matter. It depends on whether it is a grave offence or a minor one.[48]

The Court of Appeal went on to uphold the normal burden of proof in civil cases. The result is that where an employee has made a good case for equal pay or for discrimination the employer will succeed if he can show that it is more likely than not that between the two workers there is a difference other than their sex or some other reason for treating women differently from men. As has been suggested, unfamiliarity with the hidden discrimination implicit in otherwise well accepted business practices means that benefit of the doubt has been given very readily to employers in some cases. As the courts have become more familiar with how discrimination works in employment they have realized their mistakes.[49]

The accommodation of discrimination cases within a traditional civil law setting has not been without its difficulties. The statutes are so drafted that they make it impossible to fit discrimination into any previously defined legal category. Many aspects of discrimination are akin to aspects of crime. In *SRC* v. *Nasse* Anthony Lester pointed out that 'Parliament regarded discrimination as a social evil'.[50] The criminal law is the usual manner for outlawing such 'social evils'. Discrimination can be defined as prejudice in action, and while it is not the rightful role of the law to govern people's thoughts, it should act to prevent the application of such thoughts in ways which inflict social harm. The first anti-discrimination statute, the Race Relations Act 1965, started its parliamentary life as a criminal Bill and was changed only at the committee stage.[51] The links between discrimination and crime remain strong — for example, in the idea of punishment by way of damages for intentional conduct and the perceived slur cast on the employer found 'guilty' of discrimination.[52] Although the courts have soundly declared discrimination to be a tort (a civil wrong incurring only financial penalties and untainted by notions of criminality), they have found it difficult to decide on which type of civil wrong and whether the remedies provided by the legislation are most akin to contract, negligence or defamation.

There has been little difficulty with the Equal Pay Act, which is posited on contract law. It follows well established twentieth-century industrial and commercial notions of modification of contract and has a prescribed period of back pay. The tribunals have been able to assess compensation quite easily. More problems have occurred in relation to discrimination under the Sex Discrimination Act. Although tribunals have been urged to interpret the Equal Pay Act and the Sex Discrimination Act as a single code,[53] it is obviously difficult to apply contractual notions to situations where discrimination prevents a contract of employment from being made. Indeed, the Sex Discrimination Act (section 6(5) and (6) and section 8(3)) has detailed provision in relation to contractual matters, placing all such monetary matters within the Equal Pay Act. So where a woman is offered a job on a salary lower than would have been offered if she had been a man, an action under Sex Discrimination Act can be brought only if the equal pay rules apply.[54]

Since the form of the Sex Discrimination Act precludes contract, the choice of 'conceptual home' lies between negligence and defamation. The emphasis within the statute on intention militates against the former. In any event, as the above quotation from Lord Denning shows, the courts have shown little inclination to take such a strong line. The use of negligence would impose a general duty to take care that one's actions (and possibly omissions) did not have the .effect of disadvantaging a substantially higher proportion of women than men wherever it was reasonable to expect alternatives to be considered. Had this view of discrimination been fully worked out and damages been awardable in cases of indirect discrimination, as in other types of negligence, one loophole of the legislation would have been closed. The most powerful remedy of a tribunal in a case of indirect discrimination is an action recommendation (section 65(1)(c)) for a change in the practice concerned. However, under the Act a tribunal has no power to make such a recommendation mandatory. This follows the tradition of the civil law that, except in very rare cases, a court may order someone to refrain from detrimental behaviour but should not order him to take positive steps, such as re-employment, to the advantage of a complainant. The only sanction against an employer who fails to take notice of a recommendation is damages, which can be awarded only if damages could have been awarded originally (section 65(3)). Thus in the majority of cases where an employer can prove that his discriminatory practice was unintentional, no complaint to a tribunal by an individual employee can ensure that a change will be made. Only if the Equal Opportunities Commission can be persuaded, and is able to go to court for an injunction, can the practice be stopped (section 71). The Court of Appeal has shown great reluctance to use injunctions to prevent recurring discrimination, partly because of the criminal sanctions for breach of injunctions.[55] However, even if the EOC were to succeed, the injunction would be in terms only of stopping the behaviour. Any alternative practice would have to be negotiated through trade unions if the workforce were unionized. Otherwise it seems that a recalcitrant employer can substitute an alternative and equally discriminatory practice without any check other than another case brought by an employee or the EOC under its persistent discrimination powers. It is to be regretted that the courts have not interpreted the law more along the lines of negligence. In negligence the primary focus is on detrimental behaviour judged by social standards. Concentration on intentional conduct has focused on the individuals concerned, without reference to social standards. Indeed, concentration on the merits of individuals has led the judges to fail to appreciate the social importance of the law that they are applying. Cases such as *Peake* v. *Automotive Products*[56] and *National Vulcan Engineering* v. *Wade*[57] have left the impression that discrimination is a minor matter between individuals, to which little serious attention needs be given. That perception facilitates the assessment of women who bring discrimination cases as trouble-makers, abnormal women dominated by a cause, as suggested by Judge Ranking in the case brought against El Vino's by Anna Coote and Tess Gill.[58] Although perhaps most visible in that case, this perception of women complainants does appear to be a significant factor in the determination of damages in sex discrimination cases. In *Hurley* v. *Mustoe No. 2*[59] a tribunal had set damages at 50p on the grounds that the complainant did not deserve any more; not only did the tribunal consider that her past experience as a late-night waitress made her immune to the hurtful effects of sex discrimination, but it also punished her for joining a protest outside her ex-employer's restaurant. The EAT increased the award and held that such considerations were irrelevant. In *Gubala* v. *Crompton Parkinson*[60] the tribunal reduced the damages to be awarded to a woman who had been unfairly selected for redundancy on discriminatory grounds because it had the opportunity of declaring her to be of good character. This case is particularly significant because damages were explicitly said to be assessed according to defamation principles.

The parallel between discrimination and defamation was drawn in the parliamentary debates[61] and has a logical consistency. Defamation is the tort most closely linked with individual circumstances and willed behaviour, and it accommodates the punitive notions implicit in the use of intention in the Sex Discrimination Act. However, the use of defamation by analogy has had adverse consequences in the hands of both tribunals and the appeal courts. The reduction of damages because the court could declare the plaintiff to be of good character had been disapproved of by the House of Lords in 1962.[62] In any event, the tribunal in the Gubala case applied that law in a way that was significantly different from the way it had been used in the originating case. The reason for reducing the damages which might otherwise have been awarded was not that the character of the person defamed could be upheld but that the words of the judge against the person making the defamatory statement would puncture his reputation as an international businessman, giving associates notice that he was not a man of honour. It affected his pocket directly.[63] Far from fulfilling this punitive role, the tribunal's words in *Gubala* appear to have been used to rebut the presumption that Ms Gubala was in any way to blame, incorporating perhaps, in the discrimination aspect of the case, the notion that she was a 'normal' woman, a true victim, not a trouble-maker or extreme 'women's libber'.

This devaluation of the harm of discrimination has been aided by the appellate forum's willingness to intervene to reduce damages. This practice is disapproved of in proper defamation cases, in which the assumption is that the judge and jury, having seen and heard the parties to the case, are most able to assess such aspects as honesty, which may not be readily apparent on paper.[64] The courts and tribunals have taken the view that, as in other branches of law, appeal courts in discrimination cases should intervene only where the law applied by the lower tribunal was wrong or where no reasonable tribunal could have come to that decision on the true facts.[65] But the Court of Appeal in *Skyrail Oceanic Ltd* v. *Coleman*[66] said that appeal courts could interfere with damages set by tribunals '*if for any other reason* they have made a wholly erroneous estimate of the damage suffered'. 'Any other reason' appears to include the personal 'gut reaction' of the judges themselves. In that case Mrs Coleman's employer had written to her: 'Regretfully I have come to the conclusion that it would not be fair to your husband in his position to keep you employed in a similar capacity.' (This is reminiscent of the attitude of the Inland Revenue, which used to address replies to letters from married women to their husbands. The Chancellor of the Exchequer (the husband of the erstwhile deputy chairman of the Equal Opportunities Commission) was so overwhelmed by the reaction of thousands of women who complained of the offensiveness of such conduct that even though nothing has been done yet to change the substance of tax law, the practice was altered immediately). The tribunal in the *Coleman* case thought that the unfairness of such discrimination was compounded by facts which made it appear that

Mrs Coleman was being dismissed because she had leaked information. The Court of Appeal, however, made a very academic distinction between injury that was a direct consequence of discrimination and the more defamatory type of injury which, as Lord Justice Lawton said, was 'not properly attributable to an unlawful act of sex discrimination'. Lord Justice Shaw felt that Mrs Coleman's complaint was 'trivial and banal even when topped up with much legalistic froth' and that 'when she had dried her tears she would have had to look for new employment and to count herself lucky to find it'; he said, 'I would have substituted one thousand pence for the one thousand pounds the Tribunal saw fit to award.' Lord Justice Lawton did recognize that the employer's behaviour had been discriminatory. Even so the court reduced the damages further from the £250 awarded by the EAT to £100. These eminent men, accustomed to great respect, obviously found it difficult to understand the outrage of not being treated as a person in one's own right, still less to quantify that outrage in monetary terms. This lack of shared experience will be of paramount importance as long as the courts take the attitude that appeal courts can interfere with tribunal awards. Tribunal members, like juries, are more likely than judges to understand the harm of discrimination.

Statistics on levels of compensation awarded in all cases of sex discrimination (not necessarily just injury to feelings) show that in 1982 150 cases were brought, of which forty-two reached a conciliated settlement, fifty-two were withdrawn, thirty-two were dismissed by tribunals and twenty-four were successful (of these awards of damages were made in seventeen cases). In three cases the award was under £49. Three cases were under £150; three were between £150 and £300; one was between £300 and £500; two were between £500 and £750; and five were over £1,000. Of the thirty-nine cases settled with the help of ACAS, twenty-four involved sums under £300 and all but three were under £1,000. Since nearly half of the original complaints involved a dismissal and since reported cases show that it is easier to prove discrimination in dismissal cases, it is fair to assume that those levels of damages included some compensation for loss of earnings, although no breakdown is given in the official statistics. The statistics show that action recommendations were made in seven cases.[67] The figures for 1982 are slightly higher but not much out of line with those of previous years or with cases of racial discrimination. Statistics in relation to equal pay cases show that for 1980 over half the applicants were earning basic weekly wages of under £60 and that all but four of the ninety-one applicants (including two men) earned less than £90 per week. For the same year the New Earnings Survey shows the average basic weekly wage for men over 21 was £124.5; for women over 18 it was £78.8.[68] Since only a fifth of discrimination claimants each year are in professional or managerial types of occupation, it is also fair to assume that women bringing sex discrimination cases share the low pay of those bringing equal pay cases.

In such circumstances, and taking into account the general devaluation of jobs undertaken by women and ethnic minorities,[69] the tradition enshrined in the

English law, that money can effectively compensate for all harm, must be challenged. The tribunals and courts have shown great reluctance to estimate loss of opportunity in cases of discrimination in appointment and promotion, on the ground that one cannot be sure that if the discrimination had not operated, the complainant would have got the job anyway.[70] Special damages are more or less restricted to loss of earnings or other circumstances when a sum can be fixed by reference to past known quantities. Such amounts are inevitably going to be low. In most cases injury to feelings will be the only head on which damages will be assessed. So long as injury to feelings is judged by the damage to reputation of women assessed in terms of the money that their position at work can justify, it is clear that the levels of compensation are going to remain low. Since it seems unlikely that a change will be made in the law to allow tribunals to force an employer to hire, promote or retain a woman against whom he has discriminated, the English legal system should look to the USA to see how the award of damages can be changed to encourage the voluntary adoption of non-discriminatory employment practices. This will involve changing perceptions of injury in discrimination cases and adjusting the focus of attention from the person discriminated against to the person discriminating.

One tribunal has made such an attempt. In *Prestcold Ltd* v. *Irvine*[71] the tribunal was satisfied that only discrimination had prevented Ms Irvine from getting promotion. It made an action recommendation that her employers pay her the higher rate of pay until she got the promotion which she was due. The Court of Appeal firmly quashed this attempt to introduce the so-called 'front pay', which is a staple remedy of the American courts, on the ground that matters of pay belonged to the Equal Pay Act, not the Sex Discrimination Act. This case demonstrates how far the segregation of equal pay and equal opportunities under separate Acts has hindered judicial understanding of the dynamics of sex discrimination. This lack of understanding has not only prevented the effective enforcement of the law in individual cases but has also undermined the use of those strategic powers which were specifically aimed at dealing with the collective nature of discrimination.

The Limits of Strategic Intervention

Employers, aided by the fact that such cases are heard by the courts, not by tribunals, have succeeded in thwarting the efforts of the Central Arbitration Committee under the Equal Pay Act and the EOC under the Sex Discrimination Act. Although the courts recognize that it may not always be advisable to take the word of an employer at face value, they have limited the intervention of the strategic bodies in the interests of 'natural justice'. In *R.* v. *Central Arbitration Committee ex parte Hy-Mac Ltd*[72] the High Court said that the Central Arbitration Committee could not assist in negotiations between union and management on the implementation of a scheme to meet the requirements of the Equal Pay Act but were limited to amending blatantly discriminatory collective agreements which stipulated rates for men and rates for women. (It is doubtful if any of those survived 1975, all having been altered to appear sex-neutral and the jobs segregated by sex instead.)

Similarly, the House of Lords has prevented the administrative bodies, under the Sex Discrimination and Race Relations Acts, from mounting formal investigations into the general workings of organizations, limiting their scope to acts of discrimination that they suspect to be taking place and suspicions that they can objectively support.[73] The Court of Appeal has shown an open dislike of these bodies, calling the machinery of formal investigations an 'engine of oppression'[74] and not trusting them to deal fairly in a quasi-judicial capacity. In *CRE* v. *Amari Plastics Ltd*[75] the Court of Appeal held that an employer had the right to appeal to an industrial tribunal against the findings of the CRE after a lengthy and painstaking formal investigation and was not limited to appealing against the requirements of the non-discrimination notice. The purpose of the legislation was to allow the CRE and EOC to go into workplaces to discover the reality of patterns of discrimination which would not be picked up in individual action or through the artificial and limited arena of a tribunal. Yet the Court of Appeal's decision means that a tribunal will have the final say as to whether discrimination has taken place. Even though the employer investigated could challenge the actions of the EOC or CRE through an application for judicial review, and thus (one might think) the interests of justice could be satisfied, the court held that the inquisitorial nature of the administrative proceedings required that

> in fairness to the company and in justice to them, on appeal the company should also be able to challenge the findings of the fact which the Commission have already made; and to challenge them before the industrial tribunal which is the first impartial judicial tribunal to hear it.[76]

> As Sir Sebag Shaw succinctly put it in the course of the argument the Commission effectively submits that the appeal is against sentence and not conviction. If this is right, it very seriously limits the value of an appeal; which is of great importance to the employer because it is only by a successful appeal that he can remove the slur cast on him by the non-discrimination notice.[77]

Evidence given in that case and to the Home Affairs Committee on the CRE, 1981, shows the extent of distrust and antagonism felt by some targets of formal investigations. These are exacerbated by lengthy delays, which of course judicial rehearings do nothing to solve. However, as the House of Lords in *Mandla* v. *Lee* pointed out,[78] there is a danger of judicial assumption of unfair practice on the part of these administrative bodies that a close examination of the facts of the case does not bear out.

Comparison with the fate of the American Equal Employment Opportunity

Commission suggests that judicial distrust of the British Commissions arises because of their inquisitorial role and also because their appreciation of the nature of discrimination is ahead of that of many of the judges.[79] It is tempting from North American experience to believe that had the judges been given the responsibility for tackling discrimination in England, the barriers based on the concepts of individualism would have been avoided. But, of course, the comparison is not that easy. The stronger enforcement of the law by the courts in the USA cannot be taken out of the context of a society and a Supreme Court more aware of, and more committed to, civil rights. Government departments in America have strong administrative powers in relation to discrimination.[80] In England the government has delegated action against discrimination to quangos. The very department which sponsors and finances them has challenged the CRE's powers in the courts, not on the ground that the behaviour of Home Office officials was not discriminatory but on the ground that an investigation into that behaviour was technically outside the CRE's powers under the Race Relations Act 1976.[81]

Moreover, the judiciary has had an opportunity to determine policy in the way the American courts have done. European law prohibiting sex discrimination in all aspects of employment is very widely drafted. Unlike the detailed wording of English statutes, European law states the general principle and leaves judges to work out the detailed application in each case. It is law which is the exclusive province of the courts and tribunals. On Peck's analysis[82] one might expect the judiciary to have used it to override the problems in the national legislation we have outlined. A brief overview of the application of European law by the English courts indicates that this is so only for the tribunals which are already more attuned than the higher courts to the purpose of the anti-discrimination legislation.

European Law

Article 119 of the Treaty of Rome stipulates that employers must pay 'equal pay for equal work'. Unlike the Equal Pay Act, Article 119 offers no precise definition of equal pay and contains no exclusions similar to those related to death and retirement to be found in Section 6 of that Act. Stemming from the Article are two directives. One takes the definition of equal work further by including equal pay for work of equal value (Directive 75/117). The other tackles equal opportunity and treatment at work, the same field as that covered by the Sex Discrimination Act (Directive 76/207). British courts have assumed, and the European Court has now confirmed, that Article 119 is direclty enforceable through the courts and tribunals.[83] So far the European Court has refused to say that the directives go any further than requiring the member states to change their laws in accordance with the directives. The Court has been able to decide all four successful cases on Article 119 and has avoided the issue of the enforceability of the directives in the national courts. It has done so by interpreting Article 119 very widely to cover matters which had been assumed to be the province of the directive only.[84] The European Commission, whose job it is to monitor compliance with directives, has successfully taken action against the United Kingdom through the European Court to enforce reforms of the Equal Pay Act and Sex Discrimination Act.[85]

In the first few years of the operation of the Equal Pay and Sex Discrimination Acts judges referred to the European law as a means of bolstering the broad approach they wished to take in a particular case. By 1979 the Court of Appeal had clearly appreciated the potential of Community law. It is noticeable that the cases in that court which have demonstrated a wider awareness of strategic discrimination and have authoritatively pushed the law forward have made explicit, often detailed, reference to American and European cases.[86] Since 1980 both appeal courts have shown an increasing willingness, assisted by financial support of the EOC, to send to the European Court for authoritative decision cases that would otherwise have failed on the narrow and restrictive wording of the Equal Pay Act. The consequences of such referrals have been felt at different levels. In the majority of cases the individual complainants have succeeded where they would have failed under English law as interpreted in the courts. Ms Smith in the *Macarthys* case[87] was entitled to the same pay as her predecessor. Lloyds Bank were required to change the differential pension contribution rules that applied to the detriment of Ms Worringham.[88] Mrs Garland was entitled to the use of the British Rail travel concessions which applied to male employees and their dependants after her retirement in the same way as her male colleagues.[89]

But the European cases have had other effects. Their success appears to have energized the EOC in a way reminiscent of the positive approach of the American courts to the Equal Employment Opportunities Commission. Although the European Court has not been able to comment on the Commission's power in the way the American courts have done (investing the American Commission with a power in practice which it did not contain on paper), its positive policy-orientated approach has left its mark.

The effect on the courts and tribunals has been inconsistent. Indeed, in relation to European law there now appear to be three approaches. The first, exhibited by Lord Denning and Mr Justice Phillips, starts from the premise that European law overrides English law. Under this approach judges show no reluctance to modify statutes to correspond with what they see to be the wider scope of the higher law. European law in their hands becomes a tool for integrating the 1970 and 1975 Acts.[90] The second approach looks to Article 119 as an aid to the construction of the national statute only where an ambiguity exists as to meaning.[91] But, as we have seen, the ambiguities usually arise only when one contrasts the law under the Equal Pay Act with that of the Sex Discrimination Act or European law with the national legislation. The use of traditional rules of interpretation means that this second approach may be as restrictive as the third, which treats the European law as a totally separate head of law, to be applied alongside the English law in much the same way as a separate statute. Only if a woman fails under the Equal Pay Act will the tribunal consider her case under the European law.

Since those favouring this approach are likely to work to the traditional common law concepts of interpretation, which are totally unsuited to the broad and undetailed formulation of law used at European level, it is also likely that the European law will be used more restrictively in such instances. Emphasis will be placed on exact words of European Court judgments, used and applied as a House of Lords case might be under the common law doctrine of precedent. However, like European legislation, such judgments are not drafted with this use in mind; European Court judgments are binding only on a particular case, and the words used express indications of policy, not precise formulations of law.

Recent cases suggest that this third approach is now being used more than the other two. The EAT, which in the early years used European law to further the purpose of the legislation, appears now to have got cold feet. In *Southampton and South-West Hampshire Health Authority (Teaching)* v. *Marshall*[92] Ms Marshall's retirement had been postponed beyond her sixtieth birthday by mutual agreement. The Health Authority argued that it had not contravened the Sex Discrimination Act by sacking her at the age of 62, since all matters connected with retirement were excluded from the Act (section 6(4)). The EAT upheld its interpretation of the subsection. It also said that although the Sex Discrimination Act contravened the equal treatment directive in this respect, it was not prepared to give effect to the European law unless either the House of Lords or the European Court decided that the directive was directly applicable. The European Court could not have avoided making a decision on that point had the EAT referred the Marshall case to it. However, it did not.

Two other retirement linked cases indicate the extent to which the EAT is retreating from its previous position. In *Barber* v. *Guardian Royal Exchange Assurance Group* and *Roberts* v. *Tate & Lyle Food and Distribution Ltd*[93] the EAT could have decided that redundancy schemes linked with retirement age were covered by the Sex Discrimination Act. Had it used the European law either as a guide to interpretation or as the means of resolving an ambiguity, such a conclusion would have been inevitable. Instead it claimed that the retirement *exception* in section 6(4) must be given a wide interpretation. Referring to the different retirement ages for men and women, it noted: 'This differential treatment was blatantly discriminatory. However, the effect of such discrimination percolated throughout society. Accordingly, unless all this was to be swept away the Act had to exclude claims arising out of this inherently discriminatory practice.' In other words, although it could have made a start at tackling the discrimination which flowed from different retirement ages, it was not prepared to do so. We may conclude that the EAT was probably only too well aware of the Government's negotiations on the occupational pension directive and parliamentary activity in connection with retirement ages. It appears that, unlike their American counterparts, British judges do not want to take the initiative in furthering anti-discrimination legislation.

There is no evidence to suggest that there has been a dramatic improvement in women's working lives in the years since the Equal Pay Act and the Sex

Discrimination Act became law. The gap between women's and men's earnings is roughly the same as existed then. Indeed, in recent years the slight trend towards closing the gap appears to have been reversed. The majority of women remain as segregated in a small number of occupations and at the bottom end of the market as they did before 1975.[94] Given the very limited application of the Equal Pay Act, it is perhaps not surprising that very few women even attempt to use it now. One would have expected the numbers of women bringing sex discrimination cases to have increased over the years as both they and the legal system became aware of its potential, but to a large extent the traditions of both the tribunals and the courts have prevented the law from being developed effectively; the few instances in which judges have understood discrimination from the woman's viewpoint demonstrate that a lack of empathy has also played its part.

In *Gill* v. *El Vino Co. Ltd*[95] Mss Gill and Coote complained that they had been discriminated against under the Sex Discrimination Act. Women were not allowed to be served at the bar at El Vino's in Fleet Street but had to sit at the tables and wait to be served. Judge Ranking held that there was no discrimination. The plaintiffs were not frequent visitors but were interested in women's rights. Usual customers did not object; differentiation was justified because of congested conditions; and the test was 'would a *reasonable* person come to the conclusion that *lady customers*... were in *reality* less favourably treated' (emphasis added). The Court of Appeal reversed the decision on the ground that the lack of choice was less favourable treatment, a judgment which appears to go much further than the Court of Appeal had previously been prepared to contemplate.[96] Lord Justice Griffiths may have given the explanation: 'El Vino's is no ordinary wine bar; it has become a unique institution in Fleet Street. Every day it is thronged with journalists, solicitors, barristers, exchanging the gossip of the day. No doubt it is the source of many false rumours which have dashed the hopes of many an aspirant to a High Court appointment.' As Lord Justice Eveleigh said: 'It affords a unique atmosphere which is clearly greatly appreciated and is *in great demand by men and I cannot therefore assume* that there is no true demand for it by women' (emphasis added).

In *Turley* v. *Allders Department Stores Ltd*[97] Ms Turley was sacked because she was pregnant. She was unable to use the law against unfair dismissal[98] because she had not been employed for the requisite period, at that time twenty-six weeks. Instead she alleged that she had been discriminated against contrary to the Sex Discrimination Act. The majority of the EAT decided against her. They said: 'It is not on the ground of her sex that you are treating her less favourably than you would treat a man, but on the ground that she is no longer simply a woman but is a woman carrying a child.' Since there is no masculine equivalent, there can be no comparison and hence no less favourable treatment. A minority judgment is an unusual occurrence, and the strength of feeling of the dissentient woman member may be judged by that. She strongly rejected the reasoning of the majority and pointed out that there are medical conditions which affect only men. She also thought that the majority were wrong in precluding a remedy under one Act simply because a more limited remedy existed under another. Her reasoning was accepted in the case of overlap between the Equal Pay Act and Employment Protection (Consolidation) Act in *Coyne* v. *Export Credits Guarantee Department.*[99] It is open for a future tribunal to hold that the Turley case is limited to instances of dismissal only. But if the reasoning of that case is accepted, and there can be no such comparison between men and pregnant women, the Sex Discrimination Act cannot cover discrimination against pregnant women either in job applications or in promotion.

Even limited to dismissal, the Turley case results in individual injustice, heightened by changes in the law. One year's continuous employment is now required for protection against unfair dismissal instead of the twenty-six weeks then operating,[100] and two years for new employees of firms with less than twenty employees.[101] Women's working patterns for the child-bearing years, particularly in non-professional or vocational jobs, suggest that many women are outside any legal protection from dismissal because they are pregnant.[102] The Turley decision also gives rise to inconsistencies. Dismissing a woman because she is pregnant is not discrimination under the Sex Discrimination Act. Dismissing her because she has a child, and on one of the stereotyped assumptions about women with children, is discrimination within the Act.[103] Of course, the dismissal of the pregnant employee may be for reasons other than the unreliability or lack of continuous employment that tend to be the basic assumptions relating to working mothers. The reason may be appearance; an employer may object to a pregnant woman representing his business. The tribunal in *Schmidt* v. *Austicks Bookshop*[104] upheld the right of management to control the image of the establishment and the appearance of the staff.[105] The reason may be unsuitability for work — which, if assumed, would be discriminatory; if actual and fairly assessed, may not. Yet all these reasons share a common theme. They are based on a particular way of looking at motherhood and paid employment. Once the baby has arrived the law says that unverified assumptions based on this stereotyped thinking is discrimination. There seems to be no reason why the same should not apply to pregnancy.

Most women are only too well aware that the presumption of childbirth and a presumed discontinuation of paid employment is the cornerstone of all the discrimination they face at work. Slowly some tribunals are becoming aware of this fact too. In *Horsey* v. *Dyfed CC*[106] the EAT said that the assumption that a woman would follow her husband's change of employment was discrimination when the facts of the case clearly showed that throughout their marriage Mr Horsey had always sought a job in the area where Mrs Horsey had found promotion. But the hiving off of considerations relating explicitly to maternity severely limits the development of a change of thought about the position of female workers. The Employment Protection (Consolidation) Act 1978 establishes a system of maternity pay and maternity leave for women with two years' service at the time when the National Insurance Maternity Allowance is payable (i.e. eleven weeks before the expected date of the birth). It also automatically protects women workers of one year's service from dismissal on the ground that they are pregnant. Apart from detailed rules as to return to work at the end of the maternity period, which must be strictly adhered to,[107] that Act does not offer any protection to a woman who is not given a job, promotion or chance of training because of pregnancy or the presumption of a future pregnancy.

Paradoxically, the tribunals have found little difficulty in interpreting the maternity provisions of the Employment Protection Acts in ways that uphold working women's rights. Although the tribunals have introduced notions of management rights in deciding whether pregnancy has been the cause of dismissal,[108] the few maternity cases that have been heard are comparatively free from the sort of stereotyped thinking apparent in other discrimination cases. One reason could be that in maternity cases tribunals are meeting the problem head on. Yet certain cases show that tribunal members do hold sexist assumptions about pregnancy and maternity.[109] A more convincing argument is, first, that the law corresponds to unfair dismissal law and patterns of thought with which it is overridingly familiar. Second, the law is very specific. Under the 1978 Act as it was passed tribunals are not required to do any balancing act. The statute says that dismissal on grounds of pregnancy is automatically unfair. Tribunals are not required, as in other cases of unfair dismissal, to decide whether the action was reasonable. Teleological interpretation is not required. The statute lays down a clear definition of rights and a timetable for requisite action to ensure those rights. Third, the Act contains a very clear statement of principle — the *automatic right not to be discriminated* against by dismissal on the grounds of pregnancy. When a woman's job becomes unsuitable for her in her pregnant condition the law imposes a duty upon the employer to find her suitable alternative work. If this is impossible, her rights to maternity pay, to maternity leave and to the same contractual position on her return are safeguarded. Even though in the last resort the final remedy is aggravated damages, the fact that the Act is drafted in terms of positive rights and enforceable duties to take action makes it significantly different from the other two statutes.

The Employment Act 1980 made significant changes to these maternity rights which are likely to change the tribunals' approach. The periods of written notice that a woman is to leave work and that she intends to return are now three weeks in both cases (section 11). An employer can require written confirmation of an intention to return, so long as he waits for forty-nine days after the expected or actual confinement (section 11(2)). The employer must make it clear that a woman will lose her maternity protection if she fails to reply within fourteen days or as soon as is reasonably practicable.

The Act made other changes in the law ostensibly to help small employers, upon whom it was felt, the burden of maternity leave provisions fell most heavily, a hypothesis disproved in practice[110] and disapproved of by the European Court.[111] A firm with fewer than six employees is exempted from offering a woman her original position back if the employer can prove that it is not *reasonably practicable* to do so or to offer suitable alternative employment (section 12). Any firm which can prove that it is not *reasonably practicable* to offer back the original position and that the employee has *unreasonably* rejected a *suitable* alternative will be deemed not to have dismissed her unfairly (section 12(2)). We have seen the courts' notions of what is reasonable in relation to an employer's reasons for not giving a woman equal pay (see below). It has been shown that women experience a devaluation in their employment status on return to work after leaving to have children. [112] Their skills are downgraded and they are not expected to show the same commitment to work as childless female workers. There are indications that tribunals may not appreciate the sex discrimination behind the commonly held assumptions about working mothers. It is to be remembered that in the *Eley Kynoch* case (see p. 31) the EAT found the dismissal of part-timers intolerable but the dismissal of workers with shorter service tolerable. Yet part-time work and interrupted work patterns are both a predominant feature of female employment and share a common cause, children.

In recent years some feminists have begun to suggest that it is not enough to give women equal opportunities to compete on the same terms as men, according to established rules which reflect and promote the lifestyles and working patterns customarily enjoyed by men. An alternative approach involves equal recognition for the sorts of work that women do and accommodation of female working patterns within male-dominated occupations. [113] Although the direct discrimination provisions of the Sex Discrimination Act can be used only for the benefit of the woman who attempts to compete against a man, and thus can show that she has been denied some benefit because of her sex, an assertive use of the indirect discrimination provisions could change many of those practices which favour men. But there are other ways to open up greater opportunities for women. While the wisdom of introducing positive discrimination law as such is still hotly debated, the United Kingdom is committed to introducing laws which guarantee equal pay for work of equal value.

3

Beyond Equality of Opportunity

Equal Pay for Work of Equal Value

In 1982 the European Court held that workers in the Community were entitled as of right to equal pay for work of equal value.[1] The British Equal Pay Act 1970 did not conform with European law. Job evaluations under that Act were not compulsory, and no individual had the power to make an employer undertake one. Directive 75/117 made equal pay for work of equal value the primary right under Article 119 of the Treaty of Rome enforceable by judicial process. The directive required national law to forbid direct and indirect discrimination in assessments of pay. The Equal Pay Act allowed women to challenge only direct discrimination in job-evaluation schemes in which different values had been used for men and women. Indirect discrimination (for example, giving more value to physical effort than to dexterity) was unchallengeable.

The Equal Pay Act has now been amended to allow individuals to claim equal pay for work of equal value. Obviously, since it is a broader concept than 'like work' under section 1(4) and includes the job-evaluation provisions of section 1(5), it would have been possible to repeal these provisions and substitute a new equal value section. This has not been done. Instead equal value has been inserted as the third ground on which equal pay may be claimed. Moreover, it can be used only if neither of the original grounds is relevant. If a woman feels that her job is of value equal to that of a man, despite a finding to the contrary in an existing job-evaluation study, she may bring an equal value case. However, she will have to show some indirect discrimination in that job evaluation (section 2A(2) and (3) Equal Pay Act).

Under the new provisions a woman claiming equal pay for work of equal value will make a complaint to an industrial tribunal, just as with any other equal pay case. The tribunal will appoint an independent expert to investigate the claim and report back. If the expert reports that the two jobs in question are comparable and the tribunal accepts that report, the woman's claim will be upheld. The scheme appears simple, but it is beset with many procedural difficulties.

The first difficulty in an equal value case is that at the start the tribunal has to decide whether there are any reasonable grounds for the claim (section 2A(1)(a) EPA 70). In all cases before an industrial tribunal either party can request a preliminary hearing to decide if there is a prima facie case. If the tribunal decides that the case is very weak or appears spurious, it may warn the applicant that if he or she goes ahead, costs may be ordered against him or her. The normal rule in tribunal cases is that each party bears his or her own costs. The equal value pre-hearing, however, is different from this ordinary pre-hearing: it appears to be mandatory, and if the tribunal rules that there are no reasonable grounds for the claim, it can stop the case at that point. The Government sought to justify the new procedure, which is exclusive to equal value cases, on the ground that 'to allow a hopeless case to continue will be expensive and time-consuming for all concerned'.[2] However, the way tribunals deal with this problem in other cases is by awarding costs, not by preventing a hearing. Moreover, the test is one not of 'hopelessness' but of 'reasonableness'. As Baroness Seear pointed out in the House of Lords debate on the new law, what is reasonable is what

> in the light of ordinary practice...most people would do...But the whole point about equal pay for work of equal value and the job-evaluation schemes which will have to be used in order to implement it is that in some cases the results will be...quite contrary to what in the past has been normal practice. That is what is is all about...The whole point about equal value is that it will reverse the pecking order at any rate in certain cases and will not at first sight seem reasonable to a great many people.

We have already seen that the experience and philosophy of tribunal members has prevented a full awareness of the discrimination implicit in traditional labour relations. There is no evidence to suggest that in these pre-hearings they will be any more aware of how discrimination works. Indeed, all the evidence is to the contrary. In *Eaton* v. *Nuttall*[3] the EAT defined a bona fide job-evaluation scheme as one which conformed to ACAS guidelines. They disallowed the arguments which showed that these could discriminate against women. A challenge to an existing job-evaluation scheme on the ground that it is tainted with indirect discrimination is also subject to this 'reasonableness' pre-hearing (section 2A(2)). The prospect of success in such cases seems slim.

Should the tribunal decide that the claimant has a reasonable case, then it appears that the employer could still ask for a warning to be given about costs, as in the normal pre-hearing assessment, on the ground that the claim is 'vexatious' (Regulations 11 and 12 Industrial Tribunals (Rule of Procedure) Regulations 1980). This could involve allegations that the claimant is bringing her case not in good faith but perhaps for an ulterior motive.[4] It is not clear whether tribunals would tolerate such an attempt. But there is a danger that the possibility of enormous costs, raised either by the tribunal or by ACAS officers before the case was heard, would be sufficient to deter claimants. This is particularly likely when a woman brings a case without the support of her trade union. Equal value can be claimed only when there is a mixed workforce. Since many male workers will oppose the erosion of differentials in pay, it is fair to assume that many women will be in just this situation.

The third procedural difficulty has been attacked as quite contrary to natural justice.[5] In equal value claims the tribunal may hear evidence from the employer as to the differences between the employees (the 'material difference' test) *before* the tribunal decides whether the two jobs are equal. Quite obviously, the aim is to prevent a finding of equal value which could be pursued by other employees through the tribunal or be used to upset established pay structures using the usual negotiating mechanisms. There is every reason to believe that this special procedure will be successful in preventing equal value cases from going to experts for the comparative assessment.

The test of 'material difference' to be applied in equal value cases is much wider than that applied in other equal pay cases. The new provisions indicate that the employer's justification for unequal pay need not be restricted to personal differences between a man and a woman. The regulations do not specify what other justifications would be acceptable. However, Ministers introducing the amending legislation in Parliament have stated that employers could use market-forces arguments. These would include the test already rejected by the Court of Appeal in *Clay Cross* v. *Fletcher* (see p. 26), a recognition of the greater commercial benefit of one job and a higher rate for scarce skills. All three are open to criticism. The first was rejected by the Court of Appeal because the judges realized that to allow it would be to make the Equal Pay Act a 'dead letter'. The second is allowed under European law.[6] But whether one job is of greater commercial value to the employer is a matter that the expert must consider in deciding whether two jobs are of equal value. It should not be considered in isolation, particularly not by a tribunal at a preliminary stage. The Earl of Gowrie, introducing the new law in the House of Lords for the Government, gave the following example of the third type of justification: 'Local education authorities who need to attract mathematics teachers in shortage areas can offer them a lead in pay over other teachers starting their careers. This is to do simply with the shortage of maths teachers: it has nothing whatsoever to do with sex discrimination.'[7] It would seem that the Government at least is not of the opinion that European law requires such defences to be scrutinized for indirect discrimination. Because, as Lord McCarthy pointed out in the same debate, 'such shortages derive from earlier institutional or social barriers to the progress of women, their training, their appointment, their recruitment, their placement in the labour market. So behind these short-term market reasons are longer-term factors which most of us would say were at least partly sex-based.'[8]

The employer has two opportunities to put forward these arguments — before and after the case is considered by an expert. The draft procedural regulations have been amended to allow cross-examination of the expert. This at least guarantees that the decision on equal value is determined by judicial process, as required by European law. But the regulations do not guarantee the independent expert access to the workplace. Thus any expert witness called by the employer, who controls such access, can cast serious doubt on the value of the independent expert's report. The practical advantage lies with the employer all the way through an equal value case.

The last point to note is that if a woman perseveres through this obstacle course and wins her case, back pay will be made only from 1 January 1984. Since it is estimated that equal value cases will take anything from six to eight months, this may not be as bad as it first seems. However, other equal pay claimants are entitled to a maximum of two years' back pay. There is no such limit on claims of equal pay decided directly under European law.[9]

There are three general observations to be made on the new law. First, as our outline has made clear, the law is extremely complicated. It is drafted in such a tortuous way that it is almost unintelligible.[10] Second, because the change in the law stemmed from a European legal obligation, it has been possible to amend the Equal Pay Act by statutory instrument under Section 2(2) European Communities Act 1972. The debate in Parliament was thus limited to ninety minutes in each House, and there was no possibility of amending the proposed legislation. Negotiations as to the final form of both the regulations amending the Act and the procedural regulations have taken place within the Department of Employment rather than in Parliament. The lesser opportunity provided for public scrutiny has been heavily criticized. Procedural rules ensured that the amendments were approved by both Houses of Parliament. But the House of Lords was clearly dissatisfied with the proposals that they were being asked to approve and with the way in which the matter had been handled. They declared by a small majority that the changes did not bring the British law into line with European law, an opinion the European Commission may find hard to ignore. Whether the Commission takes the United Kingdom back to the European Court on its implementation of Directive 75/117 may depend on how the tribunals interpret these very complex provisions.

The third observation is that such complexity was not necessary. The Dutch and American courts are deciding equal value cases on laws which are the equivalent of the British Sex Discrimination Act.[11] The law is simpler and the scrutiny of indirect discrimination guaranteed. But it has other advantages. The comparison is not limited to one place of employment or associated employment, as under the Equal Pay Act. A woman doing the same sort of work as men working for another employer can use the law to get the rate for the job. Moreover, women in segregated occupations can compare their work with that of male-dominated occupations (for example, the work of secretaries and typesetters). Additionally, women are able to request a revaluation of their work on the male scale even where there is no exact male equivalent. In *Gunther* v. *County of Washington*[12] the American Supreme Court held that the discrepancy in the wages of male and female prison guards was greater than the difference in jobs or the difference in value could justify. The use of the Sex Discrimination Act in this way would significantly increase the effectiveness of the concept of equal value in eradicating sex discrimination in pay. The research on occupational segregation suggests that even if the tribunals interpret the law in a way most beneficial to women, the amended Equal Pay Act is not going to make much difference to women's low pay.[13]

We must conclude that the concept of equal value has the potential for improving the terms and conditions of women workers in this country. By forcing a reassessment of work undertaken predominantly by women it could begin to challenge the stereotyped assumptions about women that undermine their work and educational opportunities.[14] A female profession such as nursing could be revolutionized by recognizing that it requires specialist skills and responsibilities equal to or greater than the traditionally superior and male-dominated profession. A ward sister with many years' experience may be more skilled and have far more practical responsibility than the junior doctor who is technically in charge. Yet the pay and opportunity structures fail to recognize this fact. The only way that a woman can break into the more highly paid 'senior' service is by competing with men for a place at medical school. In the majority of cases that means using the traditional route — science A-levels and normal university entrance.

However, although the concept of equal value could fundamentally change the traditional structures of employment opportunities in the long term, it is clear that the new British law on equal value has no such potential. By contrast, positive action programmes are being implemented at present to help women overcome the barriers to wider work opportunities. We therefore turn to look at what positive action is and how the law can facilitate its effectiveness.

Positive Action

The positive action programmes operating in, or being proposed for, the United Kingdom have been developed from two sources. The first is the concept of positive discrimination developed and promoted by law in the United States. Sex discrimination is defined as unlawful only when gender is an irrelevant consideration and when the act of discrimination perpetuates disadvantage. So, for example, a decision to choose only men to do a job traditionally always done by men, when there is no objectively necessary reason why women should not also do that job, would contravene the law. However, that definition of discrimination makes it possible to envisage situations in which it might be socially desirable to take sex into account. Thus in a society pledged to improve women's employment opportunities, an employer faced with two equally qualified applicants, one female, one male, might choose the woman if women were underrepresented in that job. Because of its historical basis, this aspect of positive action still focuses on the employer/employee relationship. The law encourages or requires an employer to review employment practices and/or provide special training to ensure equality of opportunity for male and female employees. Reverse discrimination — that is, choosing a less well qualified woman in preference to a man — is usually sanctioned only where the particular circumstances make any other form of positive discrimination practically impossible. Thus the Supreme Court in the United States has been prepared to accept a scheme under which black employees junior to the white complainant were eligible for promotion training.[15] The alternative decision, to outlaw seniority as a qualification for eligibility, would have had extreme implications for the whole of American industrial relations, which are based more on seniority than is the case in Britain. In such circumstances accepting reverse discrimination as a temporary expedient appears to have been preferable to declaring the principle of seniority to be indirectly discriminatory.

The second source of positive action stems from the executive action of Governments particularly in relation to public-sector employees. This action has included special policies to promote equal access for women in public employment or publicly funded employment — for example, the Civil Service, local government or private employers enjoying public contracts. But because of the involvement of governmental bodies, these policies have not been limited to the employer/employee relationship. Policies have been developed in relation to matters which hamper the equal participation of women in paid employment, such as housing, education and child care.

In Sweden this type of positive action was introduced before, and in preference to, legislation banning sex discrimination in employment. This, it was felt, would have conflicted with positive action. Swedish policies have included the introduction of specialist staff to open up employment opportunities for women; special training for women in non-traditional areas of employment; the reservation of at least 40 per cent of jobs for the underrepresented sex as a condition of state assistance to newly located industry; state subsidies for employers who provide training for women or men in non-traditional employment; more day nursery places; the establishment of a parental leave and insurance scheme; subsidized public transport; and localized community facilities planned on the basis of two working parents.[16] Since 1967 even the United States, a country which leaves family policy much more to the individual citizens, has nevertheless required all public-sector employers and all federal contractors to submit detailed statistical breakdowns of their workforce and to demonstrate a positive action policy.[17]

The concept of positive action arose in the United States out of the civil rights movement and at a time when opportunities in employment and education were expanding. In Sweden positive action was adopted as part of a policy to encourage women to join the labour force as an alternative to a policy of immigration to solve a labour shortage. Economic and political conditions are very different in the United Kingdom of the 1980s. Opportunities for paid work appear to be decreasing rather than increasing, as is public-sector finance. New educational and training courses for women have to vie with traditional education for resources. Government policy favours the return of married women, particularly women with dependent relatives, into unpaid work at home rather than easing their participation in paid employment. In such circumstances it is not surprising that a common response to positive action is that women are benefiting at the expense of jobs for young (and, by implication, male) employees. Fear of positive action as a threat to men's opportunities is by no means confined to the United Kingdom. However, American experience indicates that positive action has a vital role to play in a recession, not least in the formulation of redundancy policies which guarantee equal distribution of dismissal and equal opportunities for retraining and redeployment. As technology reduces the unskilled and clerical work where women predominate,[18] retraining schemes and positive action in education will be significant in ensuring that there are jobs for women in future.[19]

The Sex Discrimination Act limits the scope of positive discrimination in relation to women in the UK. Reverse discrimination, implemented either by reserving a set number of previously 'male' jobs for women or even by using gender as the deciding factor between two otherwise equally qualified candidates, clearly contravenes the main provisions of the Act. Nor is it possible to use the genuine occupational qualification exemption to achieve the same ends. The very fact that a job has previously been done by a member of the opposite sex negates the requirement that being a woman or a man is essential to the effective performance of that job. Different requirements for men and women are tightly restricted to the various special provisions relating, for example, to the minimum height for police and the prison service (section 17(2)(a) and section 18 Sex Discrimination Act). The only quotas that are lawful under the Act are those which might be adopted by trade unions on their elected bodies, either by reserving a number of seats specifically for women (e.g. TUC Council) or by creating extra seats for women (section 49 Sex Discrimination Act). In relation to less contentious measures, such as compensatory training and targeted recruitment, the Act makes a distinction between measures adopted by employers and trade unions in relation to existing employees and measures adopted in relation to potential employees. In relation to existing employees, employers are allowed to offer training facilities for women (or men) only if they have been absent or underrepresented in a particular type of work during the preceding twelve months. Trade unions likewise can offer women only training courses for potential union officials subject to the same conditions. The careful wording of section 48 suggests that the reservation of a specific number of places for women on general training courses or the establishment of separate lists for access to general training, such as operated in the American *Webber* case, would not be lawful, an interpretation shared by the CRE, which has recommended changes in the law to allow preferential access to more general courses.[20]

Trade unions can act in other ways to encourage female members only to take up official posts. The National Union of Public Employees, for example, has successfully adopted the strategy of establishing all-female branches. Campaigns to attract more women to become trade unionists do not fall within the Sex Discrimination Act's positive discrimination provisions because they would not contravene the main provisions of the Act. Increased union activity related to issues such as equal pay, maternity leave, lack of promotion and the establishment of advisory committees on such matters are internal to the organization of the union itself and confer no individual benefits which could form the basis of a discrimination action under the Act. However employers' attempts to encourage women who are not already employees to apply for untraditional work could be construed as arrangements to determine who should be offered employment within the Act. Therefore section 48 allows employers to conduct special advertising campaigns directed at the underrepresented sex or promotional visits only if there has been such a shortage of such workers at some time during the same twelve-month period. Any promotional training offered by employers for prospective emplpoyees, such as the one-month practical training courses successfully initiated in Sweden,[21] will be lawful only if the employer has been designated an official training body by the Secretary of State for Employment. Apart from industrial training boards, the Manpower Services Commission and other specified governmental training agencies, any organization or educational body that wishes to put on special training courses for women can lawfully do so only if it has been through the designation procedure (section 47). Once accepted, the designation attaches to that institution, not to the particular course in relation to which approval was first sought. The conditions for courses under this section are wider than for employers under section 48. The underrepresentation in non-traditional work may be statistically proved, nationally or locally. Additionally, special courses can be put on for those persons (primarily women) who have been precluded from regular full-time employment because of domestic or family responsibilities. The Second Chance for Women and Return to Work courses increasingly being offered by educational establishments and professional organizations are covered by this provision. Once designated for the purpose, it seems that these bodies may restrict such courses to women only or may establish quotas or preferential access to more general training courses.

However, all the positive discrimination measures provided for in the Act are voluntary. There is no mandate under the Act for employers, trade unions or other organizations to make use of these exemptions or positively to promote opportunities for women. Nor does the Act contain any incentive — rather the opposite. The necessity for official designation as a training body may well deter organizations that would otherwise contemplate such courses. However, the law of the United Kingdom is not unusual in this respect. Denmark has established a similar bureaucratic system. Norway and France permit, but do not require, positive action. Sweden is the only country which has tried by legislation to make such measures compulsory.

Section 6 of the Swedish Equality in Working Life Act 1979 imposes a duty on employers to adopt an appropriate positive action programme. This should include ensuring that applications from both sexes are received for advertised jobs and also ensuring, by special recruitment or training if necessary, an even distribution of men and women across the workforce. Administrative machinery (resembling the English Race Relations Board) was set up to monitor the implementation of the law, to conciliate and, if necessary, to fine in cases of non-compliance. However, most employers have successfully avoided the operation of such mandatory policies. Section 7 of the Act allows employers voluntarily to adopt a positive programme negotiated through the traditional collective bargaining machinery and forming part of a collective agreement.[22] But the 1979

Act contains no requirement for equal or proportional representation of women on decision-making bodies or in trade union positions. Alice Cook reported in 1980 that no women held positions of authority on the national federation of blue-collar unions.[23] Even in the federation of white-collar unions, with 35 per cent female membership and approximately 50 per cent female representation on local negotiating committees, only one woman sat on the central negotiating committee, where the national agreements are formulated. Cook also cites evidence that even where a union policy takes a strong line on equality issues, the process of bargaining may result in very few proposals being adopted in the collective agreement.

By contrast, the implementation of positive action is very widespread in the United States, where the law is permissive, not mandatory. Since the UK legislation is based closely upon the American model, it is instructive to analyse why this is the case. The reasons can be summed up under four headings: the public availability of the requisite statistics; the potential imposition of extremely high damages in discrimination cases; the powerful position of the EEOC in conciliating and monitoring out-of-court settlements; the power and willingness of the courts to make positive action orders. None of these factors is present in the United Kingdom. The EOC is trying to persuade employers to adopt positive action, but it has neither the power to force them to do so nor the resources to provide technical assistance for individual employers interested in positive action. Its policy in 1983 was to call together all interested parties to facilitate the establishment of voluntary advice networks.

Without some legal structure it is unlikely that any positive action which is implemented will make a significant difference to women's opportunities in the United Kingdom. There seem to be four ways in which the present law, outlined above, could be changed to introduce the persuasive legal element which American experience has proved to be so essential.

The first option would be to introduce into the EOC's formal investigation procedure power to order positive action. At present, if after a long and complicated investigation procedure the EOC decides that an employer has contravened the law, it can issue a non-discrimination notice. This notice will require the employer to stop discriminating and to make changes in policy or practice. However, the EOC cannot stipulate the exact form that the new practices should take. The non-discrimination notice can require the employer only to inform the EOC and other relevant bodies of what changes have been made (section 67 Sex Discrimination Act), and the EOC can intervene only to modify the new practices or policies where they can be proved to cause an individual to suffer discrimination under the Act (section 71). Thus, for example, a change in recruitment policy which did not positively promote equal opportunities for women could not be challenged unless the EOC could prove that the new policy also discriminated against an individual woman.

Removing the formal barriers which have prevented women from applying for what were previously thought to be 'men's jobs' may not of itself result in women entering those jobs. A positive action programme would include such measures as special advertising directed at women likely to be interested in the new opportunities; the reassessment of qualifications necessary for entry into the job and possible alternative promotional structures; the reassessment of the conditions of work to make the job more attractive to women; the redeployment and retraining of employees from other areas of employment. Even if the EOC can succeed under section 71 — by showing, for example, that the new recruitment policy contains a requirement which indirectly discriminates against women — the court can only issue an injunction ordering the employer to stop that particular discrimination. There is no power to order remedial action. The EOC has taken preliminary action in one persistent discrimination case, *EOC* v. *Sogat* 1983. As Sadie Robarts points out, the EOC's record on formal investigation to date does not indicate that a change in the law would have a dramatic effect.[24]

However, the CRE has recently proposed changes in the law on formal investigations which, if implemented, might change the EOC's position.[25] The CRE proposes that the administrative bodies should have the power to accept, during the course of a formal investigation, binding undertakings from employers to make remedial changes. These undertakings would be registered and enforceable, as if they were non-discrimination notices. If, during a long investigation, the Commission believed that the employer was unlawfully discriminating, it should have the power to bring a case against the employer. If this were proven, the tribunal would have the power to refer the case to a county court registrar to assess the number of individuals adversely affected and to award compensatory damages. With a slight amendment, so that the employer could be made to keep to his undertaking, *without* proof that he was additionally subjecting an individual to discrimination under the Act, such a scheme would seem to fit the American criteria for the effective implementation of positive action. It combines the suggestions made by the NCCL in 1975 as to binding recommendations and their court enforcement with the financial inducements and bad publicity found to be conducive to out-of-court settlements in America. Such reforms would also be likely to reduce the length of formal investigations and to lessen the judicial distrust of a purely administrative investigative procedure.

The second way of encouraging positive action would be to amend section 65(1)(c) of the Sex Discrimination Act to give tribunals power to *order* positive action. At present tribunals can only *recommend* action likely to 'obviate' or 'reduce' the adverse effect of discrimination. The European Court has recently decided that the Sex Discrimination Act does not comply with Directive 76/207, the Equal Treatment directive.[26] Under that directive courts must have the power to order changes in discriminatory rules. It is not clear how far the directive can be relied upon to force the change in section 65(1)(c). Even if European law did demand that tribunals be given the power to order remedial action instead of merely recommending it, it is likely that the law would be of limited use. It is questionable, to judge by American experience, whether many employers would agree to go further than strictly required by the outcome of an individual complaint without the incentives of heavy damages or costs. As we have shown, damages in discrimination cases are low and likely to remain so as long as they are assessed by labour market standards. Costs are more likely to be awarded against an employee than an employer. In the USA damages are high because cases are brought on behalf of a large number of individuals. The introduction of class actions in discrimination cases in this country is currently being discussed. The weight of opinion appears to be that such actions would cut across the whole system of English law and would have ramifications far wider than those of anti-discrimination law.[27] However, Widdison has pointed out that collective action is possible under English law.[28] He suggests that the present rules should be amended to enable to EOC to bring a representative action on behalf of a group of individuals. Damages could not be awarded on that action, but a declaration that an employer's policy was unlawful would make it easy for a large number of individuals to bring their own cases for damages, as happened in the *Electrolux* cases (see p. 27). Sometimes it is possible for a number of individuals to ask a tribunal to consolidate their similar cases. The larger the number of people involved, the less likely it is that the tribunal will agree. However, our analysis shows that discrimination cases with a collective element are always more likely to succeed than those concerning single individuals. More attention should be given to representative and consolidated actions as a way of enlisting the voluntary co-operation of employers. Both types of action exist in present English law. Again, our analysis suggests that their use, rather than the American type of class action, would be better received by the English legal system.

An obvious alternative to the introduction of positive action through individual complaints of discrimination would be to use the machinery for negotiating conditions at work. In 1981 the TUC Congress formally endorsed a positive action policy, recommending the establishment of goals and monitoring machinery.[29] In the United Kingdom most conditions of employment are locally negotiated and have no legally binding effect. There is no equivalent (outside Wages Council industries) of the French or Swedish systems, whereby terms and conditions collectively negotiated at national level are legally imposed upon all employers within a particular industry. Indeed, the Fair Wages Resolution 1946, which incorporated minimum terms and conditions in the contracts of employment of employers holding government contracts, was revoked on 15 September 1983. The system of general comparison across industry established under Schedule 11 Employment Protection Act 1975 has been dismantled by the 1980 Employment Act (section 19). The general policy in relation to Wages Councils (which can impose national minimum terms and have extended their ambit to terms and conditions such as holidays and sick leave) has been one of abolition and consolidation.

In theory, the procedure by which employees lose Wages Council protection should not diminish their protection, since they will be covered by collective agreements.[30] But the position of women, and the will to implement the terms most likely to benefit women, is often extremely weak in the collective bargaining process.[31] The law has not sought to intervene in the unequal position of women in this regard, other than by allowing positive action within trade union organization (see p. 53). Section 3 Equal Pay Act allows the Central Arbitration Committee to intervene to eradicate obvious discrimination in pay structures under collective agreements,[32] but only trade unions or employers can refer the question of discrimination to the Committee. An individual has no power to do so under the law as it stands.

However, the European Court in Case 165/82 has held that the English law must be changed. Under European law pay structures and non-monetary benefits negotiated under collective agreements must be free from both direct and indirect discrimination. Additionally, an individual worker has the right to challenge the terms of such collective agreements through the Court system. The extent to which women will benefit from the European Court decision will depend upon how English law is changed to meet its requirements. It is unlikely that the Government will adopt a more positive stance than it did over the equal value reforms. It is also unlikely that the trade union movement and those involved in industrial relations are going to be as willing to give their support as they did in that case. But women workers should be aware of the opportunity that the decision has given them for increasing their negotiating power. Court action has proved useful in forcing unions to take action over demands for equal pay and for non-discriminatory structures under present legislation (see p. 32). The threat of court action may be very effective in persuading local unions to support the introduction of positive action measures into collective agreements.

The fourth way of encouraging positive action would perhaps prove the most significant if put into practice. Section 71 Race Relations Act imposes upon all local authorities the duty to make 'appropriate arrangements' to ensure that their functions are carried out with regard to the need to eliminate unlawful discrimination *and* to promote equality of opportunity and good relations between different racial groups. The wording of the section appears to require the implementation of positive action programmes by local authorities, not only in accordance with their role as employers but also in relation to the supply of such services as housing, education, social welfare. However, as drafted at present local authorities are required only to consider what the 'appropriate arrangements' might be, not to put them into practice. Since the funding for any special programmes that a local authority might decide upon comes out of discretionary rather than mainstream funding, section 71 is fraught with practical difficulties.

The CRE proposes that the wording of the section should be altered to make the duty one of implementation, not merely consideration, to be enforced through the courts by ratepayers or the CRE itself.[33] There is at present no equivalent of section 71 of the Race Relations Act in the Sex Discrimination Act, although many local authorities that have taken an active stance on section 71 in relation to race discrimination have also implemented policies in relation to women. In some cases the main focus has been employees, the provision of child-care facilities, parental leave, flexible working hours and return to work schemes. Other local authorities have instituted programmes to benefit all paid employees in their areas, such as school holiday playschools. Yet others, such as the Greater London Council, have established special administrative structures, with councillor and employee involvement, to implement positive action programmes within council employment and throughout the functions of the local authority. There is, of course, great potential for researching, establishing and monitoring positive action programmes which go wider than an individual employer but dramatically affect womens' opportunities. Initiatives in relation to science subjects and new technology education for girls in schools are at the forefront of such programmes.[34] Some local authorities are retraining adults for skilled work in the private sector. Leeds City Council, with some European Social Fund assistance, has co-ordinated the development of high-technology training for women. The courses recruit primarily unskilled women who have been at home with domestic responsibilities and skilled clothing workers who have been made redundant. The special position of the City Council has enabled it to forge links between institutions of higher education, local employers and trade unions and to offer the training centre as a resource to the community at large. This wide involvement not only leads to more opportunities for the women involved but itself promotes the concept of positive action.

As this example shows, local authorities have a crucial part to play in assisting voluntary bodies to claim the special financial assistance for positive action allocated by the European Social Fund. In order to claim this assistance a non-governmental applicant must have the support of a public body such as a local authority. Although the United Kingdom has received a large share of the general Social Fund (for assisted areas, etc.), it has received a very small share of the separate budget formerly allocated for women's projects but now subsumed under the general Social Fund. Unlike other Governments, the United Kingdom Government does not have a positive action programme for women. Projects seeking to retrain women do not enjoy direct government support and are thus heavily dependent upon the funds of other public bodies.

A study of positive action programmes was undertaken for the European Commission by Professor Vogel-Polsky of the Brussels National Centre for the Sociology of Labour Law. In 1983 its report recommended that a European directive should be drafted requiring community institutions, central and local governments and companies holding government contracts to introduce equality schemes. This approach would combine both types of positive action outlined above. It would also compel employers to produce statistical analyses of their workforces, which are essential in indirect discrimination cases. The Commission's report has not been met with much enthusiasm. The Advisory Committee on Equal Opportunities for Women and Men has rejected the proposal. The United Kingdom representative spoke strongly against any element of compulsion, preferring an 'information campaign'.[35] At present it seems that positive action will remain a voluntary option and that the European law is not going to introduce any element of compulsion. But the situation may change. A European conference on positive action attended by representatives of all member states was held in Greece in 1983. At that Conference the European Commission announced that it was investigating the possibility of drafting a code of practice on positive action. This would help to bring about the degree of consensus within and between member states which was necessary before a directive could be introduced. [36]

Pilot positive action schemes and retraining play an important part in the new action programme on the promotion of equal opportunities for women 1982—5 that was proposed by the Commission and passed by the Council on 13 July 1982 (OJ C186). Under the revised European Social Fund money will be available not only for training women for traditionally male jobs but also for ensuring a higher proportion of women on general training schemes. European interest in positive action is thus unlikely to diminish. We may well see legislation in the not too distant future which will force serious consideration of some of the law reforms outlined above.

Research shows that the unequal participation of women in paid employment is not the result of individual acts of discrimination. In order that women should have opportunities equal to those available to men changes need to be made which cannot be brought about by using the present law. Equal pay for work of equal value is extremely important because it does offer women the chance of higher pay and improved work status.

Extensive use of the new equal value provisions of the Equal Pay Act is necessary in order to educate tribunals in the importance of the new law. Only if there is a large uptake, as there was when the Equal Pay Act was first introduced, will the legal system have a chance to develop a jurisprudence which will make the law workable. Should the form of the law prevent this from occurring, then at least there will be strong evidence to support the view that the law does not conform with the European directive. Similarly, the European Court decision on discrimination in collective agreements should enable women in unionized workforces to press for changes that will benefit them. The decision comes at a particularly important time. Female membership of trade unions is increasing at a much greater rate than male membership, and women are making their interests heard at national and local levels.

The European Commission has proposed four new directives which would strengthen Britain's present law significantly. The draft directives on parental leave and protection for part-time and self-employed workers (including women working for husbands and family units, now outside the scope of many states' laws) would extend rights already enjoyed under English law. The draft directive on temporary work would restrict the increasing use of temporary workers (with lesser rights) to replace a permanent staff. Although motivated by the unemployment problem, its proposals would have tremendous implications for women, who form the majority of low-paid, seasonal and temporary workers.

Since equal pay was the only 'women's issue' dealt with the in the Treaty of

Rome itself, law on all other issues has to follow a procedure laid down in Article 235 of the Treaty. This provides that where action is necessary to further any of the Community's aims the Council of Ministers can take appropriate measures. The Commission formulates proposals and the Parliament debates them, but the Council must pass them unanimously. Partly because of its sophisticated and detailed legislation, the United Kingdom has been very influential in this process. For example, some of the most discriminatory provisions of the United Kingdom's social security system fall within the exemptions to the social security directive. The strong opposition of the United Kingdom Government to the draft directive on part-time workers casts serious doubt on its future. (The United Kingdom has the highest proportion of part-time workers in the Community, and the directive would involve change not only in employment protection legislation but also in social security law.) The Government would prefer a non-binding instrument which might result in more part-time jobs rather than improving the conditions of existing part-timers. Even if the directive were to be passed, it seems likely that a threshold clause (restricting its application to workers working over so many hours) would be included, allowing each state to fix its own threshold. Such a directive would have least effect on British women, who stand to gain most.

The second weakness of European law lies in its enforcement. The provisions of Article 119 are directly enforceable through the courts of the member states. Directives, however, operate to require Governments to alter their own laws. Individuals cannot rely on the provision of a directive in their own courts or in the European Court, except where such a provision is so clear that the European Court declares it to have direct effect. Although some commentators think that certain provisions of the equal pay and equal treatment directives fulfil the requisite criteria, the European Court has sidestepped the issue so far, deciding cases on Article 119 itself.[37] What is clear is that by allowing each member state choice as to thresholds and methods of implementation, the proposed part-time or temporary work directives could never be enforced by individuals. Should a country fail to change the law to meet the directive, it is for the European Commission to bring a case before the European Court of Justice.

The Commission, in the new social action programme, has expressed its concern at the weak enforcement machinery and the lack of any effective monitoring of how the national laws work in practice. The establishment in 1982 of the Advisory Committee on Equal Opportunities as a link between the Commission and specialist national agencies such as the EOC should provide more information on the practice. However, the minimalist approach taken by the UK Government and its literal interpretation of existing requirements suggest that confidence in Europe as an incentive for effective changes in English legislation should be tempered.

European law is not the only means for changing English law, although it has proved to be one of the most authoritative. The legal institutions, Parliament and the courts can be persuaded by the arguments of others. Both administrative bodies, the EOC and the CRE, have put forward proposals for law reform.[38]

The EOC's document reacts primarily to exclusions and loopholes already exposed in the existing legislation. The CRE tackles structural and procedural faults. However, both sets of proposals seek only to make the equal opportunity model more effective.

Positive action programmes are needed which embrace changes in discriminatory employment structures and the provision of ancillary services, like specialist training and child-care provision. The present efforts of bodies like the EOC to persuade employers voluntarily to adopt positive action may provide some women with an opportunity to work. They are clearly insufficient to provide *equal* opportunities. Voluntary efforts are not co-ordinated and are extremely piecemeal. There are no legal checks on positive action programmes adopted by employers in relation to existing employees. Positive action is being sold as a 'resource tool', a method by which employers can make the most of their workforce. There appears to be no evidence that the adoption of such positive action changes the attitude of employers, or indeed of male union members, who continue to regard women as a reserve and cheap labour force. At present it seems that women are given chances when there are few suitable men or to save employers money. Unlike the United States, where court cases can result in co-ordinated and officially monitored programmes, women workers in the United Kingdom have no power to instigate positive action.

A significant reform would be to give tribunals the power to order remedial action in cases of indirect discrimination. This could change the prospects of many women and would help to disseminate the principle of positive action. Women would be given the power to take action on their own behalf and to enlist the aid of the law in their efforts to gain equality of work. They enjoy a limited power as voters exercising democratic control over those councils who have positive action programmes, but the present Government is considering abolishing many of the local authorities which have adopted such policies.[39] It seems that education and information about law reform must be vital elements in any positive action programme.

Yet there are indications that the impetus for changes which will have most effect on women workers will not come from law-making bodies. As has been shown, the root of women's inequality in paid employment is the unequal allocation of unpaid domestic functions in the home.[40] As more men share or, indeed, reverse the traditional allocation of family responsibilities, either voluntarily or because of unemployment, the perception of women as primarily unpaid domestic workers may also change. Equal access for both men and women to this domestic work is essential to any notion of true equality. For there can be no equality as long as equality of opportunity is defined exclusively in terms of the market place, paid employment and monetary compensation. The integration of both sexes into the public sphere dominated for so long by one sex inevitably means changes in the private sphere which has been the primary reserve of the other.

The Private Domain

4

Sexuality

Sexual immorality may be 'unlawful', but it is not usually criminal. The civil law regards extramarital heterosexual intercourse as unlawful by giving priority to marriage, by penalizing adultery, by discriminating against the unmarried mother and her child and by refusing to enforce contracts which promote it. The official objectives of the criminal law are much more limited:

> to preserve public order and decency, to protect the citizen from what is offensive or injurious, and to provide sufficient safeguards against exploitation or corruption of others, particularly those who are specially vulnerable because they are young, weak in body or mind, inexperienced, or in a state of special physical, official or economic dependence.[1]

Otherwise both the Wolfenden Committee in 1957 and the Criminal Law Revision Committee in its 1980 working paper[2] and 1984 report[3] on sexual offences believe that the criminal law should keep out of matters of private morality. Clearly, however, they also include protection against unwanted sexual acts among the law's objectives.

However, the present law defines and classifies sexual offences not according to the objectives of preventing aggression, protecting the vulnerable or preserving public decency but according to the nature of the sexual act committed. This inevitably results in differentiation between the sexes because the law is dealing with acts in which their physiological differences are often involved. But such differentiation is by no means inevitable or sensible. There is no insurmountable obstacle to a sex-neutral method of penalizing behaviour which is antisocial for any of those reasons, whether committed by or against a male or a female.

The main effect of the sex-based approach to definition and classification is the continuing concentration upon homosexual acts by men with men and heterosexual acts by men with women. To almost all outward appearances, the present law takes a much more serious view of the former. In most cases the maximum penalties are higher: although at present any buggery of a woman carries a higher maximum penalty than non-consensual buggery of an adult man, this is an anomaly created when male homosexuality was selectively legalized in 1967; the Criminal Law Revision Committee (CLRC) would like to see all non-consensual buggery restored to the top of the list alongside rape.[4] Similarly, many forms of male homosexual behaviour are penalized which are not criminal at all if heterosexual — for example, whenever a third party is present or soliciting or importuning takes place in public. The CLRC clearly takes a more serious view of male homosexual approaches and behaviour in public lavatories than it does of the heterosexual harassment which many women have to suffer whenever they leave home.[5] Again, the age of consent to male homosexual acts is higher, and both parties are guilty of an offence, whereas the female victim of unlawful sexual intercourse is not. The CLRC, following the Home Secretary's Policy Advisory Committee (PAC) report on the age of consent,[6] would perpetuate this distinction. Interestingly, while there are only two female members of the CLRC, five of the seven women on the PAC could see no good reason for giving boys any greater protection against premature homosexual activity than they might be given against heterosexual activity or than girls might be given against either.

Thus the law goes to some lengths to protect women against vaginal intercourse but to even greater lengths to protect men against homosexuality. Historically, at least, the explanation must lie in the extent to which male interests are threatened by both. Men are protected against attacks and approaches by other men and even women, although they do not suffer the risks of pregnancy and childbirth. The law is anxious to preserve their freedom to determine their own sexual activity. Women are protected mainly against vaginal intercourse, which does carry the risk of pregnancy and childbirth. Their interest in being so protected is certainly great, but the male interest in protecting them against it is also great. At least until the advent of reliable contraception and blood testing for paternity it was the only means of securing legitimate heirs and bargainable daughters, let alone of protecting an exclusive sexual preserve. Those interests lay only in a limited class of females, the chaste matron and the virgin spinster, their own or their peers' wives and daughters. Even Lord Simon of Glaisdale, who dissented from the majority view in *DPP* v. *Morgan* (see p. 70), was mainly concerned to protect the 'respectable woman who has been ravished', so that she could turn to the law, her virtue 'vindicated'.

There is no equivalent male interest in protecting women whom they do not think respectable. Toleration of male promiscuity has always required the *toleration* of some women who are prepared to service them. It does not require such women to be *protected*. An astonishing but extreme illustration of this was provided by police posters warning women in northern cities of the danger of the 'Yorkshire Ripper', which pointed out that he had turned his attention from prostitutes to 'innocent' women. It is only very recently, and largely as a result of the furore which greeted the *Morgan* case, that the law has begun to subject practices which discriminate between the virtuous and the non-virtuous to a more critical scrutiny. But with the advent of contraception and blood testing, it is no longer as necessary to men's interests to keep their wives and daughters virtuous. They too can benefit from the permissive society. Active condemnation can then be reserved for prostitutes, who threaten the ideal image of relationshps between the sexes in a much more fundamental way.

Neither is there any male interest in the punishment of female homosexuality. For the most part it is an unthreatening curiosity which can be placed at the bottom of the hierarchy in relation to each of the objectives of the criminal law. It is taken much more seriously in those areas of law where male interests *are* threatened by it — for example in divorce or in custody disputes between parents. This is but one example of the difficulty the law finds in looking at sexual acts from the woman's point of view. We see considerable evidence still that her needs are defined primarily in terms of the child-bearing which is also her main wifely duty. Because that is her duty and her function, the law has also tried to deter her from committing adultery, although it has stopped short of using the criminal law to do so. But it has also stopped short of using the criminal law to deter her husband from enforcing her duty by self-help.

It is not surprising that the law should have embodied these values in the past. Far more surprising is the extent to which it still does and will continue to do even if the recent recommendations of the CLRC are implemented. The CLRC has made considerable progress in suggesting the removal of the more obvious distinctions, but the basic structure can still be seen in the laws of rape and prostitution, as well as in the family law of marriage.

Sexual Aggression

The CLRC believes that both non-consensual anal intercourse (buggery) and non-consensual vaginal intercourse (rape) are 'unique' offences deserving special condemnation. It is not in favour of extending this to other forms of penetration, whether of vagina or anus by some other organ or instrument than the male penis or of mouth by penis. At present all such attacks upon women are only indecent assaults unless other injuries can be proved. Indecent assault upon a woman, whether by a man or a woman, carries a maximum of two years' imprisonment. Indecent assault upon a man, whether by a man or a woman, carries a maximum of ten. The CLRC originally suggested a uniform compromise of five years, without distinction between ordinary and aggravated acts.[7] It has now increased this to ten years but could not agree about whether, and if so how, the offence should be divided into different degrees of seriousness.[8] Clearly, a uniform offence would remove one of the most serious examples of discrimination against women's interests. But there was little support on the Committee for defining the most serious degree in terms of penetration rather than, for example, accompanying violence. This is very curious. In its working paper it had stated that the 'risk of pregnancy' was an 'important distinguishing characteristic of rape', so that other penetrations should not be included, yet it still believes that buggery should be placed on the same level as rape, even though it carries no such risk. It is difficult to resist the conclusion that the Committee is still perceiving penetration predominantly in male terms, whereas violence is something which it finds much easier to understand.

It has been said that the unique condemnation reserved for the 'true rape' may work to the victim's disadvantage, in that the jury may be deterred from convicting the guilty. The CLRC has rejected the idea of differing degrees of rape, and perhaps this is just as well. The lesser degree mentioned in its working paper[8] was mainly to cover a 'young man of previous good character' who went 'too far with a woman who had not behaved as sensibly as she *should* have done' (emphasis supplied). By a man of 'good character' it clearly meant a man with no previous criminal convictions rather than with a good moral character, for by definition he would have participated in an act of extramarital intercourse without the woman's consent. The woman, on the other hand, is implicitly condemned as a bad moral character, but for two different reasons. Earlier the Committee talked of the

> alleged victim who has willingly allowed herself to get into a situation of a kind in which a sensible woman would have appreciated the possibility that sexual intercourse might be *expected*, as for example when she has not objected to some degree of sexual familiarity or has agreed to go to a quiet place with someone whom she does not know. (Emphasis supplied)[10]

This confuses the two separate notions of 'contributory negligence' and provocation. In the former a woman who places herself in a situation where a man might rape her is apparently thought to have caused him to do so. The Lord Chancellor has stated that he does not regard this as a mitigating factor, although others clearly do.[11] In the latter a woman who allows a degree of sexual familiarity is apparently thought to have caused the man to lose his self-control, irrespective of whether or not she has indicated her willingness to proceed to intercourse. This suggests that *he* is to be the judge of whether it is reasonable to 'expect' it, for the law does not insist that he asks. The CLRC certainly believes that allowing intimacy just short of intercourse is substantial mitigation, although not in theory a complete excuse.[12]

The Court of Appeal avoided mentioning either contributory negligence or provocation when laying down guidelines for sentencing in rape cases in *R.* v. *Roberts*.[13] Rape is always a serious crime, which will merit an immediate custodial sentence 'other than in wholly exceptional circumstances'. Aggravating features are the use of a weapon to frighten or injure, serious physical or mental injury to the victim, violence over and above that necessarily involved in the act itself, brutal threats, further sexual indignities or perversions, the youth or age of the victim, intrusion into the home, deprivation of liberty, 'gang bangs' or a series of rapes by one man, and abuse of trust. Significantly, the case involved a husband who had forced his wife to have intercourse with his uncle. The court regarded this as a serious breach of trust: if only others would display a similar attitude to the men who abuse the trust involved in accepting the offer of a lift home after a party. The court made another important point. The husband had deliberately used his uncle in order to degrade his wife. One of his grounds of appeal against a sentence of five years' imprisonment was that his wife had stayed away at another man's home for some days, leading him to believe her unfaithful. 'It seems to the court,' said the Lord Chief Justice, 'to be an extraordinary process of thought which regards this as some excuse for abetting rape'.

Roberts appears to be a significant move away from both the traditional ideas of contributory negligence and provocation. It will be interesting to see whether it has any effect upon the sentencing patterns found by Walmsley and White.[14] Custodial sentences were least likely if victims and offenders were well-known to one another, but these included some minor participants in the offence. Heavier sentences were more likely if they were strangers or well-known to one another than if they were casual acquaintances. The heaviest sentences were most likely to be imposed if they were strangers. The cases involving casual acquaintances were probably those in which the victim was most likely to be thought contributorily negligent or provocative, although the well-known may have included some of these. Only if they were total strangers could neither excuse easily be put forward.

The CLRC's concern to preserve the unique concept of 'true rape' shows also in its discussion of consent. Rape is to have unlawful sexual intercourse with a woman who at the time does not consent to it.[15] According to the Court of Appeal in *R. v. Olugboja*,[16] force or the threat of force is not necessary. Nor is mere submission to be equated with consent. Consent involves submission, but submission does not necessarily involve consent. Consent itself can range from actual desire to reluctant acquiescence, but it is a matter of fact for the jury where consent ends and mere submission without consent begins. The jury could find that the woman had not consented when she had been tricked into going to the home of two men, been raped by one of them and was to be kept there until she had intercourse with the other, even though she took her trousers down without the use or threat of force against her. This again is an important advance. *Force* is a male threat which *men* fear. There are many other less explicit ways in which men can cause women to fear them.

The CLRC agrees that the criterion should be absence of consent rather than presence of dissent, so that a man who takes advantage of a sleeping or drunken woman may be convicted. It has also been persuaded that, as at present, consent should be invalidated if the woman has been deceived as to the nature of the act or the identity of the actor. This is a welcome change of mind from its working paper suggestion that 'sexual intercourse induced by threats (other than threats of force) or other intimidation or by fraud should not be rape',[17] although procuring it by such means should be a separate offence punishable with up to five years' imprisonment. Recognizing that mistakes of identity invalidate consent reflects an important female dimension of intercourse. To men intercourse may be satisfying no matter who the woman is. For women the identity of the person is crucial to the nature of the act. Even if the law were concerned only about the risks of pregnancy, as opposed to the serious violation of the woman's integrity and personality, this must be obvious. Unfortunately, the Committee appears less sympathetic to the distinction between consent and submission drawn in *Olugboja*, for it suggests that only threats of force against the woman or another person which, 'taking a reasonable view', are capable of being carried out immediately should invalidate consent.[18] It does not like the idea of leaving it to the jury to decide whether her submission involved consent or not. This could herald a return to the threats which *men* understand rather than an attempt to appreciate the state of mind of the individual woman involved.

The Sexual Offences (Amendment) Act 1976 also requires that the man must either *know* that the woman does not consent or be *reckless* as to whether she does so (section 1(1)(*b*)). This was thought to reproduce the decision of the House of Lords in *DPP* v. *Morgan*,[19] that the man must not only intend to have intercourse but must also intend to have it without the woman's consent or be indifferent as to whether or not she consents. The majority also decided that a man cannot intend to have intercourse without the woman's consent if he believes that she has consented, even if he has no reasonable grounds for his belief. The minority held that he could displace the prosecution evidence of such an intent only by showing reasonable grounds for his belief. Curiously, one member of the majority and one member of the minority would have preferred to decide the case the other way, but each felt constrained by previous case law. As Lord Cross, in the majority, remarked,[20] 'There is nothing unreasonable in the law requiring a citizen to take reasonable care to ascertain the facts relevant to his avoiding doing a prohibited act', especially when he is engaged in the enterprise of intercourse with a woman who is not his wife. After all, he only has to *ask*. Yet, as Chambers and Millar found when studying the practice of the Scottish police investigating rape, 'There was a noticeable failure to formulate the issue of consent in bipartisan terms, that is, as one which also imposed certain obligations on the men prior to intercourse.'[21] Where some intimacy had been permitted, 'A change of mind, in effect saying no, was not seen as an acceptable course of action.'[22] A related consideration is that the higher proportion of acquittals in rape cases is the result of the higher proportion of not guilty pleas.[23] There are very few circumstances in which the defence of consent cannot at least be tried.

However, the majority view in *Morgan* seemed at the time to be more consistent with the subjective principles of criminal liability advanced in the academic textbooks upon which we had all been brought up, and feminist lawyers were inclined to accept it. Since then the House of Lords has turned its attention to the concept of recklessness. A person may be reckless not only when he is aware of a possible risk and decides to ignore it but also when he is indifferent or gives no thought to the matter at all.[24] Not only that, but the risks to which he is expected to turn his mind are those which would have been obvious to the 'ordinary prudent individual'[25] even if not to him personally.[26] This concept is very difficult to distinguish from negligence. If it can be applied to arson and to causing death by reckless driving, can it also be applied to rape?

On one view, these decisions should have disposed of *Morgan*: either the man knew that she was not consenting or if the ordinary prudent individual would have realized she was not, he ought to have done so. In *R.* v. *Pigg*[27] the Court of Appeal stated:

> a man is reckless if either he was indifferent and gave no thought to the possibility that the woman might not be consenting in circumstances where if any thought had been given to the matter it would have been obvious that there was a risk that she was not or he was aware of the possibility that she might not be consenting but nevertheless persisted regardless of whether she consented or not.

This passage comes immediately after a quotation from *Lawrence* in which the 'ordinary prudent individual' test appears. Archbold asserts that it is clear that the court meant 'if any thought had been given to the matter by the ordinary prudent individual'.[28]

However, as Temkin points out, *Pigg* did not cover the man who does think about whether a woman is consenting and carelessly concludes that she is.[29] The absurd consequence might thus be that a man who thinks about the matter and reaches a conclusion that no reasonable man would have reached is not guilty, but a man who does not think about it at all is guilty even if he would have reached a different conclusion from the ordinary prudent individual had he done so. Furthermore, academics who are opposed to the development of *Caldwell* recklessness argued against its application and extension in the context of rape. The Court of Appeal has recently adopted the view and limited reckless rape to the man who 'couldn't care less'.[30] *Morgan* is still good law. Indeed, the CLRC wishes further to limit the concept of reckless rape to the man who either knew that she might not be consenting or did not believe that she was consenting.[31] Thus, while it is important to see a decision like *Morgan* in the context of a continuing debate among the higher judiciary and academic lawyers about the philosophical basis of criminal liability in general, two things are clear. One is that there is no insuperable objection in principle to imposing an objective duty of care 'to ascertain the facts relevant to his avoiding doing a prohibited act'. The other is that some lawyers are even more unhappy about imposing such a duty in the case of rape than they are in the case of other offences.

Marital Rape

Far and away the most important remaining aspect of a wife's legal subjection to her husband is that he cannot be prosecuted for raping her. He may be prosecuted for any accompanying assault, even if this was no more than necessary to achieve his object,[32] but unless he causes her actual or grievous bodily harm apart from the intercourse itself and its effects,[33] she would have to bring a private prosecution for the minor offence of common assault. The statutory definition of rape (see p. 69) refers only to 'unlawful' (that is, extramarital) intercourse, but it is assumed that earlier cases hold good. These remove the husband's protection once there has been a decree of judicial separation,[34] decree nisi of divorce[35] or anti-molestation injunction[36] or agreement. The same would probably apply to a magistrates' order excluding the husband from the home but not to a personal protection order which prohibits only violence or the threat of violence. But there is no protection for the wife who is living apart from her husband under some other form of order or without any order at all, still less for the wife who is still living with him.

The arguments which are advanced against a change in the law are curiously weak.[37] Two of them are inconsistent. On the one hand it is said that marital rape will be difficult to prove, while on the other it is said that the threat of unjustified proceedings may be used by a wife to blackmail her husband into a favourable settlement at the ending of their marriage. The difficulties of proving rape are indeed formidable, particularly where the woman knows her assailant well; and if they are likely to deter her from prosecuting, they are equally likely to deter her from threatening it improperly or her husband from succumbing to such threats. There is no reason why the difficulties of proving antisocial behaviour should make us any less ready to acknowledge it as a crime. Two other objections assert that the criminal law should not intervene in marital relationships and that the wife will be adequately protected by her matrimonial remedies. The second cannot be right for, as the CLRC itself points out,[38] matrimonial remedies no longer depend upon considerations of conduct alone, even if all courts could be relied upon to regard a single act of marital rape in the same serious light. Even if they could, the damage would already have been done (as the CLRC again realized, this was an insuperable objection to its proposed replacement of criminal with civil sanctions against intercourse with severely mentally handicapped people).[39] The belief that the criminal law has no place in family relationships could equally be applied to familial violence. At bottom, it is a plea to the wife to put her responsibility to preserve the family unit above her wish to preserve the integrity of her person:

> Spouses have responsibilities towards one another and to any children there may be as well as having rights against each other. If a wife could invoke the law of rape in all circumstances in which the husband forced her to have sexual intercourse without her consent, the consequences for any children could be grave, and for the wife too.[40]

The fact that the victim may suffer as much as, if not more than, the aggressor does not normally inhibit the criminal law from condemning antisocial behaviour, and it will certainly be another factor deterring her from the hasty action which is so much feared. But although hasty action is deplored, so also is the risk that the victim may change her mind, which again has been much favoured as a reason for failing to respond to violence against women in their homes. The evidence on this is debatable, but in any event the fact that some may withdraw is no reason to deny the law's protection to those who continue to want it or to the much greater number whose husbands may be deterred by the knowledge that raping their wives would be a crime.

The real reason for opposing a change in the law is the difficulty which many seem to find in believing that it is indeed so dreadful for a husband to rape his wife that he should be called a criminal for doing it.[41] After all, she did once wish to have intercourse with him and may do so again. If they are still living together and sharing a bed, can he not be allowed to use a little persuasion upon her for the sake of their marriage? In the nullity case of *G.* v. *G.*[42] Lord Dunedin permitted himself to wish that the husband had used some 'gentle violence' instead of acquiescing in his wife's refusals. In *Baxter* v. *Baxter* (see p. 84) the Court of Appeal actually refused a decree because the husband had not insisted, although the House of Lords disagreed.[43]

This argument appears to have caused the CLRC to change its mind between working paper and report. In 1980 a majority thought that wives should no longer be so subject to their husbands or in a position less favourable than that of unmarried cohabitants. Nevertheless, they believed that the consent of the Director of Public Prosecutions (DPP) should be required as a check upon prosecutions which were 'not desirable in the public interest'.[44] What they meant by this was not explained. By 1984 all were agreed that the husband's exemption should go once the couple were no longer living together; but as they could not find an acceptable definition of this, they were divided as to whether the law should stay as it is or whether the exemption should be abandoned altogether. A narrow majority favoured leaving it as it is, and even most of those who wished it to go would have required the consent of the DPP to prosecution.

The majority view is clearly based on the perceived need to preserve the unique character of the 'true rape'. Although the Committee will happily contemplate an offence of indecent assault ranging from a small stroke to violent oral intercourse, it finds it hard to contemplate an offence of rape which includes intercourse between husband and wife. Yet if, as the Committee elsewhere asserts, the unique gravity of rape lies in the risk of pregnancy and childbirth, the most serious objection to the marital rape exemption ought to have been apparent. Before the advent of reliable contraception, it could effectively force a wife to bear her husband's children. Even today, unless she is a suitable candidate for oral contraceptives or an intra-uterine device, it allows him to proceed without waiting for her to take the precautions which are safest for women but which he may dislike. This objection may carry little weight with people who see a woman's prime vocation as bearing children, and particularly her husband's children. From the woman's point of view, she may indeed have the same ambitions, but she might prefer it if the law left to her the decision as to whether and when. As with the decision to prosecute, however, the law remains curiously reluctant to allow women to take responsibility for their own lives.

Problems of Proof

All persons accused of crime are presumed innocent unless and until the prosecution adduces evidence which satisfies the court beyond reasonable doubt that they are guilty. But the law gives extra protection to those who are accused of sexual offences. Corroboration of the complainant's evidence is essential to conviction in only a few offences which are rarely charged, but in all sexual cases the jury must be warned in plain language that it is dangerous to convict on the evidence of the complainant alone. Provided that this warning is given, the jury may convict without corroboration if it is sure that she is telling the truth, but it is the judge's duty to go through the evidence explaining what is capable of corroborating her account and what is not.[45] Such reinforced scepticism must have an effect on the outcome of many trials.

Complainants in sexual cases are the only group singled out as inherently unreliable because of the nature of the offence rather than their own characteristics. It cannot be a coincidence that this is the one class of offence in which complainants are predominantly female and defendants overwhelmingly male. The standard direction approved by the Court of Appeal in *R. v. Henry and Manning*[46] explains that 'experience has shown that female complainants have told false stories for various reasons, and sometimes for no reason at all.' Archbold now tactfully advises that 'it would be wise to omit the word "female" when giving the direction',[47] but the assumptions underlying this continuing discrimination remain the same.[48]

It may be thought that the complainant has a greater personal interest in the outcome of the case than have other prosecution witnesses: that she may cry rape to cover up the voluntary loss of her virginity or to extract an unpaid fee. Such fears are in any event the product of male definitions of female virtue. Nor do they reveal interests any greater than those of many other victims of alleged crimes, such as the over-enthusiastic club 'bouncer' who accuses the person he has attacked of having attacked him first, or the driver who is seeking to protect his no-claims discount. The plaintiff in any civil claim has a much greater personal stake in the outcome than does any prosecution witness. Can it be a coincidence that the only civil case in which corroboration is required as a matter of law is where the mother of an illegitimate child gives evidence against the father in affiliation proceedings?

It may also be argued that sexual cases are typically cases of 'her word against mine', for there may be no obvious damage. Yet cases abound where courts have to decide between two competing accounts of the same events for which no independent evidence can be provided — for example, where the police allege public order offences committed in crowds. In sexual cases the warning must still be given when there is no dispute that the offence took place but only as to the identity of the assailant, and even where the evidence of identity comes from someone other than the complainant.[49] Similarly, the Law Commission has felt able to recommend the abolition of the corroboration requirement in affiliation cases now that there is a 97 per cent chance of disproving a wrongful accusation of paternity by blood tests, a chance of absolute proof which is far higher than in most cases, whether civil or criminal.[50]

The real reason for the rule must therefore be the inherent unreliability of women, 'the danger that fantasy may supplant or supplement genuine recollection',[51] as it may with children. Susan Edwards has traced an interesting connection between the development of Freudian analytic theory and the explanations given in textbooks on the law of evidence, beginning in the United States and spreading here.[52] The evidence to support the 'experience' of female complainants upon which the rule relies is remarkably difficult to find.[53] Chambers and Millar found the belief in false accusation to be common among Scottish police officers; when challenged, however, the officers could produce few concrete examples.[54] If it arises simply because the police or the court have not believed a woman's story, it is a self-fulfilling prophecy. Chambers and Millar also found that many regarded the *absence* of a swift complaint to the police as an indication of a false accusation, yet the *presence* of such a complaint cannot in law amount to corroboration.

There are other ways of casting doubt upon a woman's testimony. Before 1976 the complainant in a rape case could be asked questions about her sexual relationships with other men, but traditionally the law drew a vital distinction.[55] An allegation which was relevant to an issue in the case, almost invariably consent, might be not only put to the complainant but also supported by defence evidence if she denied it. This rule was limited to allegations of 'notorious bad character', which originally meant only prostitution. If a woman was in the habit of agreeing to intercourse with total strangers for money, it could suggest that she had done so again, or at least that the defendant had thought so. There were suggestions that the rule might extend from prostitution to promiscuity in *R.* v. *Krausz*,[56] but only if she had shown a total lack of discrimination in her previous partners. Allegations of previous relationships with other men falling short of this could also be made, but these were not thought relevant to the issue of consent: 'The question in issue being whether or not a criminal attempt has been made upon her by A, evidence that she has previously had connection with B and C is *obviously not in point*' (emphasis supplied).[57] Accordingly, they were relevant only to the issue of her credibility, and the defence could not call evidence to rebut her denials.

Women and juries cannot have appreciated the law's distinction. However carefully directed, the jury must have thought that the questions *were* relevant to consent. Indeed, that was why counsel asked them. These days it is certainly not obvious that a woman is less credible in the witness box simply because she .has had sexual relationships outside marriage. The implicit suggestion was, 'Well, there you are, members of the jury: that is the sort of girl she is.'[58] In other words, if she has done it before, she will do it again, and in any event she is not worthy of the law's protection. In practice, this suggestion could often be made without running the risk that the prosecution might be allowed to make a counter-attack upon the character of the accused. Generally, if the accused attacks the character of a prosecution witness, his own character may be attacked in turn. Simply to allege that the woman consented in a rape case is not treated as an attack upon her character.[59] This does not necessarily extend to the sort of attack which is based upon allegations of intercourse with *other* men. However, the Heilbron Advisory Group on the Law of Rape[60] had evidence that in practice it was widely interpreted, and the accused was allowed to go to considerable lengths in cross-examination without putting his own character in issue. The Court of Appeal gave apparent approval to this in *R. v. Krausz.*[61]

Heilbron took the view that a woman's previous sexual relationships with other men were quite irrelevant to her credibility and hardly ever relevant to the issue of consent. Evidence of them should be allowed only when her behaviour on a previous occasion was 'strikingly similar' to that alleged by the defence on the occasion of the alleged offence or where she had been put forward by the prosecution as a woman of unblemished chastity. If she could not be attacked, it would not matter that the accused could not be attacked in return. Parliament, however, rejected the precise limits proposed by Heilbron in favour of a much vaguer rule. Evidence cannot be adduced or questions asked about any sexual experience of a complainant with a person other than the accused without the judge's leave. That leave 'shall be granted if and only if he is satisfied that it would be unfair to the defendant to refuse it' (1976 Act, Section 2(1) and (2)).

This has had an effect very different from that envisaged by Heilbron. In the leading case of *R. v. Viola*[62] the Court of Appeal distinguished between 'questions which went merely to credit and no more' and 'questions which are relevant to an issue in the trial'. The Act was intended to cut out the former, in particular the sort of 'fishing expeditions' designed to cast general aspersions upon the complainant. Although the court was reluctant to lay down any hard and fast rule, however, the latter must normally be allowed because they might cause the jury to change its mind about her evidence.[63] Indeed, if a question is thought relevant to an issue at the trial, the judge will surely have no choice, for it must be unfair to the accused to exclude it. There may be a grey area between relevance to credit and relevance to issue, but once the judge has made up his mind on which side the question lies, there cannot logically be any discretion. Some judges may be prepared to keep to the old ideas about what is relevant to consent or to limit themselves to the Heilbron ideas on the same subject. The facts of *Viola* were of the 'similar behaviour' type envisaged by Heilbron. But there is ample evidence from the observations of Zsuzsanna Adler at the Old Bailey that others are now taking a broad view of what may indicate consent.[64] Lord Coleridge's view that 'connection with B and C' is 'obviously not in point' may have given way to a rule which has actually extended rather than restricted the scope for such questioning.

The risk of this questioning is one of the many reasons why rape victims are reluctant to complain to the police. The police clearly regard it as their duty to test such complaints more rigorously than those of other victims of alleged offences.[65] They may indulge in just the sort of fishing expedition which the 1976 Act was designed to prevent. Nor are they immune from the ideas of contributory negligence or provocation which have been current in the courts. Walmsley and White found that 50 per cent of convicted rapists were strangers to their victims, 27 per cent casual acquaintances and 23 per cent well known. Yet the London rape crisis centre figures for victims who approached them indicated that a majority of assailants were known to their victims.[66] Can it be that such cases are less often reported to the police, or less often prosecuted by them, or less often convicted in court? The parallel with their figures for sentencing is more than interesting. It all contributes to the picture of a legal system which combines a high degree of protection in theory with a rather more selective degree of protection in practice.

Public Order and Decency

The official explanation for laws against soliciting or prostitution no longer rests upon morality but upon the preservation of public decency, the protection of the citizen against offence and the protection of the prostitute against exploitation. Once again, however, we see how far those laws still reflect the male interests we have defined. Far more protection is given to men against the possible offence caused by homosexual approaches, and even by some heterosexual approaches, than is given to women against any sort of approach at all. Male soliciting or importuning for immoral purposes in a public place carries a heavier maximum penalty than the street offences of the female 'common prostitute'. It is not limited to known prostitutes or to soliciting for the purposes of prostitution. It *is* limited to soliciting for homosexual purposes, unless the man was accosting girls below the age of consent.[67] The female common prostitute may be prosecuted for soliciting men for heterosexual purposes or even for loitering in order to do so. Neither of these offences requires any proof of annoyance. Yet there is no specific offence of soliciting or accosting women either for heterosexual or for homosexual purposes.

There are two obvious ways of removing the discrimination. One would be to abolish all soliciting offences and rely upon the public order, highway or road traffic offences which are arguably sufficient to cover all its objectionable aspects. Police forces who have wanted to curb the 'kerb crawler' have already found methods of doing so. The other solution would be to define a single offence. The CLRC has done neither.[68] It believes that *any* male soliciting for homosexual purposes should remain an offence because it is 'liable to cause serious annoyance, particularly to the person accosted'.[69] Apparently they do not believe that soliciting females is liable to cause such serious annoyance that it should receive blanket condemnation. They do put forward ideas for a new offence of 'kerb crawling'. This would be limited to soliciting from cars, and only in such a way as to cause fear or annoyance or possibly for the purpose of prostitution.

This might prove a more satisfactory solution to both of the evils at which the Street Offences Act 1959 is aimed. The Act's main alleged justification is the nuisance or annoyance caused to other people in the neighbourhood and in particular to the 'respectable' women there. Yet it is the prostitutes' clients who cause the nuisance to other women. Preventing kerb crawlers from causing them fear and annoyance would certainly be a possible solution to this. Any nuisance to the neighbourhood which may be caused by the practice of prostitution in the area might also be better tackled by measures aimed at the prostitutes' clients rather than at the prostitutes themselves. This certainly seems to be the experience of those places which have tried to do this.

There are many other objections to the Street Offences Act, which cannot be cured simply by extending it to male heterosexual prostitutes or by removing the pejorative adjective 'common'. The offence relies solely on the evidence of police officers, both as to the soliciting or loitering and as to the fact that the accused is a common prostitute. The court is bound to know that she is a prostitute because this is part of the offence itself. If the system of cautioning that was agreed to before the Act was passed is carried out, the court will also assume that this is by no means the first time. Such a system might have been designed to encourage the development of ground rules under which known prostitutes are regularly brought before the court for routine condemnation and financial penalties, irrespective of the actual facts, and under rather more serious threats should they fail to co-operate. Nor are the penalties only financial. The power to imprison for the offence itself was removed in 1982, but if a prostitute is fined, she will have to choose between earning the money to pay the fine or going to prison in default. If she goes to prison, her children will probably have to go into care. Once they are in care, there is certainly a risk that the local authority will assume parental rights because of her 'habits and mode of life'.[70]

In fact, there is little evidence that the police succumb to the Act's temptation to abuse it in a serious manner. There is more indication that the prostitutes themselves accept routine arrest as a fact of life.[71] It is highly doubtful whether the Act has any other effect than the expression of public disapproval, for the practice of prostitution itself is lawful and prostitutes do not regard themselves as real criminals. Yet the CLRC is reluctant to make radical changes, and some members were obviously opposed to the removal of the power to imprison for the offence.

The Act is only one of the ways in which the law operates to condemn the prostitute and her prostitution without outlawing the trade as such. Indeed, the CLRC gave serious consideration to proposals for shifting its exploitation from the underworld to the state. The law also purports to condemn the exploitation of prostitutes. Yet by making it almost impossible to carry on the trade in a lawful fashion it can drive the prostitute into the hands of unscrupulous individuals and organized crime. In practice, a great deal more attention is devoted to enforcing the Street Offences Act against one section of the trade than against the equally unlawful activities of the less obvious sections who work through contact magazines, clubs and saunas, or hotels.

In theory the law prohibits almost all methods of contacting clients. The prostitute cannot solicit in the open, or even in view of the open, or through a directory or contact magazine. The former offend against the Street Offences Act and the latter against the common law offence of conspiracy to corrupt public morals discovered by the House of Lords only shortly afterwards.[72] 'Discreet' advertising is favoured by the CLRC. In theory the law also makes it difficult for a prostitute to find premises. If she shares with another, they may be prosecuted for running a brothel, and their landlord will also be at risk. If she rents a place on her own, she runs no risk herself, but her landlord does so if he lets the room for that purpose or charges her an inflated rent, and in either event he may not be entitled to recover the rent by legal process. It is well known that debts which cannot be recovered by legal process are often collected in less orthodox ways. Together these provisions prevent two or three prostitutes from sharing for mutual comfort and protection, as many would wish to do. The CLRC would keep the offences of managing, letting or permitting premises to be used for prostitution, except where they are used as both a home and a business by only one or two prostitutes. This is certainly a step in the right direction, although it would create a new offence of letting business premises to a single prostitute and would encourage others to work from home in residential areas.[73] There is every reason to believe that this is what many of them do already.[74] In theory the law also makes it virtually impossible for the prostitute to carry on any sort of normal life outside working hours or to establish more conventional relationships if she wishes. Any man who lives with or is habitually seen with her is presumed to be living on her immoral earnings. The CLRC would like to see this presumption go, but it is reluctant to draft a general offence of coercion and exploitation to replace the present offences aimed at the pimp, the ponce and the madam. Instead it suggests offences of controlling, directing, organizing or arranging prostitution for gain. This would perpetuate the law's present focus upon the commercial exploitation of *prostitution* rather than the coercion or exploitation of the *prostitutes themselves*. The CLRC has undoubtedly been listening to the voice of the prostitutes' campaigns, but it is not surprising that its approach should remain bounded by the framework of the current law.

The current law is still trying to balance the need to control the activities of the woman who sells her sexual services commercially, rather than in the more orthodox fashion, against the need to preserve the convenience of having a class of women who are prepared to do this. But it goes deeper than that. Female prostitution challenges the gender order in a fundamental way. All the other methods whereby a woman exchanges her sexual services for financial reward take place within a familial, non-commercial context. The woman usually becomes dependent upon the man for her support. She may also be expected to bear his children. This will usually ensure that she is unable to compete in the outside world on equal terms. Whatever the reason why an individual woman resorts to prostitution, for many it is undoubtedly the only way to earn a good living in a man's world while retaining their independence.

It is also important to see the greater condemnation of the prostitute which resulted from the Street Offences Act of 1959 alongside the so-called permissive society which developed during the 1960s. This not only encouraged women to adopt traditional relationships without their traditional compensations but also encouraged the further exploitation of women's bodies for masculine profit as well as entertainment. While the Street Offences Act was increasing the censorship of women who exploited their own bodies for profit, the Obscene Publications Act 1964 and the repeal of the Theatres Act were reducing almost to vanishing point the censorship of others who sought to do so. Women are now beginning to realize that allowing them equal freedom to pursue their own sexual activities is one thing, but conniving at the horrifying abuse and degradation involved in most pornography is something quite different. Even if the recent debate about the boom in video 'nasties' has focused mainly on the threat to children rather than on the exploitation of women which they reveal, women are now beginning to protest on their own behalf as well as that of their children. Their role in bringing about the introduction of the local authority power to control the activities of 'sex shops' in the Local Government (Miscellaneous Provisions) Act 1982 is an interesting case in point.

Sex and Marriage

Traditional family law reflected male interests just as clearly as did the criminal law. Hence Parliament first began to intervene in the indissoluble marital union decreed by the Church by granting private Acts of divorce against adulterous wives in order to continue the succession to peerages in the male line. Other very rich husbands were later able to take advantage of the same principle and procedure. During the nineteenth century four private Acts were passed in favour of wives, but all depended upon more than their husbands' adultery. In 1857 the Lord Chancellor explained why:

> A wife might, without any loss of caste, and possibly with reference to the interests of her children, or even of her husband, condone an act of adultery on the part of her husband but the husband could not condone a similar act on the part of a wife...the adultery of the wife might be a means of palming spurious offspring upon the husband, while the adultery of the husband could have no such effect with regard to the wife. [75]

These same values were embodied in the Matrimonial Causes Act of 1857. A husband could divorce his wife for a single act of ordinary sexual intercourse outside marriage, whereas the wife had to show not only the intercourse but also some aggravating feature. This double standard in the grounds for divorce persisted until 1923. On the other hand, the wife could also divorce her husband for acts of unnatural sexual intercourse. Wives could not be divorced for infidelities other than ordinary intercourse until it became possible to treat them as cruelty after 1937.[76] The order of importance was thus almost exactly the same as that revealed by the criminal law.

Furthermore, save among those of more than independent means, a finding of adultery has always had more serious consequences for a wife. It has been a reason for depriving her of the custody of her children, even though this has conflicted with the value attached to mothering for a child. This persisted until the 1970s. It has also been a reason for depriving her of any economic recompense for the state of dependence produced by marriage and motherhood, irrespective of its relevance to the current marital problems. This was enshrined in the law of maintenance during marriage until 1981, although it retreated much earlier from the law of divorce. It has never entirely disappeared and is currently reappearing fast. Its reappearance is associated with the idea that maintenance is primarily the price which the guilty husband has to pay for his release. Even if that were so, the cost to him is not the same as the cost to her. Similarly, the belated emergence of the wife's right to sue for enticement should be compared with the husband's long-standing claim for damages against an adulterer for loss of his wife. These recognized her economic *value* to her husband, both in her fortune and in her services as housekeeper, wife and mother. They also recognized the injury to his feelings, the blow to his honour and the hurt to his family life.[77] Both actions were abolished only in 1970.

Between the parties themselves the law has shown more sympathy for the sexual needs and failings of husbands than for those of wives. This became apparent after 1937, when cruelty and desertion were added to the grounds for divorce, and the courts were able to develop a coherent doctrine of marital rights and duties. Women were still supposed (perhaps in both senses of the word) to be uninterested in sex for its own sake. A woman could complain of her husband's *excessive* sexual demands.[78] She might also be excused an 'invincible repugnance' to intercourse which distressed her as much as her husband.[79] She could not be excused her marital duties simply because she disliked her husband, or felt that he was not providing her with adequate support, or feared that the consequences might interfere with her attempts to support herself through her own career.[80] Yet a wife might not be allowed to complain even of an unjustified refusal of intercourse by her husband,[81] still less of a refusal which stemmed from sexual incompatibility and an inability to satisfy her.[82]

These cases might have been explained by the then prevailing doctrine that cruelty had to be 'aimed at' the other spouse. When that doctrine was abandoned in 1963, however, the discrimination became even clearer. A deliberate refusal by a wife who had no invincible repugnance to sex could certainly be condemned,[83] but so could an involuntary frigidity which stemmed from an unconquerable fear of childbirth.[84] A husband, on the other hand, could be condemned where his refusal was clearly unjustified[85] but not where he was simply under-sexed or uninterested.[86] On similar lines, the Court of Appeal refused to find a husband refusal was clearly unjustified[85] but not where he was simply under-sexed or uninterested.[86] On similar lines, the Court of Appeal refused to find a husband guilty of wilful refusal to consummate the marriage where he had suffered a 'loss of ardour' for a wife who had gone through an operation in order to enable them to do so.[87] The courts' sympathy for husbands who are unable to satisfy their wives' sexuality or, more properly, their lack of sympathy for the sexual needs of wives, has persisted into the modern law of divorce.[88] Interestingly, although it could just as easily be argued that neither a wife nor a husband can these days be expected to live with a spouse who is sexually incompatible, Bromley argues that the discrimination would be better avoided by extending equal sympathy to under-sexed wives.[89]

It seems clear that the law has still not entirely abandoned a sexual stereotype which is based upon the need to confine a wife's sexuality to her proper sphere of bearing her husband's children and a deep reluctance to recognize those other dimensions which are taken for granted in men. It takes pride of place, of course, when we come to the law's approach to fertility and childbirth.

5

Motherhood

Bearing children is the only experience which inevitably differentiates women from men. For many of us it is a uniquely satisfying experience even if it is not altogether enjoyable. It is a crucial part of our identity which we cannot ignore even supposing we would wish to do so. Because of this, as Ann Oakley has said, 'how reproduction is managed and controlled is inseparable from how women are managed and controlled.'[1] This applies both to those of us who wish to have a child and to those of us who do not. The control of childbirth is as important as the control of conception. Hitherto feminists have placed a great deal more emphasis on the control of conception, but this is natural enough. It is not only, in Glen Petrie's words, that 'the realization of an effective, cheap method of contraception readily available to women, to free them from the fear of repeated pregnancies, provides a more credible basis for progress towards genuine liberty' than the right to own property,[2] for that may only set us free to compete in a man's world. For many of us it is a matter of life and death. Advances in living standards and medical care are not the only reason why maternal deaths fell from one in every 250 live babies in 1915 to one in every 7,000 today. Seventeen per cent of the deaths which took place in the years 1973—5 were the result of 'hypertensive diseases of pregnancy', for which there is ameliorative treatment but still no prevention or cure.[3] Women who suffer from those diseases and others which make child-bearing dangerous have an urgent need to control their own fertility. Nevertheless, there is an equally important dimension in the control of the process of child-bearing itself. After child-bearing, of course, comes child-rearing, which is not biologically determined. Both men and women can experience its sorrows and its joys. But that has not prevented the society in which we live from apportioning the task between them in a peculiarly rigid way. It is also a way which makes the female portion of that task particularly vulnerable to outside control.

In this chapter, then, we shall be concerned mainly with two themes. One is the way in which the law and legal institutions have defined women primarily as child-bearers and child-rearers, a theme also of the previous chapter. Perhaps more important, however, has been the way in which the law has contributed to the control of those functions, at first by the woman's husband and later by the growing army of professional experts in childbirth and child care whose authority the courts have legitimated. Much of that control has been advanced in the name of children and their needs. We should be the last to deny that children have needs which both their parents have a duty to supply. In the past the law was content to allow the father to determine these, save in the very gravest cases of neglect or abandonment of duty. Now the initiative has passed elsewhere. At no point can we apply to mothers what was once said of fathers: 'The law does not interfere because of the great trust and faith it has in the natural affection of the father to perform his duties, and therefore gives him corresponding rights...The rights of a father are sacred rights because his duties are sacred duties.'[4] Sacred motherhood is a different concept.

Fertility and the Rights of Husbands

The law has contributed as much as any other social institution to the attempt to confine child-bearing within marriage. However, while it has shown considerable sympathy for the wife whose husband refuses to allow her to fulfil her natural functions, it has also imposed a duty upon her to do so. This notion that a husband has a right to the reproductive services of his wife, combined with his undoubted common law right to the possession of her child, have no doubt contributed to the control which the medical profession were prepared to concede to him over the process of childbirth before they took it over themselves.

Most of the English case law has concentrated upon contraception. Once wilful refusal (as opposed to inability) to consummate a marriage became a ground for annulling it in 1937, the Court of Appeal decided that barrier methods of contraception and even premarital vasectomy prevented consummation, so that the spouse concerned would be guilty of wilful refusal.[5] These decisions were in favour of wives who wanted to have their husband's children. Fortunately for those who did not, however, they were overruled by the House of Lords in *Baxter* v. *Baxter*.[6] This merely shifted the debate to the grounds for divorce. There is a long string of cases holding husbands at fault for denying their wives' natural functions through insisting on coitus interruptus,[7] or refusing intercourse despite the wife's pleas that she could 'not stand doing half the job of being a wife to you',[8] or having a vasectomy without her consent.[9]

Where the wife did *not* wish to have children, the courts were originally sympathetic to those who were afraid to do so. In *Fowler* v. *Fowler*[10] Lord Justice Denning observed that a court could easily infer that a husband who took contraceptive measures against his wife's wishes intended to inflict misery upon her, but that a wife's insistence might be due to a fear of childbirth. Once the need for such an intention disappeared, even the fearful could be divorced. The courts had very little sympathy for the wife who had no such fear but simply wished to put other interests first. In *Forbes* v. *Forbes*[11] the wife was far more interested in her painting career and had been evasive about having children before they were married. The husband, who found her 'cold-blooded preparations' repulsive, was granted a divorce. Sympathy for the husband who not only wanted children but also wanted intercourse to be pleasant for him, irrespective of whether it was pleasant for his wife, was evident.

Some decisions can, of course, be explained by the need to find fault-based grounds on which to dissolve a marriage which was obviously dead, but the consistency of the courts' approach through all these cases is astounding. Now that fault is no longer a necessary ingredient, it might be thought unreasonable to expect either spouse to live with the other where one of them wished to use contraception and the other did not. Yet in *Archard* v. *Archard*[12] the wife was advised by her doctor to avoid pregnancy after a miscarriage, while the husband was advised by his priest that it was sinful to have intercourse with a woman who used artificial contraceptives. The wife was denied a divorce on the basis that *both* of them were behaving reasonably. Later cases have emphasized that it is the effect of the respondent's behaviour, rather than the behaviour itself, which must be unreasonable. Such a wife might get her divorce today unless perhaps she had no such obviously valid reason for wishing to avoid conception.

The attitude of divorce courts, however, cannot explain the traditional medical belief that a husband had a right to prevent his wife from being sterilized or given contraceptive treatment. His powers of physical coercion lasted only until 1891, and it is doubtful whether they ever gave him power to licence or forbid what would otherwise be assaults by third parties.[13] A more convincing explanation might have been the husband's action for the loss of his wife's consortium and services, which was abolished only in 1982. But this applied only where a wrong had been done to the wife; if she had consented, no wrong would be done. In *Bravery* v. *Bravery*[9] Lord Justice Denning held that a male sterilization without just cause or excuse was so intrinsically harmful as to be an unlawful assault irrespective of the patient's consent. The other two judges, however, expressly disagreed. Nevertheless, the law has never imposed a duty upon doctors to provide treatment if they do not wish to do so, except as part of their duty to take reasonable care for the health and safety of their existing patients.

Once the wife had conceived, there was also a traditional belief that her husband was entitled to choose between her life and that of the child. It is easy to see how such a belief might be constructed out of his possessory rights over both, but rather less easy to see how it could be constructed out of the courts' approach to the enforcement of those rights. In *Paton* v. *British Pregnancy Advisory Service Trustees*[14] the President of the Family Division refused to grant a husband an injunction preventing his wife from having an abortion. Having pointed out that the child itself has no rights in civil law unless and until it is born alive, the judge regarded the husband's claim as part and parcel of his rights as a husband rather than as a father. He pointed out that the courts had long since given up any attempt to enforce the obligations of matrimony by direct order: 'no court would ever grant an injunction to stop sterilization or vasectomy' any more than it would use the old decree of restitution of conjugal rights to compel matrimonial intercourse.[15] The more interesting question today is whether the court would have granted the injunction if the husband could have shown that the abortion would be unlawful. The likely answer is that he would have found it virtually impossible to do so because control over that decision has been taken over by the medical profession.

Fertility and the Powers of Doctors

In *Paton* the judge reached a similar conclusion to the one reached by the United States Supreme Court in *Planned Parenthood of Missouri* v. *Danforth*[16] but by a very different route. In *Roe* v. *Wade*[17] the Court had held that a State could not interfere with the mother's right to decide, in consultation with her physician, to terminate a pregnancy during the first twelve weeks. This was part of her constitutionally guaranteed rights of privacy, and the State's interest in the preservation of the foetus was not such as to entitle it to intervene. If the State could not do this by direct regulation, neither could it delegate a power of veto to anyone else, whether the father of the child or the husband of the mother. The Court appreciated that it was allowing the mother to act unilaterally in a matter in which many considered that the decision should be joint. Where two disagree, however, only one can prevail: 'inasmuch as it is the woman who physically bears the child and who is the more directly and immediately affected by the pregnancy, as between the two, the balance weighs in her favour.'

In English law the decision as to whether an abortion is appropriate must be taken on medical grounds by two doctors. The abortion must be carried out by a doctor in a National Health Service Hospital or specially approved clinic. The appropriate forms must be completed.[18] The difference in approach between English law and the law in the United States is a large part of the reason why abortions are so much more readily available there than they are here, despite the fact that neither country places a positive duty upon doctors to act. The problems of interpretation are endless. They obviously allow the doctors to discriminate between deserving and undeserving cases in a way which may have nothing to do with what the law in fact allows. As Oakley reports, 'It is, apparently, unmarried women with no children whose request for abortion is most likely to be unsympathetically interpreted; as a group they are most likely to have a private instead of an NHS abortion.'[19]

Thus abortion is lawful where continuing the pregnancy would involve a greater risk to the life of the pregnant woman or of injury to her health or that of any existing children of her family than if the pregnancy were terminated. Some believe that this allows any doctor who has actually examined the woman to reach that conclusion during the first twelve weeks of pregnancy, for the risks of death from childbirth are statistically greater than those of an early abortion. Others believe that he must make a careful calculation of the odds not only of mortality but also of morbidity. All sorts of problems can enter into that calculation. Is a risk to her mental health the risk of a recognized mental illness or disorder or simply a risk to her psychological well-being? Does a risk to her health cover risks which will materialize after the birth? How can her pregnancy or confinement affect the health of her existing children?

At least the doctors are allowed simply to compare the relative risks rather than to make value judgments about their seriousness. Hence there is a powerful medical lobby in support of the current law. Value judgments are, however, involved in the second ground, which requires a substantial risk that the child, if born, would be seriously handicapped by mental or physical abnormalities. Williams regards this as an extension of the first ground, basically designed to protect the parents from the damage to their welfare that a handicapped child might cause and, secondarily, to spare the public purse.[20] Given the enormous problems which rearing such a child can bring to many mothers,[21] they would certainly welcome this view of the matter. It can, however, be looked upon as another means whereby the state is seeking to safeguard the quality of its investment in the future, a recurring theme which has much more sinister implications.

The most striking thing about the grounds for abortion, however, is that they are not expressed in moral terms. Abortion may involve a very serious moral dilemma for the mother, but the decision is not left to her. On the other hand, the state has not been prepared to make it either. One helpful way of looking at the question is to ask what *duties* the mother may reasonably be expected to owe the foetus.[22] This would make abortion available to the rape victim and to the victim of failed contraception, neither of whom is expressly covered by the present grounds. The effect of the Act is to leave the whole decision to doctors, whose opinion must be bona fide but need not be reasonable. Given the breadth of interpretation allowed, their decisions are likely to be more often moral than purely medical.

It is interesting to compare the law's approach to abortion with the reluctance of legislators to interfere in scientific advances in human fertilization and embryology. Doctors have gone to very great lengths to help women who wish to be mothers, even though this wish might not have been granted by an agency responsible for placing an existing child. In America their methods are already being used with a view to producing the best possible babies. Developments in techniques are happening all the time, and their implications are frightening. The Warnock Committee is now investigating the issues and the legislators may at last be preparing to impose a little restraint.

In the meantime the medical profession has also taken charge of the process of childbirth itself. The first legislation came about because of its sustained campaign against ignorant, incompetent and drunken 'old hags' who constituted a 'danger to the public'.[23] Hence the Midwives Act of 1902 prohibited *women* from attending other women in childbirth 'habitually and for gain' unless they did so under medical supervision or were certified as midwives under the Act. In 1926 the words 'habitually and for gain' were dropped, and all *people* were prohibited from attending unless they were certified midwives or acting under medical supervision. It may have been generally believed that this meant professional attendance. The Act, however, did not say so, and in 1982 a husband was successfully prosecuted for delivering his own child. The Nurses, Midwives and Health Visitors Act 1979 (section 17) goes further still and insists that only qualified midwives and doctors can attend women in childbirth (with exceptions for those in training and for emergencies). The upshot of this is that women are effectively obliged to have their babies where those qualified midwives and doctors are prepared to attend them. Since 1964 hospital deliveries have risen from 30 to 97 per cent.

Finch asserts that the 1979 Act is a rare attempt to use the criminal law to 'enforce an aspiration to excellence'.[24] That, of course, depends upon whose definition of excellence is used — mother's, doctor's or midwife's. The medical case for control rests on the twin assumptions that pregnancy is a disease which is almost bound to cause problems, and that the profession's methods of dealing not only with the problems but also with the disease are bound to be best. Both assumptions are controversial,[25] but we need only make three observations. First, the views of doctors are notorious for changing over time, as any reader of their instruction manuals on mothering will know. Second, they are also notorious for disagreeing with one another, as any court which has listened to their evidence will know. Third, however, in any case in which the law gives them the right to exercise their own judgment, the law will respect a view which is held by a responsible body of medical opinion, even if it is contested by another equally responsible body.[26] The implications go much deeper than the current debate about hospital and home delivery. The doctors may claim to dictate not only methods but also objectives. They have now moved beyond their former concern for maternal and perinatal mortality and are looking to produce the best possible babies. To what extent may they override the mother's wishes in order to do so?

Eekelaar and Dingwall argue that the monopoly created by the Midwives Act means that 'the mother's wishes will be relevant to the attendant's duties towards her, but cannot be uniquely determinative of his duties towards the child. It is a matter for his professional judgment as to how far those wishes should modify actions he believes to be in the child's best interests.'[27] At common law a child had no rights until he was born, but he could then sue in respect of injuries caused by a doctor's negligence during his birth.[28] The authors imply that the attendant could therefore overrride the mother's refusal to allow such things as foetal monitoring, forceps delivery, episiotomy or even Caesarian section.

Whatever the arguments against that view — and it is by no means clear that the common law would have put the best interests of the child, as defined by the doctor, above the mother's right to self-determination — the law has certainly been changed by the Civil Liability (Congenital Disabilities) Act 1976. Under that Act there is liability to the child for injuries caused before he was born only if they were caused in breach of a legal duty to his mother. There is obviously a duty to take reasonable care of her, and a failure to do so which causes harm to her child will be a ground for liability. There is almost certainly a duty owed to her to take reasonable care of her child. However, there can be no breach of duty to her if she has asked for something to be done or has refused to allow it to be done. Where she has said nothing, she must be presumed to put her own life and health before that of her child, unless she has agreed to the contrary. The 1976 Act automatically rules out any possibility that she herself may be liable to the child.[29]

Eekelaar and Dingwall agree with the Law Commission[30] that a child should not be able to sue his mother for injuries caused by such things as smoking during pregnancy. This is not so much for the mother's sake as because the child might suffer from the conflict of interest thus produced. They argue, however, that obstetric attendants should be able to intervene without the mother's consent in order to protect the baby in the womb or during delivery. They point out that this consequence of the 1976 Act runs counter to the whole trend of modern child-protection legislation, which is to allow intervention in the autonomy of parents for the good of their children. Indeed, child-care law is now prepared to allow interventions judged solely according to the 'first and paramount consideration' of the child's welfare. Taken to its logical conclusion, this could insist that there are no sacrifices, of well-being, health or even life itself, which a mother must not make to ensure the best possible life for her child. We would then be back to the choice which was once given to husbands, but this time it would be given to the doctors. Their desire to produce perfect babies for the nation's investment in the future might then tempt them to insist that certain mothers were sterilized or had abortions against their will. Eekelaar and Dingwall are against any such broad principle, arguing that the rights of children can be defined only by reference to the duties which can *properly* be imposed upon their parents or others, but *could* the law ever impose an obligation to have an abortion?

An ominous note was struck in the case of *Emeh* v. *Kensington and Chelsea and Westminster Area Health Authority*.[31] A child was born as a result of a failed sterilization operation, but the mother's damages were limited to the pain and suffering of the first four months of pregnancy and a second sterilization because she could have minimized her damage by having an abortion. This is akin to the decision of the Scottish court which refused to make an order against the father of an illegitimate child because the mother had failed to prevent the child's birth. Such decisions refuse to allow mothers to have the same doubts about contraception and abortion as have afflicted fathers, doctors and legislators.

Failed sterilization and abortion raise the more difficult problem of reconciling the belief that children are a blessing and a delight, especially to their mothers, with the undeniable costs of bringing them up. In *Scuriaga* v. *Powell*[32] a mother was awarded damages for pain and suffering, loss of earnings and earning capacity and marriage prospects, but not for the costs of bringing up the child. In *Udale* v. *Bloomsbury Area Health Authority*[33] the mother's loss of earnings was limited to that made necessary by the pregnancy and birth. Even this has been criticized on the ground that if children are indeed a blessing and delight, the law should not compensate for any losses after they have been born.[34] Astonishingly, however, a father has recently been awarded damages, apparently for the cost of bringing up the child, after a failed vasectomy.[35] The conflict between these cases will have to be resolved by the Court of Appeal. They are nevertheless an excellent illustration of how easy it is for the law to perceive the financial loss to the father, who has to provide for an unplanned child, but not to the mother, who has to bring him up. Quite apart from its view of the compensations which the child should bring to both parents, the law is not used to conceptualizing the services of a wife and mother as labour which is worthy of its hire.

Children and the Rights of Husbands

It is clear that the law regards children as a benefit to men as well as to women. In the days when legal institutions were designed for the needs of the landed and propertied classes, the reasons were obvious. The first requirement of any system of patrilineal descent is a means of discovering reliable heirs. Children are needed to carry on the family property or enterprise and to enhance its status whenever possible. However, 'motherhood, although also a legal relationship, is based on a fact, being proved demonstrably by parturition. Fatherhood, by contrast, is a presumption.'[36] The father needs the law to turn him into a father. A formal link is established between man and woman through the medium of marriage, after which it is presumed that all children born to the woman belong to the man. The corollary is the wife's obligation to remain faithful to her husband. The presumption of legitimacy was extremely difficult to rebut in English law until the Family Law Reform Act 1969 made it possible, in effect, for a husband to disclaim the relationship by evidence showing that it was more likely than not that the child was not his. By that stage the chances of his being able to do this by blood tests had become extremely good and the Act also made provision for this. By contrast, the standard and burden of proof imposed upon either a mother or a father who wishes to establish the relationship between father and extramarital child is still high.[37] The reason given for the strength of the presumption of legitimacy at common law was the courts' reluctance to impose the disabilities of illegitimacy upon the child or those of adultery upon the mother. As Engels made clear as long ago as 1884, however, the original position was the reverse: the disabilities were so great because of the need to ensure that the presumption generally reflected the facts.[38]

Once the relationship had been established, the common law was concerned mainly with defining and enforcing the rights of legitimate fathers. Blackstone saw those rights as the necessary concomitant of the father's duty to provide maintenance, protection and education for his children.[39] He also thought that the main function of marriage was to ensure that a man was there to do this, as a woman 'generally wants ability'. At that stage, however, the only system of law which made any attempt to enforce parental duties was the Poor Law. This imposed maintenance obligations upon both mothers and fathers of legitimate and illegitimate children. Its objective was to save the parish expenditure. It was also quite irrelevant to the propertied families with whom the common law was concerned. Although Blackstone laments its deficiencies in the matter of education, such families were unlikely to feel that there was a gap. Their children's needs could generally be defined by reference to the needs of the family as a whole.

The common law did provide mechanisms for enforcing the father's rights. Rights of physical coercion lasted only until the age of discretion. Interestingly, the age for girls was fixed at 16 by reference to the criminal liability of seducers. The age for boys was fixed at 14 by reference to the medieval age for taking to the field of battle.[40] The father's right to control other matters lasted until the age of majority at 21, and these were the subjects of prime concern to the preservation of the family — education, religion, marriage and the control of the child's own assets. If the father died, he could appoint a guardian to take over his powers and ensure that his wishes continued to be respected. In practice, the families who operated settlements could control their children for as long as they liked. The only part played by the mother in all of this was her right to act as the guardian 'for nurture' of a child up to the age of 14 if her husband died without appointing a guardian to supplant her.

The law began to change with the nineteenth-century triumph of middle-class individualism and self-help. The child became important not only for what he might inherit or contribute but also for the sort of person he was to become. The evolution of the human race, like that of other species, would depend upon the survival of the fittest. Later on these ideas led to an enormous expansion in the apparatus for intervening in the bringing up of children, particularly in the poorer sections of society. At first the main effect was greater emphasis on the importance of nurture and the enforcement of parental duties as well as rights. The common law courts had power to enforce a father's claim for possession and could decline to do so only in the most extreme cases of cruelty or neglect. The chancery court had jurisdiction over all aspects of a child's upbringing. It would usually employ this in order to assist the father to enforce his wishes, but it was somewhat more prepared to listen to a challenge to his authority based upon what would be better *for the child*.[41] Such a challenge, whether it came from the mother or elsewhere, could succeed only if the father had acted badly enough *as a father* to forfeit his claims. It was irrelevant that he might have acted badly as a husband. Worse still, a string of cases in the early nineteenth century revealed that he could not be prevented from separating tiny children from their mothers' care or daughters from their mothers' influence. In *Ball* v. *Ball*,[42] for example, the court was petitioned by a mother and her 14-year-old daughter. The mother had obtained an ecclesiastical decree of separation from her husband, who was living in adultery with another woman, but he had removed the daughter and sent her away to school. The court held that 'some conduct on the part of the father with reference to the management and education of the child must be shown to warrant an interference with his legal right.' As there was none here, the court had no power to award the mother access, let alone custody, 'although I know of no act more harsh or cruel than depriving the mother of proper intercourse with her child'.

These cases, together with the energetic campaigning of Caroline Norton and others, prompted Parliament to pass a series of Acts giving the court (and later the county and magistrates' courts and also the courts hearing matrimonial disputes) jurisdiction to entertain claims by mothers for custody and access. Far from legislating for mother's rights, however, these Acts simply allowed the courts to take over the father's task of deciding where the child's interests lay. It is also probable that at this period 'custody' referred to physical care only, while guardianship over matters such as marriage and property remained with the husband.[43]

The 1886 Act made a start in extending the mother's claims into the previously masculine sphere of guardianship by allowing her to act after her husband's death either alone or jointly with a guardian he had appointed, and even in limited cases to appoint a guardian to act after her own death, but it also allowed the divorce court to declare the guilty party unfit to have either custody or guardianship of the children. In 1925 masculine equivalence triumphed to the extent of giving her equal powers to act as or appoint a guardian, requiring her consent to the marriage of a child under 21 and requiring the court to put the welfare of the child before all other considerations in *any* dispute concerning upbringing or property. It was generally believed that the legislators had thereby achieved equality between husband and wife. But the husband's common law guardianship had not been abolished, so that unless and until a dispute was taken to court or one spouse died, he had the right to control everything apart from marriage and adoption. This is interesting in the light of the emphasis on mothering during the 1920s and 1930s in the fields of education and employment and the huge growth in professionals who were there to insist that it was done properly. The matter was not remedied until the Guardianship Act 1973, which gives mothers and fathers of legitimate children equal rights and authority over all matters of custody, upbringing and administration of the child's property.

Role Stereotypes in Parental Disputes

Giving mothers the right to claim custody of their children did not necessarily mean that they succeeded. It was still for the court to decide what was best for the child. In considering the courts' approach to this, it is crucial to bear in mind the very different parts commonly played by mothers and fathers in the upbringing of their children. Thus during the nineteenth century, while the mother may very well have succeeded in gaining custody, in matters such as religion she had to displace the presumption that the father knew best what was best for his child.[44] Similarly, it has rarely, if ever, been suggested that adultery makes a man a bad father, although atheism or a profligate way of life might do so. The moral purity of the mother was much more important. Adultery disqualified her entirely from either custody or access until 1873, by statute in the chancery court and in practice in the divorce court.[45] Annie Besant could be deprived of her children for publishing advice on contraception.[46] The 1886 Act placed the child's welfare top of the list of relevant considerations in a custody dispute, before the conduct and wishes of both mother and father. It was not until *Re A. and B.*[47] that it was decided that two equally guilty parents could therefore be treated equally. The children's time was divided between them, on condition that their governess went with them when they moved from one to the other. The mother was not 'mothering' her children in the modern sense. Divorce law, of course, was still governed by the principle that one party was innocent and the other guilty. Aristocratic husbands may have permitted themselves to be divorced as a matter of course, but an 'unimpeachable' father who chose to do so could divorce his wife and deny her the right even to see her children. The courts, however, became readier to grant her access after *Mozley-Stark* v. *Mozley-Stark and Hitchins.*[48] The 1925 Act made the welfare of the child the 'first and paramount consideration' in all courts.[49] As divorce came lower down the social scale, and the cult of motherhood became firmly entrenched, the courts had to accept that even an unimpeachable father should not be looking after his very young children.[50] 'In such a situation,' said Lord Justice Denning in *Wakeham* v. *Wakeham*, 'the usual order is that the father, the innocent party, is given the custody of the child or children, but the care or control is left to the mother. That order is entirely realistic.'[51] It was indeed. It reflected the distribution of parenting which had no doubt gone on during the marriage. It also ensured that the father retained the public rights while the mother retained her domestic duties. Such orders are now disapproved,[52] but the orders made by the courts reflect a very similar distribution of duties, as we shall see. However, the courts were still allowed to balance the needs of the child against the 'justice of the case'. This concept of justice sees the possession of the child as the prize to be awarded for good behaviour during marriage or, more commonly, the loss of that possession as a penalty for bad. In *Re L. (Infants)*[53] a deprivation of her children was explicitly justified as a disciplinary measure to ensure that a woman who left her husband would not succeed in having everything she wanted and to encourage her to return.

More recently, however, it has been recognized that this is inconsistent with the paramount consideration of the child's own needs.[54] In *Re K. (Minors) (Wardship: Care and Control)*[55] the Court of Appeal upheld an order in favour of a mother who had applied for custody so that she could take her children with her when she left her husband to live with another man. In effect, the court was now assisting her to have the 'best of both worlds', which had been deplored in *Re L.* This was explained not on the basis of the mother's rights, as the father's claims had been explained in the past, but by reference to the statutory criterion as interpreted by Lord Macdermott in *J.* v. *C.*[56] The child's welfare is now the first consideration because it is 'of first importance' and the paramount consideration because it 'rules on or determines the course to be followed.' Now that the father has been displaced, the courts have taken over his role.

In *Re K.* it was emphasized that there are no general rules about which parent is best suited to bring up the children, and that each case is an exercise of the court's discretion on the particular facts of the case before it, so that we should beware of generalizing from statements and decisions in any one reported case. This is certainly how the circuit judges say that they approach their task.[57] But the reported cases do give us significant pointers to the considerations which the higher courts think important, and it would be ridiculous to expect judges to approach decisions with no preconceived ideas at all. There are obvious illustrations of a preference for conventional patterns of child-rearing in which mothering and fathering are clearly differentiated.

One is the treatment of homosexual parents. Peculiar horror can be reserved for the father of boys who is a practising homosexual. Although anxious to lay down no general rules, when upholding a decision that it was unreasonable for the father to withhold his consent to the adoption of his son by another man Lord Wilberforce remarked that parliamentary tolerance of the father's activities

> [should] not entitle the courts to relax, in any degree, the vigilance and severity with which they should regard the risk of children at critical ages being exposed or introduced to ways of life which, as this case illustrates, may lead to severance from normal society, to psychological stresses and unhappiness and possibly even to physical experiences which may scar them for life.[58]

It is interesting that the belief that homosexual men may interfere with little boys seems so much stronger than the fear that heterosexual step-fathers may interfere with little girls, despite all the evidence of the latter.

This statement was quoted by the judge and upheld by the Court of Appeal in *S. v. S. (Custody of Children)*,[59] which concerned a lesbian mother. She was deprived of the custody of her children, although the court welfare officer and two psychiatrists thought that their sexual identity was now firmly established and there was no risk of their being led into sexually deviant ways. The judge preferred the view of a psychiatrist who had not seen either of the parties, that the children might suffer social embarrassment and hurt if their mother's lesbian relationship became known locally. This outweighed not only the children's wishes but also the difficulties which the father might have in caring for their material needs. In many such cases, however, the court has been torn between disapproval of the mother's sexual orientation and the assumption that children should be looked after by women. There are certainly cases in which the latter prevails over the former. Presenting the children with women who adopt some features of the male role may be thought preferable to leaving them with no woman at all to care for them or expecting a man to adopt the female role.

Custody disputes are usually presented as disputes between mother and father. Those studies which purport to discover the extent of the courts' alleged 'maternal preference', whether through examining the decisions of the Court of Appeal which happen to have been reported[60] or through examining the actual practice of the divorce courts,[61] perpetuate this impression. They indicate that, although the mother obtains custody in roughly three-quarters of the cases, and actual care in rather more, this is usually because the parties themselves are content for her to have it. Only a small minority of cases are contested, and in both contested and uncontested cases the court is more likely than not to confirm the child in his existing home. Changes in the status quo are so rare that even in the large-scale study carried out by Eekelaar and Clive (1977), only thirteen out of 652 cases resulted in a move.[62] In a later study Eekelaar observed that if the mother challenged the father's custody, she was rather more likely to win than was the father who challenged the mother, but that it was still more likely than not that the children would stay where they were.[63] Maidment's study of Court of Appeal decisions suggests that the higher court is rather more prepared to upset the status quo in order to reunite mother and child, sometimes in circumstances where the author could find little justification.[64] Otherwise the researchers tend to the view that there is little evidence of a judicial bias in favour of *mothers*.

None of these studies quite addresses itself to the question of how far the courts may be biased in favour of *female care*. Maidment does mention that the 'father's ability to provide suitable care for the child(ren), in particular a female influence in the form of a grandmother, other relative, cohabitee' may load the balance in his favour.[65] In fact, reported instances in which the father intends to carry out the mothering role himself, particularly where the children are young, are very rare. If he has been left to look after the children after the separation, we usually find that he has done so with the help of a female relative or friend. If he wishes to keep or regain the children, he has generally found a new partner to care for them. Thus the cases which both courts and commentators find most evenly balanced are those in which the dispute is between the step-mother and father who are at present looking after the child and the natural mother (and sometimes step-father) who would like to do so.[66] A good illustration of the difficulty in interpreting decided cases lies in *Re D. W. (A Minor) (Custody)*.[67] When the parents divorced, the father and step-mother retained his 4-year-old son. Six years later their marriage broke up, and the court removed the boy from his devoted step-mother and returned him to his natural mother. But this was not a case of maternal preference. Now that the natural father was no longer there, the advantages of being brought up in a stable two-parent home with step-father and siblings outweighed the admittedly excellent home which his step-mother could provide.

There is nothing in such cases to contradict the assumption that women are best placed to fulfil a child's physical needs. All children need to be fed, cleaned, clothed and guarded against those dangers from which they cannot protect themselves. The courts are rarely faced with a proposal that the father should cook their fish fingers, wash their hair and their nappies or compromise his employment in order to supervise them. In making such an order in *Y. v. Y. (Custody)*,[68] Lord Justice Cumming-Bruce observed that 'the court did not reconcile itself with equanimity to the solution of a custody case whereby a young man had to give up his job to look after children and might be tempted to *look forward* to living on social security for the next twelve years' (emphasis supplied). Yet the courts regularly reconcile themselves to mothers doing so, and Parliament has changed the supplementary benefit rules to enable a father to do the same.

Thus the disputed evidence about maternal preference is more probably evidence about the choice between the 'real' and 'substitute' mothers or about the relative importance to be attached to 'mothering' and 'fathering' at different stages of a child's development. While the child is very young, of pre-school or kindergarten age, the psychological aspects of mothering may be thought just as important as its material aspects. It is usually believed that the 'real' mother can provide for her child's emotional needs more satisfactorily than can a substitute. When the child grows older, the psychological aspects of fathering may increase in importance. The courts are reluctant to generalize, but the need of older boys for the part-time companionship and guidance of a father is certainly felt to be an important factor. For older girls the need for a mother's guidance through puberty is also mentioned. Once again this reflects the conventional distribution of roles between the sexes.

It is also consistent with the law's approach to access. Once upon a time it regarded access as the right of the parent, which might be forfeited by a guilty mother or, later, by any parent who had behaved particularly badly towards the child. Nowadays access is said to be the right of the child: thus 'to deprive a parent of access is to deprive a child of an important contribution to his emotional and material growing up in the long term.'[69] Hence particular importance is attached to persuading the custodial parent to co-operate with access, to the extent of threatening to remove (or even removing) the children if she does not. This can certainly be justified by reference to the child's needs, not only for the part-time aspects of parenting which a visiting father may well be able to supply but also for the knowlege of both sides of his parentage which will help him to build his own sense of identity and personal worth as time goes by. Fathering is thus seen as important function, but one which it is possible to perform at a distance and at part-time meetings. Mothering, by contrast, depends upon continual interaction between mother and child. Yet, as we have already seen, although mothering is supposed to be instinctive, it is also something that girls have to be taught to do. Boys do not have to be taught to be fathers.

Nor indeed, does the law make much sustained effort to encourage fathers to maintain even this attenuated role. The child's 'right to access' is a means of persuading the custodial parent to co-operate with something which is often highly stressful. It is rarely a means of encouraging the reluctant absent parent to remember his children's needs and to take some of the burden from the custodial parent. Despite some extremely persuasive psychological and social arguments in its favour,[70] courts do little to affirm a concept of shared responsibility. Although the law assumes that every child whose parents divorce is at such risk that expensive judicial time must be spent in checking upon their welfare, it makes little attempt to use that opportunity to encourage parental co-operation.[71] Joint custody orders are made more often when the parties are in dispute than when they have settled things amicably.[72] Even if they are made, they rarely mean what they say. The children do not divide their time between their parents,[73] but spend it much as they would have done under an order for sole custody to one parent with reasonable access to the other. The absent parent simply has a greater right to be consulted about the major decisions in the child's life, the public aspects associated with fathering. Indeed, in *Dipper* v. *Dipper* the Court of Appeal suggested that even without a joint custody order, the custodial parent did not have the right to take major decisions if the other objected. This looks regrettably like enhancing the right of the absent father to interfere in his child's upbringing without at the same time enhancing the mother's right to some practical help. Exactly the same could be said of the Law Commission's proposals to enhance the claims of fathers of illegitimate children. At present, the mother has sole parental rights over an illegitimate child, subject to the father's right to seek custody or access in the courts. The child's exclusion from his parents' lineage for the purposes of succession has already been largely abolished, even though this was the original rationale for the distinction. This reflects the decreased importance of inherited property and the modern emphasis upon equality of opportunity, which places great weight on the right of a child to a loving relationship with both parents. It therefore seemed unjust to the child to deny him a legal relationship with his father while he was growing up but to recognize it the moment either of them died. The Law Commission originally suggested that the status of illegitimacy should be abolished.[74] They also suggested that the only way to do this was to remove all the differences between the legal consequences of a birth in wedlock and a birth outside it. Instead of considering whether this might be better done by equating the status of all children to that of the illegitimate, however, they suggested that the inevitable consequence would be to recognize the automatic parental rights and duties of all fathers. Yet they clearly could have considered an alternative model, for they suggested that a child's domicile should invariably be that of the mother. One Parent Families riposted that the Law Commission's scheme would cause difficulties, doubts and insecurity for the majority of mothers who were trying to bring up their children alone, while the benefits to the child were by no means obvious.[75] It did, however, suggest that parents should be able to make a joint declaration of paternity and parental rights, which would encourage the sharing of responsibility between cohabiting parents. The Law Commission reacted by abandoning the idea of automatic paternal rights.[76] It also rejected One Parent Families' simple suggestion in favour of a complex scheme for applying to the courts. If fathers were not to be given rights by law, mothers were thought to require the protection of the courts in overseeing their agreement to share. Fatherhood is to remain a legal concept, defined by marriage or by the courts, rather than the product of the parents' own care and concern for the child. On the other hand, the Law Commission has proposed improvements in the mechanisms for obliging parents, but predominantly fathers, to make provision for their children. Interestingly, the defects in those mechanisms were described as 'procedural discrimination' against the child rather than as the discrimination against the mother that they undoubtedly are.[77]

All this contributes to what we have come to expect as the typical picture of the one-parent family. Whether single, widowed or divorced, the mother will usually have custody, either by right, or by consent, or by court order. The case in which she is most likely to lose is where she has left her children with their father for any considerable length of time and another woman has taken her place. There is implicit and sometimes explicit condemnation of the mother who is prepared to leave her children. Even if it is realized that she would have liked to take them with her but was prevented by their father or had nowhere suitable to take them, it may be too late to disturb the status quo. An over-ready preference for the status quo without a careful examination of the evidence is another of the many ways in which the law can work to the disadvantage of the home-maker spouse. Not surprisingly, Eekelaar and Clive found that mothers were more persistent in trying to recover their children from their husbands than were fathers in trying to recover them from their wives.[78] They attribute this to societal pressures which the mother is likely to share. For some women, those pressures have unfortunately meant that their children are all they have to give meaning to their lives.

Unless the father can afford to maintain them all, mother and children will then have to subsist on means-tested benefits. Fewer lone parents than married mothers are in employment, although more work full-time.[79] It is much more difficult for a single parent to arrange to go out to work than it is for either of united parents to do so. The father's role is that of visitor and provider. Sooner or later it is likely, and even hoped, that a mother will solve her problems by marrying again. The man she marries may well have left his own children in the care of their mother and be happy to take on the fathering role for his wife's children.

It seems that if her new husband's children are with him, she will not feel any great need to cement their relationship through adoption. Both she and her new husband, however, are likely to feel the need to provide him with some outward symbol of his relationship with her children, either through adoption or at least through changing the children's surname to his. At that point, however, they come up against the fact that the children's father also needs such a symbol. It is the last link with his children and his only guarantee of survival. The courts are very reluctant to dispense with his agreement to their adoption. Even if he has agreed, the Children Act 1975 sought to discourage it, but the courts have adopted some very inconsistent attitudes and practices.[80] They are similarly divided about the question of a change of surname. Unless the father has agreed, the mother cannot change it without the leave of the court. The decision should again be governed by the child's welfare, but the judges hold very different views about this. Some think that the reality of the relationship between father and child is more important, so that he should be encouraged to take a relaxed view and not to object when mother and children find it more convenient to be known by the name of the new 'head of the family'.[81] Others, who are now in the ascendant, think it a serious matter, in which the wishes and convenience of both mother and children are of less account.[82] There was no significant difference between the facts of these two cases to indicate that the needs of the *children* involved were any different. Interestingly, in another case the mother had left the father before the child had been born and had decided to call him by another name. The Court of Appeal allowed her to do so, but the trial judge did not, and throughout referred to what she had done as *changing* the name.[83] If mother and father have equal rights, it may be wrong for one of them to act unilaterally, but there can be no presumption that the child automatically starts out with the father's name. There is obviously a persisting fear that without this outward expression, the relationship will somehow be threatened. As Burgoyne and Clark observe, 'there is considerable evidence that the obligations and responsibilities of fatherhood are very diffusely defined in our society.'[84] The same is not true of the obligations of motherhood. Even if she is separated from her children, or living with someone else's, there is no call for a metaphorical bond to seal their relationship.

Mothers and the State

The explosion of concern for the needs of children, which undoubtedly led to a great improvement in the legal status of mothers, has also led to a huge increase in the apparatus of the state for controlling their activities. Procedures for compulsory intervention between parent and child can now be invoked not only for physical neglect or ill-treatment but also because of the mother's inability to cater for the child's emotional needs.[85] Children who have been placed voluntarily in the care of local authorities or private organizations may be withheld not only when parents are physically or mentally unfit to care for them but also when the parent's 'habits or mode of life' are thought to make her so or when the child has been in care for three years.[86] Children may be adopted without their parent's consent not only where the parent has been guilty of some culpable conduct in relation to the child but also where her agreement is unreasonably withheld.[87] If a child is in care, agreement may be dispensed with before the child is placed with a substitute family.[88] Above all, the courts have encouraged local authorities which feel that the statutory schemes do not give them sufficient powers to protect children to make them wards of the High Court where the issue is governed by the 'first and paramount consideration' of the child's welfare.[89] They have not been able to give the same encouragement to parents who feel that the statutory schemes give them too little voice in their children's future.[90]

All of this is evidence of a concern for the needs of children which spread far beyond their physical health and welfare and is aimed particularly at those aspects of child-rearing which are traditionally associated with mothering. At the same time as the powers of the state to arrange substitute mothering for those children whose own mothers are judged inadequate have been increased, the rights of parents to make their own arrangements for their children have been greatly eroded. Private placements for adoption have been outlawed, even where these are made by the mother herself.[91] Private fostering has long been subject to official control, through a system of notification and inspection, because of the horrific revelations of the Victorian baby-farming cases.[92] Private day care for the under-5s is controlled by a system of registration and inspection.[93] Both these measures were originally designed to protect the physical health of the children involved. Both are widely ignored. In practice, the law can discourage parents who know about it from making perfectly proper arrangements, while it deters illegal minders from coming forward for help and advice. Public day care for children concentrates upon expensive facilities for the priority few, leaving the great mass of women workers without provision or forcing them to rely upon their families or illegal and often unsatisfactory arrangements.[94] Mothers are thus left with a responsibility which only a few of them can lawfully delegate — to relatives, registered minders, nannies or au pair girls. There is an obvious class distinction here. Further, the group that is accorded priority in public day care comprises single parents. Where a mother has a man to provide for her the official assumption that she needs no assistance can reinforce the divisions between them in the labour market.

The law has now reached a state of such complexity that its effectiveness in protecting and helping the children involved can be seriously called in question. We must also begin to question how much of that protection is based upon, and reinforces, conventional assumptions about the proper way to bring up children. Our natural concern for the nation's investment in the future could lead us to impose an ever greater burden of expectation upon the nation's mothers, with an ever greater power to condemn those who fall short. Alternatively, it could lead us to realize, as many fathers are now beginning to do,[95] that there is nothing inevitable about the current division of parenting tasks and a great deal to be said for encouraging more flexible patterns of upbringing and care.

6

Breadwinners and Homemakers: Partners or Dependants?

The actual or expected polarization of roles between breadwinner and homemaker is the central feature of women's lives. Laws which expect or assume that the breadwinner is male and the homemaker female are now disappearing from the statute book. The roles themselves are in no danger of disappearing, nor is the fact that one is adopted by the overwhelming majority of men and the other by a rather less overwhelming but still substantial majority of women. As Mary McIntosh has said, 'The very construction of men and women as separate and opposed categories takes place within, and in terms of, the family.'[1]

There are many variations of the domestic role. It can cover, for example, the hard labour of housework and child care, with an obvious economic value;[2] the more managerial, decorative and supportive functions of some middle-class housewives; the purely ornamental and sexual services of the old-style mistress. There is a perceived hierarchy of merit within such variations, but all share the same relationship with the normal methods of distributing income and wealth. All are labelled 'economically inactive' and are denied an independent place in that system. The assumed justification for this is dependence upon some economically active breadwinner. Only if the breadwinner does not exist or has disappeared without fulfilling his functions properly, may an independent claim be grudgingly recognized. It may well be that 'the role of wife, mother, homemaker is valued perhaps more than any other single role in our society',[3] but if the value is an economic one, it is payable primarily to someone else, to be distributed by him within the home. For many people, indeed, the prime merit in the role is its dedication to values other than the purely economic. It is certainly deeply embedded in women's ideas about themselves.[4]

There is a considerable body of research which points to the 'characteristic satisfactions and strains' associated with adopting the conventional breadwinner/housewife pattern.[5] While there are clearly a great many contented housewives, happy with their lot and the way in which it is defined by society and the law, there are equally clearly a great many who are oppressed by it. Even among those who do not feel oppressed, the demands of the breadwinner's employment are likely to take first place in the family's decisions.[6] More and more women are turning to work outside the home. In some families this is essential; the number of families in poverty would be much higher if there were not two incomes.[7] As well as that, however, employment outside the home can bring companionship and satisfactions which are not available to those who work within it.

Most of these women are not setting up in 'dual-career families' but seeking to balance their contributions in and outside the home. Over the last sixty years the economic activity rate of married women in the relevant age group has risen from less than one-tenth to more than a half. But in recent years most of the rise has been among those holding part-time jobs or seeking work. From 1973 to 1981 the proportion of married women with full-time jobs remained steady at around a quarter. The proportion with part-time jobs or seeking work rose from 30 to 36 per cent. There is a close correlation between the economic activity of married women and the age of the youngest child. Three-quarters of those with children under 5 in 1981 did no outside work, compared with less than one-third of those whose youngest child was at least 10. Even so, most of the jobs were part-time.[8] It has also been estimated that something like one-fifth of the economically inactive married women who have no dependent children are living in households containing an elderly or disabled person.[9] Despite changing patterns and attitudes, therefore, there is no evidence that married women are forsaking their domestic and familial responsibilities in large numbers. Indeed, the trend towards employment has recently levelled off.[10] There is some evidence that there are working wives, particularly in the lower-income groups, who would like to work a little less outside the home in order to achieve a better balance between their multiple functions as workers, wives and mothers.[11] This is scarcely surprising if they are still required to shoulder those burdens largely alone. A UNESCO study concluded that 'in no country do employed men spend more than half an hour a day on housework, and employed women less than an hour and a half.'[12]

We have already seen that the law of employment does little to help the woman who compromises her position in the market place for the sake of her home and family. At almost every turn it has discriminated against the part-time worker. It attempts, however ineffectually, to grant equality of opportunity, but that has amounted to opportunity to compete upon terms which are compatible only with the male lifestyle. It is generally unlawful to discriminate against a woman on the mere suspicion that sooner or later she will put her domestic concerns before any others. In some respects, but by no means all, it can be unlawful to discriminate against her *now* because she has done so in the past. But patterns of employment which are designed to enable her to combine her responsibilities have justified discriminatory treatment. We are only now, and without much enthusiasm, beginning to recognize the right to equal treatment for work of equal value, as opposed to identical or equivalent content.

Nor is the small but increasing proportion of women who are willing to enter the market place entirely on male terms well served by the present position. Laws against discrimination will not assist them if they are still expected to expend a large part of their energies in servicing their competitors. As the Rapoports remark, 'though there is a substantial basis in social values, particularly middle-class values, to support the pattern as an expression of egalitarian orientation, the observed behaviour of husbands leads to the conclusion that this is often lip-service.'[13] There is a considerable gap between what these husbands say and what they in fact do to replace the time which their wives are unable to devote to household tasks. Many may choose the more entertaining activities while leaving their wives with even less satisfying housework.[14] The wives are nevertheless grateful for the concessions their husbands are prepared to make.

The old alternative of forgoing marriage or intimate relationships altogether is unacceptable to women who recognize that men have traditionally been able to enjoy both. Despite conventional male complaints about the burdens of matrimony, on most scales of well-being the balance of advantage in conventional marriage is clearly on their side.[15] The chances of women being able to enjoy those benefits are still remote. The genuine role-reversal family is extremely rare, for to all the disadvantages experienced by the female homemaker are added the astonishment and disapproval of a society which still expects its men to adopt their traditional careers. Fundamental changes in men's attitudes towards their own lives are necessary before this could be possible, but there would also have to be changes in women's attitudes towards men. Women still tend to 'tone down their own achievements out of deference to male self-esteem'.[16] Nor is the reversal of two equally rigid roles necessarily the right way forward.

These matters raise many questions about the organization of work, the current system of distributing resources outside the home and, above all, the distribution of roles and resources within it. The notions of 'domestic duties' or 'domestic responsibilities' are part of common speech as well as common experience. They could suggest a matter of legal obligation. Yet it is almost unthinkable to hear them used by or applied to a man. We will find, here as elsewhere, that the law is becoming more and more sex-neutral, but that it has hardly begun to accord equal treatment to the respective roles of homemaker and breadwinner or to encourage flexibility between them. There are many who believe that it should never do so, for every advance in the treatment of homemaking may retard its eventual abolition. Unfortunately, society cannot renege on its responsibilities to children, the sick and the old, who are still tended more frequently by their relatives than by any one else.[17] Society could more readily ignore the responsibilities of homemakers towards the breadwinners themselves, but encouraging the *breadwinners* to do so could be a long and difficult struggle. The question is: what part should the breadwinner's resources play in compensating the homemaker for her role?

Private Law and the Private Domain

Katherine O'Donovan has argued that 'legal institutions support the ordering of society on a gender-role basis.'[18] They are certainly a vital part of the process of separating the public and private domains. The law finds it difficult to recognize domestic labour as work unless it is performed on a commercial basis. Yet it is quite well aware of how valuable such labour can be to the people who benefit from it. We have seen that a mother who cares for a child who should never have been born cannot claim the value of her services. On the other hand, a child or husband who is wrongfully injured may claim the value of her services and hold it upon trust for her.[19] Kemp and Kemp find this 'hard to support on strict legal principles' because it is taken for granted that such services are rendered gratuitously.[20]

Similarly, the law refuses to acknowledge that domestic labour is a valuable contribution to the acquisitions of the household. Even where it is quite clear that the labour has added to their value, it has taken the law a long time to recognize that fact: is the cake which the homemaker bakes with the breadwinner's materials his, hers or theirs? On the other hand, the law has for centuries been prepared to grant compensation to a husband against a wrongdoer whose actions have deprived him of the services of his wife. In *Best* v. *Samuel Fox*[21] the House of Lords refused to extend a similar remedy to a wife whose husband had been made impotent in an accident at work, on the ground that the action was an anachronistic survival of the wife's chattel status at common law and better abolished than brought up to date. The effect was to reinforce the view that husbands are important to their wives primarily for their earning power, for the wrongful loss of which the husband must be compensated directly, whereas wives are important to their husbands primarily for their domestic services, which have a clear market value to husbands but not to wives. Now that it is almost certainly accepted that the wife is entitled to be compensated directly for the wrongful loss of her capacity to perform her chosen role, to allow the husband an independent claim for the same loss would be absurd. The husband's action has been abolished by the Administration of Justice Act 1982.

Nevertheless, the same ideas live on in claims under the Fatal Accidents Act 1976. Kemp and Kemp list the items which a husband may claim as pecuniary gains and losses against a wrongdoer who has killed his wife: the loss of her earnings, the expense of having to provide a housekeeper, including board and lodging and her own television, sending the children away to school, buying their clothes instead of having them made by the wife, having his own clothes mended and cleaned, eating meals out and the loss of the married man's tax allowance.[22] Against these must be set the savings in not having to maintain the wife or give her pocket money. It can safely be assumed that the cost of replacing her services will work out at a figure greater than the cost of maintaining her. However, it is also usually assumed that the husband will fairly swiftly replace her with another. The law can recognize that it pays a man to have a wife.

A widow's dependency is normally financial. Since 1971, in assessing her fatal accident claim, the courts have had to ignore her remarriage or prospects of remarriage, although these can still be taken into account in assessing the dependency of children. Many women felt degraded by the judicial appraisal of their chances in the witness box. Perhaps more important, it offended against masculine gallantry. The damages awarded can be very substantial, for the law does not require the wife to give credit for no longer having to perform her domestic services. She will usually have to go on doing so for the children.

Similarly, if a young woman is injured in such a way as to reduce or destroy her chances of marriage, she can usually claim damages for loss of amenity and possibly for the financial loss of the prospect of being maintained by a husband.[23] Both in claims against the wrongdoer and under the criminal injuries compensation scheme, the level of compensation payable to a woman for facial scars is far higher than that payable to a man. Indeed, her beauty is ranked higher than her chastity, for rape compensation is lower than both. Yet in view of the approach to the husband's dependency after his wife's death, the law might have decided that marriage involves a wife in financial loss. The better analogy, however, is employment, for in compensating for loss of earning power the courts do not inquire whether or not the employer was making a profit out of the worker's labour.

The Concept of Dependence

Three broad approaches to the economic relationship between breadwinner and homemaker have competed for acceptance by the law. The first is the concept of maintenance, which regards the breadwinner's assets as his and his alone but places him under an obligation to expend some of those assets in supporting his dependants. Those dependants are his wife and the children of their family, although he will also have an obligation to an illegitimate child of whom he is adjudged the father. During the post-war years this concept was increasingly thought both to offend against the more egalitarian ideals of modern marriage and to devalue the contribution made by the homemaker to the assets of the household and the earning power of the breadwinner. Considerable efforts were therefore made to replace the idea of maintenance with a concept more akin to matrimonial partnership. This never gained complete acceptance in principle and was extremely difficult to apply in practice. In recent years the law has been struggling to achieve an adjustment whereby the one who has gained most economically during the relationship provides some compensation for the losses suffered by the other. Unfortunately, English law remains confused about what it is trying to achieve in this area. All the signs at present are that the concept of maintenance is re-emerging, but in a form which is in many ways even less favourable to the homemaking spouse than it was in the past.

The common law insisted that a wife became dependent upon her husband. All her assets, including the product of her labour, became his property or subject to his control. In return, he had to maintain her, but decisions concerning their standard of living and the method of maintenance lay with him. He might allow his wife to have some of his money to spend on the household, but it remained his, as did anything she bought with it.[24] Indeed, that remained the law until the Married Women's Property Act 1964 gave wives equal shares in money derived from a housekeeping allowance made from husband to wife (but not vice versa) or things bought from it. Alternatively, the husband might allow his wife to pledge his credit with local tradesmen for housekeeping expenses. Wherever a man and a woman are living together there remains a presumption that he has done this, although he can readily rebut it by proof that he has not. Equally, however, a husband might maintain his dependants by providing for everything himself and allowing his wife no choice in the matter at all. It followed that he was under no obligation to maintain her in a separate household unless he chose to do so. If they separated by agreement, he might be liable (not to her directly but to tradesmen with whom she pledged his credit) to the extent that he had agreed to maintain her but had failed to do so. If he had deserted her without just cause or driven her from the home, he was liable to an extent appropriate to their standard of living. But where the separation was the fault of the wife, or where she was later guilty of adultery, he was under no obligation towards her, even though the common law refused to give her the right to acquire any resources of her own. Not until *Brannan* v. *Brannan*[25] was it recognized that his obligation remained during an enforced separation which was the fault of neither party.

Since the sixteenth century families with property had been able to retain assets for the benefit of wife and children through the medium of the marriage settlement. The Married Women's Property Acts of 1870 and 1882 allowed all married women to retain and acquire assets as if these had been settled on them for their separate use. This marked the end of the wife's automatic dependence upon her husband and allowed her to participate in the market place if she could. However, it also coincided with the entrenchment of housewife marriage across all sections of society. This had started in the agrarian revolution of the eighteenth century, with the progressive withdrawal of the farmer's wife into the drawing-room,[26] to be followed by the urban wives whose middle-class status was defined by the possession of a servant. Lower down the social scale breadwinning was also now done for money outside the home. The disciplines of the factory conflicted with the housewife's domestic duties, and there was no incentive for the employer to make concessions. As Tilly and Scott point out, 'The resolution of the conflict was for married women not to work unless family finances urgently required it, and then to try and find work which conflicted least with their domestic responsibilities.'[27] Her connection with the generation of the family's resources became much less direct than it had been in the days of agricultural production and cottage industry. No longer was her husband deemed as a matter of law to be the owner of her product outside the home, but as he was the owner both of his own wages and of her product within it, the result was the same — indeed worse. The obligation of the breadwinner to support the homemaker became increasingly prominent both in his wage negotiations and in family law.

Remedies were provided in the magistrates' courts (and later in the High Court) to oblige the husband to support his family, but they suffered from two defects. First, magistrates' orders could be enforced only after the couple had separated. The law was reluctant to intervene where husband and wife were still together or even to enforce the agreements which they had made between themselves.[28] Second, they depended upon the same principles as the common law duty and thus upon showing that the husband was, and the wife was not, at fault. No matter how great her dependence over how long a period, or how relatively unimportant her conduct had been in the context of the marriage or their separation, the guilty wife was unable to seek support while the marriage subsisted. That remained the law until 1981.

The law governing the financial consequences of divorce, nullity and judicial separation has always been rather different. Judicial separation, which relieves the parties of the obligation to live together but leaves the marriage intact, originated in the ecclesiastical courts. Alimony would be granted to a wife who could prove that her husband had been guilty of cruelty or adultery. As in the magistrates' courts, therefore, it was possible to regard the husband's duty to pay it as the price he had to pay for breaking his matrimonial obligations, her damages for his breach of their life-long personal contract and his punishment for the matrimonial offence.

This is how the Law Commission explained the persistence of maintenance after divorce when considering the matter in 1980.[29] Such an analysis obviously lends great weight to what it saw as a 'fundamental' criticism. Once divorce law abandons its reliance upon the concept of matrimonial fault, as it did in 1971, there can be no breach of contract and no matrimonial offence. Damages or penalties are therefore inappropriate. However, this analysis leaves out of account the fact that Parliament has always recognized that there may be an obligation to compensate for the economic consequences of marriage, irrespective of who was to blame for its eventual ending. Parliament itself had initiated the practice of divorce, by private Act, and had always required the outraged husband to make at least some provision for his guilty wife, to enable her to live quietly, as the price of his freedom to marry again. The Matrimonial Causes Act of 1857, which transferred this jurisdiction and that of the ecclesiastical courts to a new divorce court, allowed the court to award financial provision to both innocent and guilty wives. At first it followed the ecclesiastical practice, but

> by about the 1880s...the guilty wife, as under the old parliamentary practice, would have some modicum awarded to her; the innocent wife, as under the old ecclesiastical practice, would be granted a proportion, almost always one-third of the joint income, and, in addition, an amount in respect of any children committed to her custody.[30]

Lord Justice Lindley listed the relevant factors as the parties' 'conduct, their position in life, ages and respective means, the amount of provision actually made, the presence or absence of children and who was to care for them, and any other important circumstances in the particular case'.[31]

Over the period between then and the 1971 divorce law the courts attached increasing importance to the degree of dependence and the needs of the children. They also began to realize that the moral blame, if any, to be attached to the breakdown of a marriage did not invariably coincide with the crude findings in the divorce suit. A wife guilty of adultery might be entirely deprived of support, 'for example, where it broke up the marriage, where it is continuing and where she is being supported by her paramour',[32] but 'the court must always take into account how long the marriage has lasted and to what extent the wife has rendered her domestic services to her husband', especially if he wished her to do so to the exclusion of anything else, and also that where the children are with her ('If she suffers they will suffer').[33]

This development is passed over very swiftly by the Law Commission in pursuing its contractual analogy,[34] but it is evident that the courts at least had ceased to regard the husband's duty to provide for his wife after divorce as the price to be paid for his breach of contract. More properly, the husband was regarded as having a life-long duty to support his wife, which duty might be reduced or extinguished to the extent that she was to blame for their marital breakdown.[35] Issues of conduct have hardly ever been raised in relation to financial matters in order to increase the 'damages' payable by the husband. They are almost invariably raised by him in order to decrease what his wife would otherwise be entitled to claim. The divorce court may have been reluctant to diminish her claims entirely, but it was certainly prepared to reduce them to the extent that she had been less than perfect in relation to the marriage.

Quite apart from the importance of conduct, however, the concept of maintenance suffers from the difficulty that it can work satisfactorily only in one direction. It depends upon the premise that the innocent wife has the inalienable right to her husband's support until his death (and even beyond if he has the means to pay). Until 1971, he was not absolved even by her remarriage, for if her second husband was a poorer man, she might continue to receive something from her first. Nor was she under much obligation to mitigate her damage by attempting to support herself. Her fortune was relevant and her earnings might be taken into account, but he could not evade his responsibility entirely by expecting her to get a job after he had left.[36] The wife herself had very little obligation to maintain her family.

These principles served to reinforce the individualism of the few women who had, or could acquire, sufficient resources of their own and the subordination of those who could not. It was even possible to combine individualism with dependence on the husband for basic support. The charge, at least, was common that the wife could take the view that 'what's thine's mine and what's mine's my own.' For the great mass of wives and mothers who were unable or unwilling to compete in the market place on equal terms the concept of maintenance could clearly be an instrument of oppression. The separate property system refused to recognize the value of their contributions to the family's assets and to the bread-winner's earning power. His duty to expend some of his resources in providing for those who were dependent upon him could be reduced if they remained less than wholly faithful to the marital commitment which it was much easier for him to repudiate, should he so wish. Meanwhile, everything was under his control.

The Ideal of Marital Partnership

During the twentieth century, as prosperity has increased, so has the family's surplus above bare subsistence. The emphasis on the family as a unit of consumption has become greater. The family itself has tended to shrink to the couple and their young children, who will expect to leave when they are able to become self-supporting. It has also become more private, with the members spending a great deal of their time together. But, for a while at least, the differentiation of roles between breadwinner and homemaker became even greater. Increased expectations and technological change combined to make the homemaker's task less arduous but more complex. Labour-saving devices did not reduce the time spent in looking after the home but raised the levels of comfort and cleanliness expected. The developing sense of what was due to a child also played a part in determining how the housewife was expected to spend her day. These expectations remain, even though married women are returning to the labour force in greater numbers. Many are doing so, indeed, because the money is needed to maintain these standards.

During those same post-war years legal writers and some legal changes began to develop the idea of an economic partnership in marriage. This sees the marriage as a common enterprise to which the parties make different but equally valuable contributions, which should be rewarded with an equal share in its assets. Advocates of this view undoubtedly had in mind the more egalitarian attitudes which had been developing within middle-class marriage, although the potential for making some improvement in the status of the oppressed housewife was also there. But it is probable that the concept would never have gained currency had it not been for the acceptance in some very influential circles of the argument that the homemaking role has a genuine economic value. Professor Kahn-Freund, for example, saw the idea of shared ownership of the family's assets as the natural extension into the law of property of the efforts made by the law of maintenance to redress the 'natural inequality' in the functions of husband and wife.[37] When Sir Jocelyn Simon advocated the idea in his famous statement, 'The cock bird can feather his nest precisely because he is not required to spend most of his time sitting on it,'[38] he was pointing specifically to the economic contribution made by the housewife's work.

This is a complex of several factors. Her work clearly has a straightforward economic value because it consists of products and services which can be bought and sold on the open market. Their value is not diminished simply because she does not trade them in this fashion, although their cost to the husband is certainly reduced. The economists' emphasis on the consuming role of the family has also tended to obscure the fact that a great deal of added value can be contributed to the raw materials by the housewife's skill, as any dual-career family casting envious eyes at the cooking, baking, decorating, dressmaking and other home comforts provided by the housewife will understand. Moreover, the subtle skills of turning a house into a home, along with the comfort and support which the homemaker can offer to the breadwinner, enhance his ability to compete in the market place. In some occupations the possession of a wife who is capable of supporting her husband's career in this way is an essential qualification for the job.[39] In others she participates directly.[40]

This partnership principle has the great advantage of living happily with a system in which the spouses adopt varying career patterns to suit their own wishes and circumstances. Gray quotes McDougal, Lasswell and Chen: 'To achieve genuine equality between the sexes, it is vital that "nobody be forced into a predetermined role on account of sex, but each person be given better possibilities to develop his or her personal talents"'.[41] He then goes on:

> In view of the current movement away from the culturally defined allocation of spousal roles towards sexual equality and self-determination, it is of paramount importance that the apportionment of matrimonial property on divorce should not favour one conjugal role in preference to the other. A formula must be sought which will remove the odious discrimination between the financial and domestic roles performed by the spouses.[42]

The essential feature of the partnership concept is reciprocity: each partner is expected to make a contribution, but the nature of that contribution is not predetermined by sex and can vary over time. Husbands can become homemakers as well.

However, it also suffers from two main disadvantages which have impeded its full acceptance. First, the emphasis upon contributions, with the suggestion that these invariably have an economic value of some sort to the couple, can be very unconvincing. As Clive has pointed out:

> Some wives do less work in the home than they would if they were employed and live at a higher standard of living than they would if they were employed. Generally speaking the wealthier the husband the less housework the traditionally oriented housewife does, so that the effect of this proposal [for automatic co-ownership of the matrimonial home] is that the housewives who work most get least and those who work least get most — a curious form of justice.[43]

Clive himself prefers the principle of fair sharing, which he believes underlies most marriages, at least while they remain intact.[44] However, there is little doubt that the picture of the leisured lady who does least and gets most lies behind much of the lack of enthusiasm for imposing any sort of co-ownership during marriage or any sort of equal sharing of the family's assets when the marriage comes to an end.

The second objection to the partnership principle is more formidable. Partnership is easier to apply to tangible assets than to any other aspect of a couple's resources, such as their earning potential or ability to bring up children. Its adherents also assume that the distribution of those tangible assets should take place when the common enterprise ceases on divorce or death. Taken to its logical conclusion, therefore, the principle would force a sale of the matrimonial home irrespective of whether that would in fact maximize the housing available to the parties, a division of all their other family assets and the complete parting of the ways. Many of the opponents of continuing periodical payments after divorce do indeed envisage this, for they are not opposed to the principle of fair sharing of family property.[45]

For a while English law came close to adopting some of the principles of partnership. In retrospect, the high point was the decision of the Court of Appeal in *Wachtel* v. *Wachtel*.[46] This was preceded by a period during which the limitations of the separate property system became steadily more apparent. A wife's right to live in a home belonging to her husband ended when the marriage did. Unless the home had been conveyed in their joint names, therefore, she stood to lose not only the roof over her head but also any share in the proceeds of sale of their major asset.

This was first thought to be unjust to those women who had made some financial contribution to the acquisition of a home which had been intended for their common use but conveyed to the husband alone. Faced with the uncontemplated breakdown of the marriage, the courts began to impose a trust upon the proceeds of sale by asking themselves what the parties must have intended when they bought the house. Had house prices been going down, the courts might instead have decided that the wife intended only to lend the money to her husband, so that she would be entitled to be repaid with interest, while he had the house encumbered also by the mortgage debt. But as house prices were rising, there was a much greater incentive to decide that they had intended to share beneficial ownership, even though chance, habit or the insistence of the building society might have led to the conveyance of the whole legal estate to the husband.

The courts began by recognizing the wife's direct contributions to the initial deposit and legal fees,[47] then took into account her substantial payment of mortgage instalments,[48] then her payments into an actual pool of joint resources from which mortgage instalments were paid.[49] Lord Denning also favoured the concept of the 'notional pool', whereby one spouse undertook responsibility for mortgage instalments and the other for day-to-day expenditure on food, cleaning, utensils and the like.[50] Others were less attracted by this idea of indirect contributions.[51] Discriminating against them almost inevitably discriminated against the wife. Todd and Jones found that the husband more often actually paid the housing bills when it was owner-occupied, and even more often when he was paid otherwise than in cash. [52] Where the husband has the larger and more regular income which is paid into a bank account, it makes obvious sense for him to pay the larger household bills by standing order from that account. At least English law assumes that a joint account is jointly owned unless there is good evidence of a contrary intention. Where there is no such account, the value of the wife's expenditure upon food and other items will be lost unless the law is prepared to call them indirect contributions. Todd and Jones found that the wife was overwhelmingly responsible for buying food, whether or not the money derived from her earnings, [53] and the Hunt Committee found that this sort of expenditure was the usual use to which the wife's earnings were put. [54] The eventual conclusion of the House of Lords in *Gissing* v. *Gissing*[55] seemed to recognize indirect contributions only if these could be related to the acquisition of the house — for example, by allowing the husband to reduce the housekeeping money so that he could afford the instalments. [56] The mere fact that the wife had been employed full-time throughout the marriage and had spent her money on furniture, the garden, clothing for herself and the child and family holidays was not enough. Thus she *had* to expend all or most of her money on housekeeping in order to gain an interest, whereas her husband could readily retain a surplus for his own entertainment. It is small comfort that Jephcott, Seear and Smith found that this was in fact what tended to happen. [57]

Although Lord Denning was still prepared to take a broad view of indirect contributions, even he had to accept that the law could not recognize any contribution other than in 'money or money's worth'. A husband who used specialist skills in renovating a tumbledown cottage[58] or converted his wife's property into money-earning flats[59] might gain an interest, but he certainly would not do so by decorating or putting up a shelf or working in the garden. [60] A wife who worked unpaid in her husband's business might gain an interest in a home bought from the profits, [61] perhaps even in the business itself. But looking after the home and the household budget, doing the decorating and other routine household tasks, did not count as 'money or money's worth'. [62] For a while, however, the law gave indirect recognition to the spouses' different career patterns, through the maxim 'Equality is equity'. Provided that she could show some contribution — and many post-war wives who gave up work only when the first child came along could do this — then, unless it was clear what the couple had intended their shares to be, the court might conclude that they intended them to be equal. Once again, however, the House of Lords in *Gissing* v. *Gissing*[63] emphasized that the court must do its best to quantify the precise financial contribution made.

None of these principles was capable of recognizing the wife's domestic work as *work*. They were simply translating traditional concepts into a 1960s setting. This has continued now that the emphasis has shifted to extra-marital cohabitations. The courts can recognize a contribution which has clearly added value to the property[64] but not the value of her other work. Indeed, the emphasis on financial contributions may recently have increased. [65] There used to be a presumption that a house conveyed into the joint names of husband and wife belonged to them equally, but such presumptions have been discounted.[66] The court must deduce from the behaviour of both parties what their real intentions were. This applies to both married and unmarried couples.[67] The behaviour in question, however, is almost invariably their respective contributions in 'money or money's worth'. Although Lord Denning mentions cash, kind or *services*, these services cannot include looking after the home and bringing up children.[68] Even wives, therefore, should take care to insist that both the legal and the beneficial interests are clearly stated whenever a house is bought in joint names.

Although these concepts are clearly inadequate to recognize the wife's role as a genuinely equal contributor to the family economy, they do have the merit of entirely ignoring her matrimonial guilt or innocence, at least in theory. The cynical might suggest that even these advances would never have been made had the wives in question been manifestly to blame for the breakdown of their marriages. There is certainly some evidence for a tendency to try to reintroduce conduct when the wife wished to force a sale of the jointly owned home[69] or when considering whether credit should be given for mortgage payments made by the husband after he had been left there.[70] But the attempts generally failed because they were inimical to the principles of property law, which concentrate upon the purpose for which the trust was set up (providing a home for the family)[71] and the apportionment of liabilities between co-owners.[72]

During the 1970s the Law Commission gave serious consideration to introducing a system of community of matrimonial property into English law[73] but concluded that it was necessary only to insist upon automatic joint ownership of the matrimonial home.[74] In 1980 Lord Simon of Glaisdale (as Sir Jocelyn had since become) attempted to implement this by Private Member's Bill but encountered resistance from the Lord Chancellor. Perhaps it was just as well. The complex scheme recommended by the Law Commission depended upon the wife registering her rights if she was to gain protection against third parties to whom her husband disposed of the home. A wife who had not insisted upon the conveyance of the home into joint names in the first place would be unlikely to protect herself by registration. Since then the House of Lords has held that her beneficial interest is protected if she is in actual occupation of registered land.[75] Introduction of the Law Commission's scheme[76] would probably be a retrograde step. On the other hand, the difficulties caused to lending institutions by that case may also result in their insisting that most matrimonial homes are now bought in joint names.

The Scottish Law Commission has recently shown a marked lack of enthusiasm for introducing automatic co-ownership there.[77] One of its reasons is that any injustice can more easily be cured by the discretionary powers of the courts once the marriage has ended. As the spouses' strict property rights would have to be subordinated to those in any event, there is little reason to interfere with their existing arrangements while the marriage subsists. Such arguments not only ignore the majority of marriages which end in death rather than divorce but also discount the very real importance of property rights in determining the power structure during marriage.

The courts' discretionary powers on divorce, nullity or judicial separation were revised and extended at the same time as the divorce law which came into force in 1971. There were three main changes. First, all their powers were made entirely reciprocal, so that they could be used for or against husband or wife, as well as for the benefit of their children. Secondly, the courts were given power to adjust the strict property rights of either spouse in almost any way they wished, in addition to their existing powers to award periodical payments, with or without capital security, and a lump sum of unlimited amount.[78] Thirdly, the statutory instructions guiding the exercise of their discretion required them to have regard to the contributions made by each spouse to the welfare of the family, including any contribution made by looking after the home and caring for the family.[79] At last domestic responsibilities were recognized as a contribution to welfare, if not as work.

At the first opportunity the Court of Appeal, under Lord Denning's leadership, sought to translate these new features into something very like the concept of partnership. Reciprocity means that the courts are no longer obliged simply to consider how much of what is his should be expended by the husband in maintaining his former family. All the assets of both parties can be placed in a notional pool and shared out between them. The powers of property adjustment mean that this can be done with both income and capital, including the matrimonial home. The contributions and shares of the parties can be approached on a footing of equality, irrespective of the purely financial value of those contributions. Above all, perhaps, if the resources are to be shared between two equal partners, their matrimonial conduct will hardly ever be relevant. Under the maintenance concept the wife might suffer a discount from her 100 per cent entitlement if she was less than 100 per cent innocent in the marital breakdown. Under a partnership concept, if the partners are equally to blame, they are still entitled to an equal distribution. Only if one is very much more to blame than the other should it affect matters at all.

This, in effect, was the approach adopted by the Court of Appeal in *Wachtel* v. *Wachtel*.[80] This middle-class marriage had lasted some eighteen years. There were two teenage children, a boy remaining with the father during his holidays from boarding school and a girl living with the mother. The parties were equally to blame for the breakup. It was a copybook example of a marriage to which breadwinner and housewife could be assumed to have made their differing contributions over a number of years. Their combined resources were sufficient to enable the court to grant the wife a share in the value of the matrimonial home in order to provide a new home for herself and their daugher, without depriving the husband and son of theirs. Their combined incomes were just about sufficient to enable each new household to function independently, albeit at a reduced standard of living.

It looked, then, like a case in which a new norm of equal sharing could be applied. The trial judge awarded the wife a lump sum equivalent to half the equity in the house and the wife and daughter an income equivalent to half the couple's combined incomes. The Court of Appeal adopted much the same reasoning but reduced these proportions to a third, for two reasons. First:

> When a marriage breaks up, there will thenceforward be two households instead of one. The husband will have to go out to work all day and must get some woman to look after the house — either a wife if he remarries, or a housekeeper, if he does not. He will also have to provide maintenance for the children. The wife will not usually have so much expense. She may go out to work herself, but she will not usually employ a housekeeper. She will do most of the housework herself, perhaps with some help. Or she may remarry, in which case her new husband will provide for her. In any case, where there are two households, the greater expense will, in most cases, fall on the husband than the wife.

Quite apart from its sexist assumptions about who can do what about a house, this reasoning can apply only where the husband's contributions towards the maintenance of the child in the wife's custody are sufficient to defray all the costs of keeping that child and where the wife does not work full-time outside the home whereas the husband does. Otherwise a mother who is in full-time employment is just as much entitled to seek help in the house as is a father. There can be no justification for reducing the wife and child to living on an income which is little more than half that of the husband. Nor can it apply to capital. The fact that a man may feel obliged to pay directly or indirectly for tasks which a woman is prepared to do does not explain why he should be entitled to a home and savings which are twice as valuable as hers. Secondly, however:

> If we were only concerned with the capital assets of the family, and particularly with the matrimonial home, it would be tempting to divide them half and half, as the judge did. That would be fair enough if the wife afterwards went her own way, making no further demands on the husband. It would be simply a division of the assets of the partnership. That may come in the future. But at present few wives are content with a share of the capital assets. Most wives want their former husbands to make periodical payments as well to support them; because, after the divorce, he will be earning far more than she; and she can only keep up her standard of living with his help. He also has to make payments for the children out of his earnings, even if they are with her. In view of all these calls on his future earnings, we do not think she can have both — half the capital assets, and half the earnings.

In other words, one-third represents a compromise between dissolving the partnership in order to share out its existing assets and keeping it alive in order to share out its future income. The court was obliged to look to the future because of the statutory objective laid down for the exercise of its discretion. Having taken all the circumstances into account, it was to try, so far as it was practicable, and having regard to the conduct of the parties just to do so, to place each of them 'in the financial position in which they would have been if the marriage had not broken down and each had properly discharged his or her financial obligations and responsibilities towards the other'.[81] The lifelong commitment to maintain the standard of living established during marriage was thus preserved.

Once again, this provides no justification for the one-third approach. Had the marriage not broken down, the couple would have continued living together and enjoying a similar standard of living (although it must be said that many husbands and wives do *not* enjoy a similar standard of living, particularly in respect of the amount they can spend on personal entertainment). In reality, the *Wachtel*[82] approach demonstrates a perceived incompatibility between the attempt to share out tangible assets equitably on the basis of past contributions and the attempt to provide roughly equal standards of living for both parties in the future. This incompatibility arises because it is still not accepted that the homemaker's contribution to those tangible assets is indeed as valuable as that made by the breadwinner's hard-earned money, while her contribution to his earning power, both in the past and in the future, is not recognized at all. If those points had been genuinely accepted, the approach of the trial judge in *Wachtel* would have been upheld.

The Principle of Equal Misery

The main obstacle to achieving even the limited form of partnership envisaged in *Wachtel*, however, has been its sheer impracticability in the great majority of cases. The resources of housing, income and potential income which previously supported one household cannot maintain the same standard of living in two, whether or not they are shared out in proportion to past contributions. More and more, the courts have departed from the concepts laid down in *Wachtel* and have attempted to return to the precise words of the Matrimonial Causes Act 1973 guidelines.[83]

The most frequent reason for departing from the one-third share of income is that the husband simply cannot afford to pay it. If he is made to pay a sum which will depress his income below subsistence level, the state will not make up the difference. In general, it will also take away any widows' or means-tested benefits which it was formerly paying to any woman with whom he cohabits. On the other hand, if the sums he pays are not enough to raise his former wife and children to subsistence level, the state will do so. The courts do not take all of their supplementary benefit entitlement into account as a resource available to them, for in many cases this would enable the husband to throw the whole burden of supporting his former family on to the state. Instead they accept that the state's assistance means that they can cease to ask, 'How much do the wife and children need?' and ask merely, 'How much should he be allowed to keep?'[84] The only live issue has been whether he should be able to keep a margin above subsistence level for himself and his new family, so as to maintain his work incentive, or whether he should be reduced to a standard equivalent to that of his former family. The latter view has won the day.[85]

Because the only benefits available to the former family are means-tested, whatever the husband does pay is of no advantage to it at all. It is usually paid into the magistrates' court, which then pays it direct to the DHSS, so that the family can collect the same amount of benefit each week irrespective of how much has been paid in maintenance. The problems of one-parent families subsisting in this way are well-known,[86] but a recent study of divorced people with children has re-emphasized some important points about the relationship between private support and their circumstances.[87] *Fewer* mothers were in employment after the separation than had been before.[88] It is more difficult to find work, especially the part-time work which is so crucial to the domestic economy of many two-parent families, to fit in with child-care responsibilities when there is only one adult in the household. It is also difficult to find full-time work which will pay the mother enough to lift her above supplementary benefit level *and* to compensate her for all the other benefits which are linked to it *and* to take account of the extra costs to her of going out to work. The supplementary benefit rules already incorporate a more generous disregard of part-time earnings for one-parent families than for other claimants. From their point of view, as Maclean and Eekelaar suggest,[89] far and away the most useful reform of the law would be to provide for an equivalent disregard of maintenance payments. The payer would also know that his payments were doing some good.

Davis, Macleod and Murch also found a positive correlation between the payment of maintenance and the mother being in employment.[90] An obvious reason for this is that while few ex-husbands can afford enough to keep their former wives and children above subsistence level, they can afford enough to make it economically feasible for the mother to go out to work. Not only this, the higher the husband's socio-economic class, the more likely is his ex-wife to continue in employment. She may be able to command an income high enough to escape the poverty trap, while he may be able to afford enough to make it worth her while. The tax system undoubtedly contributes to this by allowing the custodial parent the equivalent of a married man's personal allowance and a full single person's allowance against payments ordered to be made direct to each child, and by allowing the non-custodial parent full tax relief on all payments made by court order. The calculation has, as far as is known, not been done, but it is interesting to speculate upon whether this indirect subsidy to the better-off costs more than would a limited disregard of maintenance against means-tested benefits to the less well-off. It is even more interesting to speculate upon whether the withdrawal of maintenance payments to those mothers who are able to go out to work would result in far more of them becoming caught in the poverty trap, and whether the means-tested benefits then claimed would cost the community more than the tax relief they enjoy at present. Certainly, the financial consequences of divorce cannot be understood in isolation from the laws of tax and social security, which at present enhance the distinctions of social class.

Even among divorced mothers the proportion whose largest source of income is maintenance is low and the proportion who subsist on maintenance alone even lower.[91] The reason is almost certainly shortage of money, for 'a dominant theme in our interviews concerned both parents' continuing sense of obligation to maintain their children.'[92] Less is known about the circumstances of childless divorcees, including those whose children have grown up, but Eekelaar and Maclean found that in only a very small proportion was there any provision for continuing periodical payments at the divorce and that in no case were payments in fact being made at the time of the research interviews.[93] Alimony drones are very hard to find.

The most frequent reason for departing from the share-out of capital is the need to preserve the home for the children and their custodial parent.[94] Occasionally the custodial parent may be in a position to buy out the interest of the other. More often, until quite recently, the house would be resettled so that it could not be sold and the proceeds divided until the children grew up or the custodial parent wished to move.[95] But then the custodial parent may find it difficult to obtain alternative accommodation, and so the court may allow her to stay on after the children have grown up, paying rent to the other co-owner who is thus being kept out of his money.[96] Another solution to that problem, which is particularly appropriate where the husband will not or cannot pay substantial maintenance, is to transfer his whole interest in the home to the custodial parent outright, in return for reduced or extinguished financial provision.[97]

In Eekelaar and Maclean's small-scale but representative study of the financial consequences of divorce,[98] the effects of children upon the disposition of the matrimonial home were obvious. Financial problems might force a sale of the house, but if it was not sold, the wife stayed on in more than half the cases, undoubtedly to provide a home for the children and irrespective of legal owner-ship. Where there were no children, disposition of the home depended upon legal ownership. If it was jointly owned, it would either be sold and the proceeds divided or one of them (almost always the husband) would remain in return for a lump sum to the other (save in a few cases where the wife left to live with another man). If the house was in the husband's sole name, the wife never stayed there and hardly ever received a share in its value. Although these childless marriages tended to be shorter, there is no indication here of the acceptance of a norm of matrimonial sharing by these couples or by the courts which settled their affairs. The wife may even have been deprived of her beneficial interest under the principles of property law discussed earlier.

These studies indicate a sharp distinction between divorces where there are children and those where there are none. The case law, however, tends to rely upon other concepts to justify departure from the statutory objective. The House of Lords promoted the objective of the 'clean break' in *Minton v. Minton*[99] but partly in order to prevent the wife from reopening an agreed settlement. Since then the courts have shown considerable reluctance on both points. A settlement which has not been embodied in a court order can always be reassessed, and even those where an agreed order has been made can be overturned if the wife was suffering from great emotional distress at the time,[100] although elsewhere it has been held that undue influence is not sufficient.[101] It has also been decided that a wife's claim for periodical payments cannot be dismissed out of hand without her consent[102] and that where an order for continuing periodical payments has been made she cannot be prevented from coming back to court and asking for more.[103] These cases may perhaps be related to the view that an enforced clean break is not appropriate where there are children, especially if they would otherwise have to be supported by the state.[104]

There undoubtedly are cases where the courts are prepared to enforce a clean or cleanish break. Both divorce and magistrates' courts may make an order for a limited duration, and in *H. v. H. (Financial Provision: Short Marriage)* it was said:[105]

> where one has...a very short marriage between two young perons, neither of whom has been adversely affected financially by the consequences of the marriage and each of whom is fully capable of earning his or her own living, the approach which the court should normally adopt is to allow the party who is in the weaker financial position (usually, as here, the wife) to adjust herself to the situation....

Despite the doubts expressed by the Law Commission,[106] this principle has been applied to both magistrates' and divorce courts.[107]

Exactly the same approach has been taken to capital. In *Churchill v. Churchill*[108] the Court of Appeal set aside a lump-sum order in a very short childless marriage precisely because 'neither of them have suffered any economic damage as a result of the marriage. The wife is working successfully in her career which has not been in any way adversely influenced.... They acquired between them no assets to which they contributed.' In *Potter v. Potter*[109] the marrige had lasted six years, but again there were no children and both parties earned good incomes. The wife had remained in the home, which was transferred to her. She claimed not periodical payments but a lump sum. This the trial judge calculated by adding up their assets and giving her a one-third share, which included the house. Lord Justice Ormrod remarked that, had it not been for the statutory objective of placing the parties in the same financial positions as if they had remained married, he would not have thought this a case for any lump sum at all, and the order was more than halved.

This case indicates how far the courts have moved from the partnership principle laid down in *Wachtel*. If they had believed in that principle, they would have shared out the assets on an equal basis, instead of relegating the wife to much less than one-third. On the other hand, they might have asked how much of those assets were indeed attributable to the partnership, for a great deal was the result of the husband's unaided efforts in his business. They have been much more generous to wives of longstanding who have contributed towards the establishment of a successful business as well as bringing up their husbands' children,[110] although not always to the extent of giving her one-third.

Incidentally, the cases in which wives have been ordered to make provision for their husbands have also involved family businesses to which the husband has made some contribution.[111] These awards have been for the purpose of buying a home. The courts still do not take kindly to husbands living on their wives' resources unless their earning capacity is obviously impaired by disability.

All of this indicates that two principles have been competing for the courts' attention. They know that the statutory objective cannot usually be attained, but where there are children they are still trying to achieve roughly equal standards of living for both households after the marriage has broken down. They seek to affirm the father's prior responsibility to his first family. Nevertheless, they have to take his *responsibilities* to any new family into account in deciding how much is available to support the first.[112] Contrary to popular belief, the *resources* of a second wife cannot be used to support the first. But they are relevant in so far as they prevent the husband from arguing that he needs to keep all his own resources in order to support her.[113] If, therefore, the relationship is established *after* his liabilities to his first family have been determined, his second wife may find that she cannot give up work and become dependent upon him. The difficulty is less likely to arise if she has become dependent upon him *before* his liabilities to his first family are decided, for then her needs can be taken into account from the outset.

Where there are no children the courts have been groping their way towards a policy of attempting to compensate for the economic disadvantage resulting from the marriage, but no more. Even in a short marriage the wife may have lost a widow's pension or given up a secure home,[114] and the courts try to compensate for this. In a longer marriage they may allow the wife to remain in the matrimonial home if the husband is adequately housed.[115] There is not much evidence of continuing periodical payments, and every case has indicated a willingness to take the wife's potential as well as her actual earning capacity into account. But if she has none or very little, the court may only be able to achieve equal misery, or to compensate her for the effects of the marriage, by awarding some maintenance. Save in the case of the marriage which has done little or no economic harm to either party, the courts are still concerned with their *future* positions. However, this may no longer be the case, when the Matrimonial and Family Proceedings Act 1984 becomes law.

A Step in the Dark

The main purpose of the Matrimonial and Family Proceedings Act is to repeal the statutory instruction to place the parties in the position in which they would have been had the marriage not broken down. Marriage will no longer involve a life-long economic commitment. Although the courts will still be directed to take into account the parties' resources and responsibilities, their ages and any disabilities, the length of their marriage and their standard of living during it, as well as their respective contributions and prospective loss of benefits because of the divorce, there will be no indication that the courts should attempt to achieve rough equality in living standards after the break. There will be little to indicate that they should seek to share out the assets accumulated during the partnership, for this was always the creation of Lord Denning in *Wachtel* rather than the result of the statute. There will be nothing to suggest that the courts should seek to compensate for the economic disadvantage resulting from the relationship.

Instead the courts will be directed to give first priority to the welfare of the couple's children for as long as they remain under the age of 18. They will also be instructed to consider whether it would be appropriate to end the adults' financial responsibilities towads one another as soon as 'just and reasonable' or to require periodical payments 'only for such term as would in the opinion of the court be sufficient to enable the party in whose favour the order is made to adjust without undue hardship to the termination of his or her financial dependence on the other party'. They will be able to dismiss an application for such payments without consent. When assessing the parties' resources they will have to take into account increases in earning capacity which it would be reasonable to expect them to acquire. They will also have to take into account the conduct of each of the parties if it would be 'inequitable' to disregad it.

It is tempting to conclude that these changes will make very little difference in practice. The courts already try to do their best for the children. They will probably continue to disregard the conduct of the custodial parent, on the ground that 'if she suffers, they will suffer.'[116] The second family will presumably still be subordinated to the needs of the first unless there is clear evidence that the custodial parent could increase her earning power. The changes may therefore do little to meet the wishes of the Campaign for Justice in Divorce.[117] That campaign was launched mainly by husbands and their second wives, who objected that the dependency induced by the first marriage prevented the husband from making a second family dependent upon him. Equally, however, the changes will do nothing to mitigate the hardship suffered by most one-parent families or the discriminatory results of the present policies of the tax and social security systems. That hardship undoubtedly means that the best way in which most one-parent families can lift themselves out of poverty is through remarriage.[118] It could be thought that the only way to break into this vicious circle of marriage and remarriage would be to re-examine social policies which might have been designed to throw the divorced mother straight into dependence upon a second husband.

Nevertheless, the changes clearly represent a major rewriting of the marital bargain. The problem case is obviously the wife whose children have grown up or who has had no children but has devoted her life to being a wife. For her the courts will have to consider how soon they can end her support, possibly by making a rehabilitative award, possibly by making none at all. It is not clear whether the court should be aiming at the self-sufficiency of the wage packet or of the dole queue. Nor is it clear what the effect upon capital adjustments will be. The Bill was the result of Law Commission discussions[119] which concentrated almost entirely on maintenance payments. Yet the changed guidelines apply just as much to capital and property. They give not a hint of the partnership ideas which were such a prominent feature of the earlier debates about family property. The Government, which has been quick to implement these proposals, has been strongly opposed to implementing the scheme for co-ownership of the matrimonial home or any other form of sharing during the marriage. The Law Commission's discussion document[120] contains a powerful section on the effects of marriage and family responsibilities upon the position of women in the market place. Unlike the Scottish Law Commission,[121] however, it did not discuss whether the attempt to redress those disadvantages could provide a satisfactory model for reform.

There may be no obvious reason why a breadwinner should have to compensate a homemaker for the disadvantage suffered by all woman in the market place.[122] Perhaps we should not visit the sins of the male-dominated world on the individual men whose marriages break up. But there is no good reason why she should not be entitled to compensation for the disadvantages which are clearly the result of their common expectations and behaviour during the relationship. We may all hope that eventually women will gain an equal right to compete in the market place, although the idea that employment should be the only meritorious method of distributing wealth is already beginning to wear an old-fashioned look. But the main reason why a wife cannot do so lies in those domestic responsibilities which both she and her husband expect her to perform. If all husbands were prepared to asume an equal share of household tasks and child care, there might be no disadvantage suffered and no corresponding obligation to provide compensation.[123] At present, however, while men can choose whether or not to marry a wife who wishes to pursue a career outside the home, there is usually only one form of husbandly lifestyle on offer to women. The loss which she suffers as a result of that can often be permanent (think, for example, of state and private pensions). Expecting her to mitigate that loss if she can is not the same as depriving her of any right to compensation for it. The courts had been feeling their way towards some principle of compensation before Parliament intervened.

The model which is about to be adopted looks very different. The spouses will remain under a duty to provide for one another during the marriage. In practice, the breadwinner must support the homemaker while she is supplying him with services, but it will still be largely on his terms. Once the marriage ends, the breadwinner will remain under an obligation to provide for the homemaker for as long as she is looking after his children. Anything more is beginning to look doubtful. The risk of a discount when a wife has been less than wholly blameless is in danger of re-emerging.[124] The opportunity of developing the law towards a more egalitarian framework which could be applied to both marital and non-marital unions has been lost.

7

Power and Violence in the Home

Interpretations

We do not know how much violence goes on between men and women who live together. There is no representative study of modern marriage in this country, still less of modern cohabitation. What evidence we have suggests that some degree of violence is common and that overwhelmingly its victims are women. Almost one half of wife petitioners for divorce rely upon their husbands' behaviour, either alone or in combination with other facts. Because of the high proportion of wife petitioners, this amounts to around one-third of all divorce petitions (husbands' behaviour petitions are around 4 per cent). When Chester and Streather studied a sample of 125 wives' petitions for cruelty, filed during 1966 to 1968, they found that 101 relied upon repeated physical abuse and a further twelve upon one or two incidents, along with other things.[1] The courts' readiness to expand the concept of cruelty was not generally reflected in these petitioners' choice of allegations. Fifteen years later, of course, the proportion relying upon violence may well have fallen from 90 per cent. But in Davis and Macleod's study of the special procedure in divorce, conducted between 1979 and 1981, 40 per cent of their sample of recently divorced men and 40 per cent of the women reported that there had been some violence in the marriage.[2] Only 20 per cent of the women used that violence in support of their petitions.

If these figures are at all representative, something between one-third and two-fifths of all divorcing couples have experienced violence in their relationship. Extrapolation of current trends suggests that one third of all marriages now taking place will end in divorce.[3] Although one explanation for the rising tide is that couples will now separate for reasons which have little to do with the old ideas of matrimonial misbehaviour, putting these two proportions together would indicate that there is violence in around 13 per cent of all marriages. To these must be added the relationships which do not end in divorce, which carry on despite all, or those in which separation does not lead to dissolution or where there is no marrige to dissolve. There is little reason to suppose that violence between cohabiting unmarried couples is either more or less than that between the married.

These speculations tell us nothing about the type and severity of the attacks, although there is plenty of evidence of a pattern of escalation from a first blow, which may be treated as an isolated and shocking event but is then repeated and intensified until it becomes a regular feature of the relationship.[4] Overwhelmingly, of course, the victims who come to the attention of refuges, the police, the medical and social services and the legal profession, are women.[5] However, a representative sample of 2,143 American families was studied during 1976:[6] 16 per cent of couples reported some violence during the marriage, but slightly more men than women said that they had been victims of severe attacks. One of the authors has himself pointed out how misleading this can be. The study dealt only with the type of act and not with the injuries received: 'when men hit women and women hit men, the real victims are almost certainly going to be the women.'[7] Nor were the acts examined in their context: as many men may be killed by their wives and wives are killed by their husbands, but in America at least the wives are seven times more likely to kill in self-defence.[8] While the possibility that women may abuse men cannot be denied, the context and consequences of their use of physical aggression will usually be quite different from those of a man's.

That is one reason why the hunt for figures is not an empty exercise. But another is the pointer they might give to causes and cures. As Elizabeth Wilson has pointed out:

If you are one of only 500 women in a population of 50 million then you have certainly been more than unlucky and there may perhaps be something very peculiar about your husband, or unusual about your circumstances, or about you; on the other hand, if you are one of 500,000 women then that suggests something very different — that there is something wrong not with a few individual men, or women, or marriages, but with the *situation* in which *many* women and children regularly get assaulted — that situation being the home and the family.[9]

There is, then, a clear link between the explanations suggested for violence in the home and the ideology of the family.

Many writers have found causes for wife-beating which in themselves cast no aspersions on the institutions of marriage and the family. Men may become violent because they have themselves witnessed or experienced violence in childhood,[10] or because of their own psychopathology,[11] or because they have drunk too much.[12] Alternatively, it may be a response to the social pressures to which they are exposed through bad housing, financial difficulties, unemployment and a generally impoverished existence;[13] this may include socialization in a community which takes some types of violence for granted.[14] Further, the victim may have brought the violence upon herself through her own psychological needs for domination, excitement or attention.[15] Such theories not only legitimate the efforts of professionals to cure the individual deviants or to remove the stresses upon the family; they also enable those efforts to take place in the name of saving and supporting the family so that it can carry on with its essential tasks.

However, other writers have found explanations in the man's inability to live up to the traditional stereotype of male superiority. He may be an under-achiever in education or employment;[16] he may find it impossible to tolerate superior achievements in his wife,[17] so that violence may actually increase as women's desire for equality, freedom and independence increases.[18] On the other hand, he may be denied access to power and prestige outside the home and so resort to violence in order to assert his superiority within it.[19] The last is an echo of John Stuart Mill:

> how many thousands are there among the lowest classes of every country, who, without being in a legal sense malefactors in any other respect, because in every quarter their aggressions meet with resistance, indulge the utmost habitual excesses of bodily violence towards the unhappy wife, who alone, at least of grown persons, can neither repel nor escape their brutality.[20]

Some of these explanations, like the earlier ones, are still focusing upon the individual man, but this time upon the problem which he may have in reconciling what he has been led to expect with the reality of his situation. Individual factors may indeed be necessary to explain why some men react with violence and others do not. But the women's movement would argue that the inferior and dependent position of women within the household is a large part of the explanation for the maltreatment which they experience there. The opposed roles of men and women within the family are part of what produces the ideology of male superiority. At the same time they afford an unrivalled opportunity for expressing that superiority in physical terms. Dobash and Dobash have described how commonly violence results from some supposed challenge to the man's authority, whether as head of the household, or as arbiter of how his wife should behave both inside and outside it, or as the primary recipient of her services and attention.[21]

The legal system, of course, purports both to condemn the violence and to provide the woman with remedies against it. But Freeman has argued that it is the legal system itself which constitutes the problem.[22] Even if it no longer forces men and women to adopt opposed roles within the family, it is still a vital part of the ideology which defines and promotes their separate spheres of activity. Can the laws of crime and the family, which explicitly set out to deal with the problem of violence, themselves contribute towards the expectation of male domination? No one can deny that important advances have been made in recent years, but the practical benefits resulting from new legal remedies have always been less than was hoped. One reason for this is that the law still accords some degree of recognition to the authority of the male bread-winner. Another is persistent ambivalence about solutions which could threaten the privacy and stability of the family, both as an individual unit and as an institution.

The Breadwinner's Lawful Authority

Where two people are one in the eyes of the law, whatever the degree of formal authority enjoyed by one over the other there can be no remedy between them should a husband abuse it. The secular courts began to allow a wife to 'swear the peace' against her husband early in the seventeenth century. Originally, as with child-beating today, there was an exception for *moderata castigatio*, but towards the end of the century it was held that this meant not beating but only admonition and confinement in cases of extravagance.[23] It was still admitted that 'where a wife makes undue use of her liberty, either by squandering her husband's estate or going into lewd company, it is lawful for the husband to preserve his honour and estate to lay her under restraint.'[24] A similar view appears in Blackstone.[25] But the 1832 edition of Bacon's Abridgement was still quoting the earlier statements allowing moderate punishment, along with the right of restraint. It is scarcely surprising that courts and people alike were confused as to the extent to which husbands could enforce their commands.[26]

There was no doubt during most of the nineteenth century that a husband could use self-help to enforce his wife's primary obligations towards him. In *Re Cochrane*[27] a wife was refused habeas corpus to enable her to escape from a husband who had trapped her in his apartment and confined her there in order to prevent her living separately from him. Courts had earlier refused to grant habeas corpus to two husbands who wished to force their wives to return, but in each case the wife had some excuse for her departure. One husband had agreed to her living apart in consideration of a large sum from her separate propety.[28] Another had treated her with cruelty.[29] Not until *R. v. Leggatt, ex parte Sandilands*[30] was habeas corpus refused to a husband on the clear ground that he had no right to the custody of his wife, so that even if she had no good cause for living apart, his remedy was in the ecclesiastical or matrimonial courts rather than at common law. and in *R. v. Jackson*[31] the court took away the husband's right of self-help and granted habeas corpus to release a wife whose husband had behaved in almost exactly the same way as had Mr Cochrane half a century earlier. Even then the court reserved the possibility that restraint might be lawful in extreme situations, as where she was just about to leave him for another man. The best part of another century elapsed before a husband who behaved as Mr Cochrane and Mr Jackson had done was convicted of the common law offence of kidnapping and sentenced to three years' imprisonment.[32] There are still circumstances in which a husband is entitled to use self-help to enforce the wife's duty to have sexual intercourse with him.

Thus the husband's rights of coercion went hand in hand with his rights of possession. A striking feature of many of the reported cases in criminal and family law is the continuing desire of the husband to possess a wife who has made it quite clear that she wants nothing more to do with him. Where they were still together, Dobash and Dobash found that 44 per cent of the arguments which preceded a violent attack were triggered by the husband's jealousy. [33]

Husband and wife remain under a mutual duty to live together unless released. Although the strict scheme of matrimonial rights and duties has now been abandoned, a wife's reasons for wanting to live apart from her husband will be relevant to the regulation of their rights to occupy the matrimonial home, to any claim for financial relief or personal protection and to the ground for divorce. Hence it is one thing to deny the husband the right to coerce his wife and another thing to grant her the right to escape from him. As Mill commented, 'it is contrary to reason and experience to suppose that there can be any real check to brutality, consistent with leaving the victim in the power of the executioner.' [34] Thus, although physical violence has long been a valid excuse for the wife to leave and a good ground for obtaining relief, the courts' approach to its interpretation may still be relevant.

First is the question of the risk that the offending behaviour will be repeated. Under the old law one act was sufficient for the rich to get a judicial separation or, later, a divorce, while the cruelty required for a magistrates' order had to be 'persistent'. More insidiously, if marriage is a life-long commitment, it could be argued that there is no justification for releasing the wife if her husband's violence is unlikely to recur. This indeed was part of the reason for the decision of Mr Justice Henn Collins in *Meacher* v. *Meacher*. [35] The Court of Appeal disagreed: there was 'nothing in the legislation or authorities to justify the view that a wife who has suffered assaults cannot get a decree unless the assaults are likely to continue'. Yet as late as 1976 this decision was criticized in the leading academic textbook on family law: 'no spouse ought to be allowed to rely on the other's past conduct as a justification for living apart' where there is no probability of recurrence. [36] That passage has disappeared from the most recent edition, but the values which it represents may not have entirely disappeared from the thinking of the courts. It is evidence of some reluctance to give a clear statement that the battered woman is entitled to escape from her relationship once she has decided that enough is enough.

A second and related feature is the question of toleration. Under the old law a wife could not complain of behaviour which she had condoned. Unlike adultery, however, cruelty which had been condoned could be revived, but only by a fresh act of cruelty. Reaching the end of her tether after a long history of assaults, covered up or forgiven in the vain hope of improvement, she would have to wait for a fresh incident to give grounds for relief. Further, while the courts have been tender to the susceptibilities of gentlewomen, there is a long-standing belief among legal writers that the lower orders take a certain amount of violence for granted. Blackstone may be forgiven his belief that 'the lower rank of people who are always fond of the old common law, still claim and exert their ancient privilege.' [37] More than two centuries later a practitioners' textbook on matrimonial offences observed: 'some justices are inclined to interpret "wear and tear" of married life as "rough and tumble" and allow considerable latitude to husbands, particularly if the parties come from the poorer classes.' [38] The author cannot entirely disapprove, for he subscribes to another popular view that 'there are some people who regard horseplay as a natural part of married life and some wives who regard an occasional thrashing as a sign of their husband's affection.'[39]

The effects of such atittudes are shown all too clearly in the recent case of *Bergin* v. *Bergin*,[40] in which the wife sought financial relief from the magistrates on the ground that her husband had behaved in such a way that she could not reasonably be expected to live with him. The magistrates refused her. They found that she had indeed been hit in the face three times in six months, twice suffering from black eyes, but thought that she had 'accepted the situation as part of their married life' because she had neither gone to the police nor sought medical attention. No doubt, as Mrs Justice Heilbron remarked on appeal, she thought that she could attend to a black eye for herself, and it is not every wife who wants to get her husband into trouble. The appeal was allowed on the ground that the magistrates should have applied the same criterion as the divorce courts in assessing behaviour (see p. 155). Nevertheless, the President of the Family Division observed that she might have been debarred from relying upon violence which she had tolerated, and even covered up, in an effort to make her marrige work had it not been for a final incident in which she was terrified by her husband coming home drunk and starting to throw the furniture about. This is a clear echo of the old law on condonation (although divorce courts are now instructed to ignore the fact that the couple have lived together for a total of less than six months after the last act complained of and are at liberty to ignore a much longer period in deciding whether it is reasonable for her to live with him now). Yet even if the battered woman has, for a host of reasons, tried to make the best of her situation in the past, the law could make it quite clear that she is under no duty at all to do so: to deny her relief because she has put up with it for the sake of her marriage suggests that she is expected to do so.

The most insidious concept of all to emerge from the cruelty cases, however, is provocation. The earliest reported case held that 'a wife was not entitled to a divorce for cruelty unless it appeared that she was a person of good temper and had always behaved well and dutifully to her husband.'[41] Later, Dr Lushington declared that 'if a wife violates the rules and regulations of her husband (provided they are not absolutely absurd or irrational) he has a right to complain of it.'[42] For years the leading case was *Waring* v. *Waring*,[43] in which Sir William Scott remarked:

> I do not mean by this that every slight failure on the part of the wife is to be visited by intemperate violence on the part of the husband. . . . But if the conduct of the wife is inconsistent with the duties of that character, and provokes the just indignation of the husband, and causes danger to her person, she must seek the remedy for that evil, so provoked, in the change of her own manners.

There was a direct echo of this decision in that of Mr Justice Henn Collins in *Meacher* v. *Meacher*.[44] He held that it was not cruelty for the husband to beat his wife because she had disobeyed his orders not to visit her relations, for she had it in her own hands to prevent a repetition. As Dobash and Dobash found, even today, the wives did indeed seek to confirm their behaviour to their husbands' expectations in the vain hope of averting further attacks.[45] However, the Court of Appeal held that a wife was not disentitled to a decree simply because she could have put an end to the cruelty by obeying unreasonable orders from her husband. The report does not reveal what their lordships would have thought had the orders been, in their view, reasonable. It seems unlikely that the courts would nowadays use the concept of provocation to legitimate the husband's use of force to compel his wife's obedience to any of his orders, reasonable or unreasonable.

Nevertheless, the concept of provocation undoubtedly survives. The alleged provocative act is usually an affront to the husband's exclusive rights of possession. Examples abound in the criminal cases where the issue is not total but partial justification. The divorce courts may be prepared to hold him justified, but only if the violence used is in proportion to the provocation offered. It seems that unfaithfulness will rarely be enough these days. In *McKenzie* v. *McKenzie*[46] a confession of adultery did not excuse the 'hardest smacked bottom she had ever had', although it might have justified 'no more than the punishment which a parent might have meted out to a naughty child'.

More significant, however, is the courts' treatment of nagging and neglect of household duties. The courts were at first reluctant to find that a bad or sluttish housewife was guilty of a matrimonial offence, but the law is now quite capable of condemning such behaviour (one of the allegations against the wife in *Stanwick* v. *Stanwick*[47] was that she had left her husband to fend for their three young children as well earning his living). In *Stick* v. *Stick*[48] Mr Justice Karminski held that the wife's withdrawal from sexual intercourse and neglect of her household duties did not justify the 'very considerable violence'. But he considered it a borderline case in which his sympathies were with the sorely tried husband. Nagging, on the other hand, being obviously 'aimed at' the husband, became a possible matrimonial offence as soon as husbands were able to divorce their wives for cruelty.[49] And in *Douglas* v. *Douglas*[50] the Divisional Court rejected the argument that words could never justify violence. A wife who nagged and abused her husband might be the authoress of her own wrong.

Perhaps, after two decades and considerable publicity for the plight of battered women, things have changed. But the 'behaviour' fact is undoubtedly capable of incorporating similar ideas. In *Ash* v. *Ash*[51] Mr Justice Bagnall put it thus:

> I have to consider not only the behaviour of the respondent as alleged and established in evidence, but the character, personality, disposition and behaviour of the petitioner. . . . if I may give a few examples, it seems to me that a violent petitioner can reasonably be expected to live with a violent respondent. . . . if each is equally bad, at any rate in similar respects, each can reasonably be expected to live with the other.

Even if the courts would no longer hold that non-violent behaviour could ever be a complete excuse for violence, they have been prepared to extend equal condemnation to the bullying husband and the nagging wife. The concept of cruelty was first extended beyond physical violence in the case of a husband obsessed with the belief that it was his religious duty to make his wife completely subservient to him.[52] Domineering husbands who broke their wives' spirits recur in several cases.[53] It was in these cases that the courts first began to emphasize the need to consider the effect of the respondent's behaviour upon the particular woman to whom he was married and to show their sympathy for the delicate and sensitive soul whose husband abused his dominant position, whether or not through physical means. It could be that the wives whose nagging they were also ready to condemn were similarly abusing their position, but to regard the subtler means which women must use to get their own way as just as blameworthy as the cruder methods employed by men ignores the structural inequalities in their situations.

There are two aspects to this. The first is strength. Where men and women disagree, the woman must always 'plead, cajole, beguile and hope that he will be convinced'.[54] She cannot coerce by physical means, for she has neither the strength or the technique, nor has she been brought up to think in those terms. Men have usually been brought up to abhor the use of violence against the defenceless woman but not as an instrument of settling other types of disagreement. It might be thought that it is the socialization of men, rather than that of women, which is defective in this respect.

The other aspect is dependence. Where roles are divided into breadwinner and homemaker, the law decrees that the breadwinner is owner of their resources. He can decide how these are to be allocated. In particular, he has first call upon any surplus over the family's immediate needs. He has automatic access to the outside world, not only through his employment but also through his ability to spend what he likes on transport and entertainment. She by definition has none of these things and is further confined by her prior responsibility for household tasks and child care. At every turn, therefore, she has to negotiate for what she needs to fulfil her housewifely duties, let alone for less immediate wants such as clothing, entertainment or a night out. But unless her husband is content to allow her to be an equal partner with an equal voice in their affairs, she will have to resort to the stratagems of the underdog if she is ever to get her own way. To suggest that a wife has no right to nag her husband is to suggest that she has no right to set herself up in opposition to his decrees. To suggest that the means which she employs can be compared with a breadwinner's abuse of his already dominant position is to deny her right to an equal voice in their affairs.

Whatever the law may have to say on this subject, there is certainly evidence that this is how a great deal of violence within the home arises. Incidents are commonly triggered by disagreements, arising primarily out of the husband's jealousy but secondly out of food or money. A meal may not be ready when he comes home late or may have burned to a cinder in the oven. The breakfast eggs may be greasy. The children's toys may be lying around or the mantelshelf may not have been dusted. A grandfather may be given a slice of the child's birthday cake before the husband. The catalogue of such events is endless.[55] Whether or not the wife's shortcomings are regarded as provocation, her dependent status certainly legitimates the husband's assumption of authority. Whatever tips him over the edge into abuse, it is impossible to deny the role which dependence can play in bringing that about.

Most of the law we have been discussing is relevant only between husband and wife. But the themes of toleration, of making the best of a bad job for the sake of the family and, above all, of provocation can certainly influence the approach of those agencies which should be providing remedies for both married and unmarried victims of violence. Dependence is the same, or even worse, if the dependant is not married to the breadwinner, for then the law gives her no right to ask for his support.

Why were the Obvious Remedies not Enough?

Despite the problems just discussed, violence is almost always a ground for matrimonial relief, a civil wrong for which compensation or other remedies may be claimed and a criminal offence. Nevertheless, these remedies have proved quite inadequate to solve the problem. All three of them have been bedevilled, first, by a competing commitment to the preservation of the family unit and, second, by a failure to understand and to cater for the woman's own ambivalence about using them. Nor do they provide for her main needs, which are either to exclude the aggressor from their common home or to acquire a new home and protection for herself.

Matrimonial relief in the divorce courts was dominated by the concept of the matrimonial offence until 1971 and in the magistrates' courts until 1981. That doctrine was itself dedicated to the prior value of the sanctity of marriage. Its abandonment certainly involves an important shift in values away from the preservation of the family at all costs and towards the protection of individual members. But that shift has been accompanied by an apparently greater emphasis upon attempts to reconcile the parties.[56] Such attempts have largely been useless.[57] Nevertheless, both divorce and magistrates' courts have power to adjourn proceedings for divorce or financial relief respectively if they think that there is a reasonable possibility of reconciliation.[58] Magistrates, indeed, have a positive duty to consider whether reconciliation may be possible, even in cases such as *Bergin* v. *Bergin* (see p. 129). This does not apply to their new powers to grant personal protection and exclusion orders in cases of violence, but it did apply to all types of order under the old law. Wives who were about to complain of a long list of beatings were solemnly asked whether there was any chance of reconciliation. The clear suggestion that they ought to return was added to all the other pressures upon them to do so.

There has been a recent shift in official thinking away from trying to reunite the parties towards trying to get them to adjust to the fact that their relationship is at an end and settle the legal consequences by agreement rather than by litigation. If the legal system is indeed trying to help people to separate rather than to put obstacles in their way, the change is revolutionary. But a commitment to conciliation can easily be turned into an excuse for denying immediate relief to those who sorely need it. The Booth Committee on matrimonial procedure was worried that injunctions can be sought without any attempt to seek the co-operation of the other party, which 'inevitably engenders great resentment and bitterness after which any attempts at conciliation may be doomed to failure'.[59] But if an injunction is granted, this must mean that the court has come to the conclusion that, for the time being at least, the protection of the applicant (or a child) is the overwhelming consideration. To deny her the opportunity to make her case would be to put other values before her protection. Enthusiasm for the undoubted value of conciliation in some cases cannot justify reducing the scope of a remedy which is essential in others.

That enthusiasm is a modern manifestation of the law's respect for family privacy. In 1957 the then Master of the Rolls warned of the dangers of intervening between husband and wife: 'among themselves they can claim a kind of sacred protection behind the door of the family home which, generally speaking, the civil law may not penetrate.'[60] At that time husband and wife could not sue one another in tort. Having been one in the eyes of the law, there was no machinery and (until the Married Women's Property Acts) no point. It was the anomalies thrown up by that legislation which persuaded the Law Reform Committee to suggest change.[61] But the legislators were haunted by the spectre of marriages destroyed by litigation between the spouses. An action in tort can still be stayed if the court considers that 'no substantial benefit' will accrue to either party from continuing it.[62] The intention was that they should not be allowed to proceed with actions for 'trivial' injuries. The serious problems of marital violence were not considered. Yet the fact that assault and battery are torts has important implications for the availability of injunctions where no matrimonial proceedings are contemplated. Luckily, there is no evidence that any point on this provision has been taken in this context. Equally, however, it seems that tort law was very little used before the Domestic Violence and Matrimonial Proceedings Act 1976.

The main object of the tort system, however, is financial compensation. There is no excuse for denying this to the woman who is otherwise entitled to it, but in most cases the effect will be to reduce the resources available to maintain the family and so she is unlikely to apply. Violence is also a crime, and for more than twenty years public money has been available to compensate the victims of criminal injuries. Until 1980, however, victims who at the time were living with the aggressor as members of the same family were excluded. The ostensible reasons were the problems of proof, the risks of collusion and the possibility that the proceeds might find their way into the hands of the offender, bringing the scheme into disrepute. Problems of proof are always raised as objections to providing remedies between husband and wife. Yet when a woman has obviously been injured, it is not clear why her account of the incident should be any less easy to assess than that of the victim of an unwitnessed assault in a lonely street or park.

The Criminal Injuries Compensation Board may now accept this point, following the extension of the scheme, but this still discriminates against family victims in important ways. Originally, the injuries suffered had to be twice as serious as those of other victims before a claim could be entertained. Even now the scheme allows the Board to reduce compensation because of the victim's conduct or way of life. This could give ample scope for the display of attitudes to both provocation and toleration which are similar to those displayed in the matrimonial and criminal courts.[63] More important, although a general requirement of co-operation with the police is imposed upon all victims, only in family cases is prosecution usually an essential prerequisite to compensation. Yet it is in just these cases that both co-operation and prosecution present so many problems for even the most meritorious of victims. It seems unlikely that the Board wishes to see more prosecutions in these cases. The same may be said of the last unique requirement, which is that the victim should no longer be living with the aggressor. This was not to encourage her to leave but to ensure that the award would not benefit the aggressor and to reduce the chance of collusion. The idea that a woman would willingly suffer £500 worth of injuries in order to gain compensation is frankly bizarre. The idea that the husband might benefit may owe less to the assumption that she might be terrified into handing it over (for there are ways of preventing this) than that any money which is payable to a non-breadwinner is not in reality hers but his, for he is responsible for all the family's expenditure. Once again, the scheme contributes to the dominant values of family stability and privacy.

The same values have been even more apparent in relation to prosecution for crime. In the mid-1970s the police explicitly rationalized their reluctance to take action in 'domestic' cases in terms of the sanctity of marriage: 'we are, after all, dealing with persons "bound in marriage", and it is important, for a host of reasons, to maintain the unity of the spouses.'[64] Jan Pahl's study of women who used a refuge indicated that the police were much more helpful to women who were either not married to their attackers or had already taken the decision to leave.[65] Closely associated with this is the problem of withdrawal: 'I only know how frustrating it is for a police officer who has taken so much care and trouble in the preparation of the presentation of the case at court to be let down because his principal witness has "second thoughts".'[66]

Yet in 1979 the House of Lords appeared to go out of its way to sanction withdrawal in the interests of the preservation of the marriage. At common law a husband and wife could not give evidence either for or against one another. But it had long been admitted that a wife could testify against a husband who had attacked her, and it was assumed that if she were competent, she could also be compelled to do so. In *Hoskyn* v. *Metropolitan Police Commissioner*,[67] however, their lordships decided by a majority that, though competent, she could not be compelled. This was, according to Lord Diplock, because of the 'identity of interest between husband and wife' and because 'to allow her to give evidence would give rise to discord and to perjury and would be, to ordinary people, repugnant'. Lord Edmund Davies disagreed:

> Such cases are too grave to depend simply on whether the injured spouse is, or is not, willing to testify against the attacker. Reluctance may spring from a variety of reasons and does not by any means necessarily denote that domestic harmony has been restored. . . . it may well prove a positive boon for her to be directed by the court that she has no alternative but to testify. But, be that as it may, such incidents ought not to be regarded as having no importance extending beyond the domestic hearth. . . .

This is a rare but clear statement that such violence should be unequivocally condemned irrespective of the effect upon the particular marriage. Yet even he was only referring to serious cases: the authorities, he thought, would not and should not be too anxious to intervene in the 'trivial'. But the need for a clear and unequivocal condemnation of violence may be even greater at its 'trivial' beginnings than when it has escalated to a level at which almost anyone would be prepared to intervene. At all events, compellability removes one of the pressures upon the woman to withdraw and one of the excuses for failing to intervene. It is to be introduced for assaults or threats of violence against a spouse (as well as for similar acts or sexual offences against a child under 16 in the same household) by the Police and Criminal Evidence Bill 1983—84.

It would be absurd to suggest that this in itself could solve the 'problem' of withdrawal. This is often stated to be a problem for the police and other agencies whose task it is to protect the victim of aggression. In reality, it is *her* problem, and the agencies could instead be prepared to adapt their own expectations to accommodate it. The courts and police see success in terms of an arrest, charge, trial, conviction and sentence. Only then is the effort worthwhile. But that process is fraught with difficulties for the victim.

If the police are called and do arrest, the wife has 'shopped' her husband or the father of her children. Her feelings about that will be highly ambivalent. She may have been brought up to believe that a woman is not complete without a man, that marriage and childbirth are her main sources of satisfaction and that she will live happily ever after. She wants to believe her husband when he says that he is sorry and will make amends. She does not want the shame and stigma of confessing that all is not well with her marriage. Perhaps, she feels, it really is all her own fault. There are often great difficulties in getting her own family, friends and neighbours to see things her way, let alone the forces of law and order. After a long period of oppression she may be unable to cope with the pressures of making her own decisions. She may believe her husband's threats to deprive her of home and children should she take action against him. All of these provide ample explanation for the difficulty which so many women experience in breaking free, without any need to resort to theories that they may need the violence in some pathological way.

These apply, of course, to any form of initiative against a husband, but prosecution adds some peculiar difficulties of its own. If the police are called to the house, they may be reluctant to gain entry if the husband tells them to go.[68] Yet in *R. v. Thornley*[69] it was held that a licence to enter premises given by a wife in the course of a domestic dispute could not be revoked by a husband who had been subject to a complaint: the police were not trespassers because they had been invited to enter by the wife. The right of a wife to invite whomsoever she pleases into her home, whether or not she is its legal owner or tenant, should be beyond question, but apart from this case, there is no unequivocal statement of it.

If the police do gain entry, they may restrict their intervention to separating the combatants and warning the husband about his behaviour. This is a great deal better than nothing. Better still may be to make use of their common law power to arrest for breach of the peace and to bring before a magistrate as soon as possible. This removes the aggressor for a short while, is not technically a conviction and results in his being bound over to keep the peace unless further charges are preferred. It provides a clear, instant warning, coupled with the possibility of further action should that warning be ignored. If the officer has himself intervened between them, it does not require the co-operation of the victim. Nor does it leave a substantial gap during which she may be terrorized or cajoled into changing her mind or come to see the enormity of what she has done. Yet it seems that the police make little use of this possibility. Even if it has occurred to them, they are very dependent upon the attitudes of their local Bench. Magistrates may not welcome being troubled by these 'trivial' cases or may be reluctant to take action against a man who has disturbed the peace of his own home. The solution has much to commend it in those early stages before the woman has decided to bring the relationship to an end. It can only hope to succeed if there is no equivocation and all are committed to making it work.

From the woman's point of view, the difficulties of proceeding with a more serious criminal charge may seem terrible. Arrest cannot guarantee a remand in custody, so that she may have much to fear during the interim period. Trial cannot guarantee conviction, so that she will have to give evidence unless he pleads guilty. Conviction certainly cannot guarantee an immediate custodial sentence. Despite all this, there is some evidence that withdrawal is more of a myth than a reality. The Dobashes' study of 1,000 Glasgow police files for 1974 indicated that only 6 per cent of the women in fact withdrew, but in all instances after considerable postponement of the proceedings.[70] Wasoff's study of Scottish prosecution practice suggested that if anything this was an over-estimate.[71] It may be that, like the sanctity of marriage, withdrawal can be used by the police as an excuse for discriminating between 'domestic' and other violence.

The Scottish studies also indicated that as a group domestic cases received lower sentences than others. A large part of the reason for this lies in the attitude of police and prosecutors. Police perceptions of the seriousness of an assault are often different, so that the degree of harm which they require for a charge of 'actual' or 'grievous' bodily harm in a case of street violence can be less than they would require in a 'domestic' case. The court can sentence only for the offence before it. Similarly, if (as the Scottish studies indicate) domestic cases are frequently allocated to the lower courts even where they might be sent to the higher, the tariff is inevitably lower.

There is no comprehensive English study of sentencing law and practice in domestic cases which might tell us whether the tariff itself is lower for them, as many suspect that it is. The suspicion arises for several reasons. The Court of Appeal has made it abundantly clear on numerous occasions that unprovoked street violence resulting in appreciable injury will always merit an immediate custodial sentence.[72] They have also said that the 'courts cannot regrettably be deflected from their duty of imposing sentences appropriate to the gravity of the offence when crimes of violence of this nature are committed against a domestic background.'[73] Their regrets were related to the fact that the victim had now forgiven her attacker and was willing to have him back. The contrast with the attitude displayed by the House of Lords in *Hoskyn's* case (see p. 135) leads us to suppose that other courts may not always share this view.

In any event, it is so much easier to suggest that a domestic incident has been provoked than it is when victim and assailant are unknown to one another. Provocation can provide a partial defence to murder and a reason for mitigating sentence in other charges. In murder at least, it should be judged by the standards of the 'reasonable man' (Homicide Act 1957, section 3). Logically, of course, if the reasonable man would have used violence in the circumstances, this should be a complete rather than a partial excuse. If so, its scope would be a great deal more limited. Ashworth has convincingly argued that its real purpose is to supply an objective criterion for regarding the act as less blameworthy.[74] But the end result is to suggest that the reasonable man will, on occasions, resort to violence even when it is not completely necessary.

Indeed, Thomas describes several cases where the provocation was non-violent.[75] The most common case is not a provocative act at all, but the jealousy of the person provoked. Men who find their wives or cohabitants in bed with another man are definitely included, but so are those who go round and attack the woman or her new partner after the first relationship has clearly broken up.[76] It is hard to see what possible objective justification there is for killing in such cases, or how they can be reconciled with the statement in *R. v. Duffy*[77] that 'circumstances which induce a desire for revenge are inconsistent with provocation since the conscious formulation of a desire for revenge means that the person has had time to think.'

That was a case in which a wife had killed her husband while he was asleep, after a long course of brutal treatment from him. Although there is no doubt that prosecutors, juries and judges often take a lenient view of such cases, Wasik has pointed out that there are still doubts about whether, in law, they should do so. [78] No matter how cruel it has been, the 'cumulative' provocation may lead to counter-measures which are at least partially planned. This may explain why other courts have been far from lenient. In *R. v. Owen*, [79] for example, Lord Justice Roskill suggested that as the wife had gone on living with her violent husband, she had assumed the risk that the provocation would be repeated, so that a sentence of four years' imprisonment was entirely justifiable.

Concidentally, a sentence of four years' imprisonment was also held to be justifiable in the case of *Mason*. [80] Here the husband had killed the wife following a period of non-stop nagging, neglect of her household duties and allegations that his inability to work was due to malingering when in fact it was caused by heart trouble. The momentary loss of control in such cases may be easier to reconcile with *Duffy* than is the wife's response to her brutal husband. The 1957 Act meant that the types of conduct capable of amounting to provocation could be extended indefinitely, but Wasik argues that the *Duffy* approach is still theoretically good law. The husband who kills his non-violent wife could therefore be thought less blameworthy than the wife who kills her violent husband. In practice, courts are probably equally tender to both.

Obviously a criminal court should be able to mitigate punishment in circumstances in which a matrimonial court would still grant the victim relief. But the actions of criminal courts are among the most potent reinforcers of dominant ideologies. If they listen too uncritically to pleas of provocation based on 'flightiness', they unconsciously endorse male possessiveness, as well as the view that a flirtatious woman gets what she deserves. If they listen too uncritically to pleas based on nagging, they forget the fact that many women have to resort to such techniques in negotiations within the family. The 'reasonable man' test contributes to the view that there was some objective justification for what was done. This is quite different from mitigating the sentence of a man of otherwise excellent character who has indulged in a sudden and uncharacteristic excess of passion, for that is based upon the subjective merits of the offender and the unlikelihood of his offending again.

Even if the tariff for wife-beating were the same as that for street violence, the criminal law could never solve all the victim's problems. That is not its purpose. Its main object is the clear affirmation of society's most important values and the deterrence of those who might be tempted to follow suit. Despite this, there are some who believe that it has little part to play in most 'domestic' violence. Susan Maidment, for example, argues that although police reluctance to prosecute arises for all the wrong reasons, it is nevertheless evidence of a belief in society that these cases should not be dealt with by the criminal law. [81] As well as the disadvantages for the individual complainant, she suggests, it contains no facility for treatment, for understanding the aggression, for trying to improve the marital relationship or for developing mutual respect between husband and wife. Although not opposed to prosecution in serious cases, she argues that the choice of remedy should depend not upon where the woman goes for help but upon a 'professional, principled decision'.

It could be just that 'belief in society' that lies at the root of the problem of violence in the home. It perpetuates the notion that 'domestic' crime is somehow not real crime, that the fact that victim and aggressor are bound together by ties of law and emotion makes it better rather than worse, that it can properly be described by the cosy and comfortable word 'domestic'. It refuses to place the value of protecting the victim above the value of preserving the relationship. Above all, it assumes that others will know better than she what is the proper solution to her problems. It is another example of our recurring theme that women cannot be trusted to use the law to their real advantage. Professionals must do this for them. Yet many professionals who might be involved, such as social workers or probation officers, may be devoted to the values of preserving the family even if it is clearly destructive of the interests of some of its members. There would, indeed, be something to be said for giving the woman more rather than less control over the way in which the process operates to protect her.

The Search for New Solutions

The Domestic Violence and Matrimonial Proceedings Act 1976 refers to four types of injunction which may be available between husband and wife or a man and woman who are living with each other as such in the same household. These may restrain the respondent from molesting the applicant or from molesting a child living with the applicant, or may exclude him from their home or part of it or from the area where it is, or may require him to allow her to enter and remain in the home or part of it. Orders of this type can serve two rather different functions. One is to encourage the respondent to refrain from violence or other forms of molestation (such as pestering, threatening or forcing his attentions upon her).[82] The sanction is punishment for contempt of court, either at the request of the applicant or in some cases after arrest without warrant by a police officer. The effect is to combine many of the advantages of civil and criminal proceedings. This explains both the attraction for battered women and the reservations felt by many legal authorities. The other function is in practice more useful, for it enables the court to decide, at least in the short term, which of the parties should remain in their common home and which should leave. The importance of this to the battered woman who is afraid to return to the same house as her aggressor is obvious, but the courts have experienced considerable difficulty in reconciling her need for protection with the law's respect for rights of property. They may not quite have shaken off their old perception of wives as a form of property in themselves.

There has been considerable confusion about whether the 1976 Act was intended to grant a new and unfettered discretion to county court judges or whether it simply extended their jurisdiction to deal with cases according to existing principles. An injunction is in any event a discretionary remedy, but it is axiomatic that it can be granted only in support of a legal right or claim. Injunctions against violence present fewer problems than those against wider forms of molestation or excluding people from their homes because women have a right not to be beaten or assaulted.

The anti-molestation injunction was originally developed to protect a wife pending the hearing of her claim for divorce, judicial separation or other matrimonial relief. The object was to prevent her being influenced or terrorized out of her remedy. It could, however, be continued or even made after the decree, presumably to restrain a husband who had a tendency to behave as though he were still entitled to her society. Ouster injunctions were also developed for the purpose of protecting the wife pending matrimonial proceedings, but the husband could no longer be kept out of his property once the decree had been made.[83] That is still the case, at least where the wife has no property right in the home and there are no children whose welfare requires protection.[84] Before divorce proceedings were started, a wife might found her case upon her right to live in the matrimonial home. As Lord Denning said in *Gurasz* v. *Gurasz*:[85]

Some features of family life are elemental in our society. One is that it is the husband's duty to provide his wife with a roof over her head; and the children too. So long as the wife behaves herself, she is entitled to remain in the matrimonial home. The husband is not at liberty to turn her out of it, neither by virtue of his command, nor by force of his conduct. If he should seek to get rid of her, the court will restrain him. If he should succeed in making her go, the court will restore her. In an extreme case, if his conduct is so outrageous as to make it impossible for them to live together, the court will order him to go out and leave her there.

The basis of this, of course, was the husband's common law duty to maintain his wife, which gave her a right to live in the matrimonial home even though he was its sole owner, but only so long as she behaved herself. The wife in that case was also joint tenant of the home, so that the claim might have been put on the need to protect her rights of property against a co-owner who was effectively prohibiting her from exercising them.

An unmarried woman, however, had no matrimonial remedy pending which she might be protected against molestation. Nor had she any equivalent right to live in her cohabitant's home. The only possible foundation for an ouster order, unless the home was hers alone, was that the man's behaviour was effectively depriving her of a contractual licence which he had given her to live there, or of her rights of occupation as a joint owner or tenant. There was no clear statement of either of these before the 1976 Act. There are, however, some references in husband-and-wife cases to a broad inherent jurisdiction in the High Court to protect the well-being of children, which might be equally applicable to the unmarried.[86]

Thus there were obviously substantive limits on the courts' powers before 1976. There were also problems relating to the jurisdiction of the county courts. The High Court has a general power to grant both final and interlocutory (interim) injunctions (under what is now the Supreme Court Act 1981, section 37). A county court can do so only 'as regards a cause of action for the time being within its jurisdiction' (County Courts Act 1984, section 38). This meant that the woman generally had to undertake to begin some such proceedings, either for a divorce or judicial separation, or for a proprietory remedy, or in tort. Allied to this was a long-standing principle, developed in other contexts, that a county court should not grant an injunction if this was the main relief wanted but only where it was ancillary to some other claim.

Section 1 of the 1976 Act gave county courts 'jurisdiction' to make the orders listed whether or not any other relief was sought in the proceedings. A narrow interpretation would have held that this was simply intended to solve the jurisdictional problems in the more convenient and accessible county courts, but not to change the substantive principles upon which such relief was available. However, in *Davies* v. *Johnson*[87] the House of Lords took a broader view. Parliament must have intended to enhance the courts' powers to interfere with property rights for the purpose of protecting the fundamental right to integrity and safety of the person. The case concerned an unmarried woman who was joint tenant of the home along with the man who had battered her. Lord Diplock would have decided it on the narrow basis that to exclude him for a while could be a justifiable protection for *her* rights of property. But the majority held that the power to grant an exclusion order under the Act was not limited to women who had such rights. It must have been intended to grant a limited occupancy right even to non-tenants, although in most cases this would last only for as long as was necessary for her to make alternative arrangements. Lord Scarman did suggest that, in some cases, this might last a long time. Unlike the Matrimonial Homes Act, however, it could not protect her against the risk that a man who was solely entitled to the home might dispose of his rights to third parties who could evict her.

This was a bold decision in the circumstances. It raised a number of technical problems in property law which need not concern us. But it also raised a difficulty which was illustrated by the case of *Spindlow* v. *Spindlow*:[88] section 1 of the 1976 Act made no reference to violence. Did it then give the courts a wide discretion to decide the occupation of the unmarried couple's home when their relationship broke down? After all, there is no other power to 'divorce' them and adjust their property rights. The courts had already begun to develop this line of approach in applications made by wives, both under the 1976 Act and pending matrimonial causes. In a series of cases they had taken the view that the court had to balance the relative hardship caused to each party in having to leave the home for a short while.[89] They should attempt to make an order which was 'fair, just and reasonable' as far as possible to all parties.[90] In particular they should consider the needs of the children.[91] These judges found it difficult to believe that a woman would leave her home and go to live in grossly overcrowded and unsuitable accommodation without a good reason for doing so, and hence preferred to take that as read and to concentrate upon the practical problem of accommodation for the time being until matters could be properly sorted out.[92]

This approach was well on the way to redressing the imbalance between the respective powers of breadwinner and homemaker to bring about a separation if they so wished. Logically, it applied just as much to a wife who had no good reason, in the eyes of the law, for wanting to separate from her husband as it applied to one who was suffering serious violence from him. But there was a different line of cases in which the courts had emphasized that she had to show reasonable grounds for saying that she was unable to live in the same house with him before she could seek an order getting him out.[93] One might have thought that a battered wife would inevitably have been able to do so. In *Myers* v. *Myers*,[94] however, the Court of Appeal allowed the husband's appeal, even though the wife had alleged three specific instances of violence, a 'tendency to violent outbursts' (which they took to mean verbal abuse), heavy drinking and the taking of soft drugs. The last incident was a textbook example of a husband blaming his wife for 'flighty behaviour' after an advance made by a man at a dance, an attempted reconciliation when they got home and a 'thumping' when the wife decided that she no longer wished for intercourse. Despite this, the county court judge did not believe her when she said that the marriage was over, a fact which appears to have weighed heavily in the Court of Appeal.

The conflict between these two lines of approach in the Court of Appeal has recently been resolved by the House of Lords' decision in *Richards* v. *Richards*[95] that neither is right. The lower courts had erred in seeking principles for the exercise of their discretion in isolation from the substantive law involved. An application for an ouster injunction between spouses, whether in pending matrimonial proceedings or under the 1976 Act, is in essence an application to decide their respective rights of occupation in the matrimonial home and is therefore to be governed by the principles laid down in the Matrimonial Homes Act (now 1983). This originally applied only where one spouse was entitled to the home in law and the other was not and gave the court no power to exclude the owning spouse completely.[96] It *cannot* have governed all the ouster orders which were made before the 1976 Act. But that Act amended the Matrimonial Homes Act so as to allow the court to rearrange both parties' rights of occupation in almost whatever way it wished (1983 Act, section 1(2)) and applied the same procedure where the couple were jointly entitled to the home (1983 Act, section 9). This means, said their lordships, that Parliament must have intended that all these cases be decided according to the guidelines laid down in the Act. This allows the court to make such order as it thinks just and reasonable, having regard to the conduct of the spouses in relation to each other and otherwise, to their respective needs and financial resources, to the needs of any children and to all the circumstances of the case (section 1(3)). Once again, therefore, personal protection may be subordinated to property rights, and the court may look at the wife's faults before it looks at her needs or those of the children.

It seems unlikely, to say the least, that when Parliament passed the 1976 Act it intended at one and the same time to *increase* the courts' powers in relation to cohabitants (as decided in *Davis* v. *Johnson*: see p. 143) but to *restrict* them in relation to the married (as decided in *Richards* v. *Richards*). The case is evidence of a stricter line in re-emphasizing the importance of marital conduct, even when dealing with the short-term issues arising from the spouses' disagreements. It will make it more difficult for the wife who has children to look after to break away from a marriage which has become intolerable to her — unless, of course, she is prepared to abandon the children. It should not affect the position of the seriously battered woman. But there is always the possibility that if the court thinks the incidents trivial and is not convinced that the marriage is over, she will be denied this relief. By increasing the issues to be canvassed by the court, it will certainly add to the opportunities for delaying tactics on the part of the aggressor, which are already considerable (evasion of service, delaying of legal aid applications, seeking of adjournments for legal advice and the like).

The court must also decide how long an exclusion should last. If divorce proceedings are pending, the court may be prepared to continue it until these are resolved. Otherwise an injunction is normally a short-term remedy.[97] Up to three months is recommended.[98] Considerable pressure is thus exerted on the woman to decide whether to get a divorce, leave home for alternative accommodation or allow her husband to return. Yet she may have very good reasons for wanting to do none of these, at least for some time to come. She may be in no condition, physically or mentally, to make up her mind once and for all what she wants to do. The courts undoubtedly prefer it if the long-term disposition of the home can be decided in divorce proceedings, but the Matrimonial Home Act allows them to make orders which can last indefinitely and to make any appropriate financial adjustments. There seems to be no reason why the court should not be prepared to allow them to live separately while remaining married, if that is the right solution.

The court can now attach a power of arrest to any injunction restraining the use of violence against applicant or child or excluding a husband from the matrimonial home or area, provided that the respondent has already caused actual bodily harm to the applicant or child and is likely to do so again (1976 Act, section 2). A policeman can then arrest without warrant on reasonable suspicion of a breach of the order. The person must then be brought before a judge, who can impose a penalty on his own initiative. The cases display a marked lack of enthusiasm for powers of arrest, regarding them as akin to a suspended sentence of imprisonment.[99] They are reserved for the most serious cases and not thought appropriate where the last act of violence was some time ago. A practice direction in 1981[100] indicated that the court should normally place on the power a time limit of not more than three months, even if the injunction is to continue for longer. This is a law which had to be passed because the police would not interfere, yet the courts hesitate to use it because the police *remain* reluctant to interfere.

The courts appear to have accepted the police viewpoint rather than that of the victims or Parliament.

The proportion of 1976 Act injunctions to which a power of arrest is attached has remained remarkably constant (according to the Judicial Statistics for 1977 to 1982) at around one quarter. But although the numbers of orders, and thus powers of arrest, have risen dramatically, the numbers of arrests have remained the same. This confirms the melancholy finding of Binney, Harkell and Nixon that the Act has had little effect upon the police approach.[101] Their survey certainly does not suggest that a power of arrest is sufficient to persuade a man to obey an injunction. It is unlikely that marital behaviour has changed so quickly, particularly as fewer than half the arrests result in a committal to prison. Here again, in *Ansah* v. *Ansah*[102] it was said that this was to be done 'very reluctantly and only when every other effort to bring the situation under control has failed or is almost certain to fail'. On the facts of that case, committal was undoubtedly absurd, but the court's words can be used to justify a reluctance to take action even in the most serious cases.

All this has the unfortunate appearance of an attempt to stem the tide of a remedy whose very popularity indicates how much it was needed. Applications for injunctions under the 1976 Act rose from 2,612 in 1977 to 7,691 in 1982. Despite all the obstacles, a very high proportion succeed. The failure rate fell from 8.4 per cent in 1977 to 2.8 per cent in 1982. Whatever else this may mean, it undoubtedly means that fears of a rush of unjustified claims are quite unwarranted. Yet that such fears exist is shown not only by the attitudes reported here but also by the courts' repeated condemnation of those who apply for injunctions as a tactical move to improve their position in the final divorce settlement.[103] The remedy for that problem is simply to refuse the order to the unmeritorious rather than to make it more difficult for the meritorious to get one.

Magistrates' courts seem to be approaching applications by wives for personal protection or exclusion orders under the Domestic Proceedings and Magistrates' Courts Act 1978 (sections 16—18) in a rather different way. Overall, only 66 per cent of the 3,600 applications made during the first half of 1983 were granted. But getting on for half were for expedited protection, without giving notice to the other party, and over 94 per cent of these succeeded. It is not known how many 'ex parte' applications for injunctions are granted. There is certainly evidence of extreme reluctance to grant ex parte ouster injunctions,[104] but magistrates are not permitted to grant expedited exclusion orders. Magistrates may be more prepared to react strongly to an urgent need for protection. They are certainly more prepared to attach a power of arrest, for this was done in more than half the expedited orders and almost one third of the others.[105] They have not been immune to the 'wear and tear of married life' view of marital violence, but their associations with crime (so much deplored in other contexts) may contrast with the habitual respect which judges show towards civil litigants.

With or without ex parte protection, many women can pluck up courage to apply only once they have left the home. However, most of those who have left for a refuge do not want to return, even if the man can be removed. Binney, Harkell and Nixon found that only 16 per cent of their sample wanted to go back home to live there alone; only 8 per cent did so; and a year later only half of those were still there.[106] Like the 1976 and 1978 Acts, the Housing (Homeless Persons) Act 1977 was thought to herald a new era by obliging local authorities to provide them with alternative accommodation. However, a woman who has a home is not 'homeless' unless violence from another person living there is *likely* (1977 Act, section 1); she does not have a 'priority need' for accommodation (section 2) unless she has children who live with or might reasonably be expected to live with her, although the authority should not insist that she gets a custody order first;[107] and she may be excluded as 'intentionally' homeless if it would have been reasonable to remain (section 17). In *R. v. Wandsworth London Borough Council, ex parte Nimako-Boateng*[108] Mr Justice Woolf stated that 'in many cases, even where a husband has been violent, it would be reasonable for the wife to continue to reside in the matrimonial home but to seek a court order restraining the husband's violence or barring him from the home.' This may be attractive to local authorities with a housing shortage which do not wish the husband to remain as a secure tenant in a family home. But the courts may not co-operate with such a scheme, particularly if the wife has no intention of returning.[109] The woman may thus be caught in a 'catch 22', where the authorities refuse a home because she could get an injunction and the courts refuse an injunction because she could be rehoused by the authorities.[110] Certainly, the criteria obliging the authorities to rehouse her are more restrictive than those allowing the courts to grant her protection, and many authorities appear to have adopted an unhelpful approach.[111]

Three themes have cropped up again and again in this chapter: provocation, the 'there but for the grace of God go I' reaction which can so easily contribute to the trivialization of family violence; privacy, the reluctance to intervene in the family for 'trivial' causes; and toleration, the belief that women can and do tolerate a level of violence and, having done so, may be denied a remedy. Taken to extremes, these place women in an impossible circle: family violence is understandable and relatively unimportant compared with the 'real' problems of escalating violence on the streets; it is certainly not important enough for us to intervene in a trivial case, although we must obviously do so once serious injuries have been sustained; but a woman who has gone on living with relatively small-scale injuries over a period of time must clearly have accepted it and unless things go on getting worse may do so again; it is not worth helping a woman who is so bound up with her home that she is quite likely to abandon the attempt to break free. What is clearly needed to break this vicious circle at the outset is an unequivocal statement from the law that *all* family violence is to be condemned and that the victim is always entitled to the law's protection.

We could, of course, go further and insist that the family itself is the source of the problem. Wherever women are trapped with men in a relationship which denies them access both to resources and to the outside world, there will be men who abuse that position. An attack upon family violence can easily became an attack upon the family. Hence there are powerful forces ranged against it in the name of preserving that useful institution. Just as there are those who would destroy all happy families in the name of preventing abuse, there are those who would preserve all unhappy families in the name of upholding the institution. The last ten years have seen the beginnings of a remarkable change in English law. It is slowly being acknowledged that unhappy families do not have to be preserved. The main beneficiaries of this have been those civilized couples who can agree both that their marriage has broken down and upon how to solve the practical issues which result. At the very least, the law could do the same for those who are locked into the vicious circle of a much less civilized relationship.

8

The Case Against Marriage?

Marriage or Cohabitation?

There is a well-developed feminist thesis to the effect that family law helps to bring about and reproduce a particular set of relationships between the sexes in the crucial domestic sphere. The mechanism blamed for this is formal marriage, which is therefore unfavourably compared with other types of intimate relationship. Marriage is clearly the relationship preferred by the law, for although overt sanctions against fornication have been abandoned, extramarital sexual intercourse is still termed 'unlawful'; contracts designed to promote it are 'illegal'; and its offspring are 'illegitimate' and thereby disadvantaged. Marriage itself, however, is said to consist of an implicit and non-negotiable contract whose terms entrench the respective roles of breadwinner husband and dependent wife. The fullest exposition of this thesis can be found in the work of Lenore Weitzman.[1] She argues that the marriage contract contains four main terms. First, the husband is head of the household. Second, he is responsible for support. Third, the wife is responsible for domestic services. Fourth, the wife is responsible for child care, the husband for child support. Surprisingly enough, she leaves out a possible fifth term, which is the most oppressive of all: the wife owes her husband her sexual and reproductive services. For most couples today it is the birth of children which leads to the polarization of roles, although its prospect can lead to very different attitudes and expectations well before that time.

But Weitzman is writing about the United States of America, and many family lawyers in this country would see several objections to her views. These lawyers tend, as Freeman has pointed out,[2] to assume that the law plays little or no part in regulating how people behave towards one another within the family. Only when things go wrong, they say, can the law step in to solve the conflict. In one sense, of course, that must be true. Glendon has described how legal systems have evolved two basic approaches to family politics:[3] 'Laws of the continental European type plunge directly into the question of whether one spouse should predominate in the decision-making process of the family. Anglo-American common law on the other hand traditionally stays away from interspousal disputes unless and until they reach the divorce court.' Nowhere does English family law contain any blatant statement that 'the husband is head of the household', such as might once have been found in the Continental civil codes.

That, however, does not mean that the statement cannot be made in other ways. The very fact that the law keeps out of relationships within the united family can itself be a powerful factor in determining what those relationships are. If the law refuses to say how the resources brought into the home should be distributed by the breadwinner, it is reinforcing the unequal treatment of domestic labour. If the law refuses to protect one family member against the physical aggression of another, it is reinforcing the authority of the aggressor. If the law refuses to punish a husband who has intercourse with his wife against her will, it is not only reinforcing his authority but also subordinating her reproductive capacities to his will.

Quite apart from that, the way in which the civil law generally seeks to encourage particular types of behaviour is through the determination of those disputes which are submitted to its arbitration. The courts do not interfere with the smooth running of commercial contracts any more than they interfere with the smooth running of personal relationships. But they do have a fairly clear set of rules about what will happen if those contracts are broken and the parties do not sort out the resulting problems for themselves. The prospect of a breach of contract action is only one among many factors which may incline a businessman to keep his bargain, just as the prospect of an unfavourable outcome to matrimonial litigation can be only one among many factors which might incline a husband or wife to keep his or her side of the contract. We do not for that reason argue that the law plays no part in regulating how business is conducted.

Family laws goes further than that. Businessmen are allowed very considerable freedom to write their own contracts without interference from the law in the precise content of the undertakings given. Husbands and wives are allowed to write their own contracts about some matters but not about others. The law certainly no longer insists that they adopt the Weitzman terms. While the marriage is a going concern, each has the right to live in a matrimonial home belonging to the other (Matrimonial Homes Act 1983), and each has a duty to make reasonable financial provision for the other and for their children (Domestic Proceedings and Magistrates Courts Act 1978, section 1; Matrimonial Causes Act 1973, section 27). Otherwise the law no longer dictates what the terms of their private bargain are. They may conduct their affairs jointly or as two separate individuals. They may adopt whatever lifestyles they please. The wife need not assume her husband's surname,[4] and he has no lawful claim upon her obedience or services. Once the marriage comes to an end, however, the law reserves the right to rearrange all their affairs and to vary whatever bargains they may have made at the outset of their relationship. There is remarkably little evidence that the law uses that opportunity to penalize those who have adopted an unconventional division of labour. Career women appear to suffer very little, although househusbands have certainly not gained equality with housewives.

Despite the increasing neutrality of family law, for most couples marriage still involves something very similar to the Weitzman exchange. Diana Leonard concludes her study of courtship and marriage with the suspicion that most people would be surprised that Mary Stott protests when 'intelligent women' agree to a ceremony involving virginal white, a wedding ring, and a change of name for the woman, since for them marriage *does* involve submission for the woman. Liberal intellectuals are resorting to wishful thinking. . . if they try to pretend that what the rituals say no longer holds for the majority most of the time, or for themselves some of the time.[5]

Furthermore, all couples will encounter laws of tax and social security far more frequently than they encounter family laws, which are applied only at the end of a relationship. These are still structured on the assumption that marriages are conducted upon Weitzman lines: a wife can claim a retirement pension or widow's benefits on the basis of her husband's contributions because of her actual or assumed dependence upon him, but for the same reason she is denied invalid care allowance or (in practice) independent access to means-tested benefits.

This is why legal scholars are so divided on the proper approach to cohabitation outside marriage. There is one school of thought which would resist very strongly any attempt to impose the legal consequences of marriage upon cohabitants.[6] There is evidence from studies in the United States that those who cohabit have deliberately rejected marriage. Marriage should therefore not be thrust upon them. They should be permitted to arrange their affairs according to the ordinary laws of property and contract. At the end of their relationship they should be held to the bargain which they made at the beginning. It is insulting to women to suggest that there is any inequality in bargaining power when they embark upon these relationships. The one concession which should obviously be made is to remove the risk that the contracts by which they regulate their affairs are held to be tainted with an immoral purpose and therefore unenforceable.

It may be that the law is already adequate in the last respect. It can enforce any contract provided that the terms are clear, the parties intend it to be binding and each has given valuable consideration for the other's promise. Sexual services alone cannot count as valuable consideration for this purpose, and it is highly doubtful whether they should.[7] The notion that any person, male or female, should be bound in law to deliver sexual services, even if he or she has previously agreed to do so, has little appeal. Child-care services have been held sufficient to support an agreement to maintain an illegitimate child,[8] although doubts have been expressed because the mother is already under a public duty to do this.[9] Domestic services are clearly adequate. If an agreement is made for purposes which are not entirely immoral, therefore, the law may be prepared to enforce it. In *Tanner* v. *Tanner*[10] the Court of Appeal spelt out a contract that the woman should be entitled to remain in a house owned by the man for as long as their children were of school age. They were negotiating at arm's length after their relationship had ended, and the woman gave up her protected tenancy to move into the house with their daughters. In *Horrocks* v. *Forray*,[11] however, the court could find no contract when a married man bought a house for his long-standing mistress and their child to live in, mainly because it was impossible to work out what the terms would have been and whether he intended to be bound.

There are several problems with the contractual approach to cohabitation. It is likely that cohabiting couples are to be found at every point on a continuum starting at the clear-sighted rejection of marriage and ending at the 'would-be-married-if-we-could' (Burgoyne's and Clark's research into step-families certainly suggests something along these lines).[12] It is also likely that these relationships do not stand still. Where two people live together for any length of time, the process of role polarization is insidious. Career choices have to be made; location has to be decided; children have to be considered. At each point adjustments may have to be made in the lifestyle of one or both parties. The social and cultural pressure, to say nothing of the institutional pressure, upon the woman to define her primary role in terms of home and children is still enormous. The pressure upon a man to avoid doing so is even greater.[13]

Given that the welfare state is one of the prime institutional pressures, class differences in the attitudes of cohabitants are more than likely. As a matter of policy, the laws of tax and social security extend to extramarital cohabitation all the disadvantages attached to marriage (such as aggregation of income for the purpose of claiming means-tested benefits and non-eligibility for invalid care allowance) but none of the advantages (such as higher tax reliefs, albeit on the degrading assumption that the husband must have a wife to support, and benefits based upon the other's contributions). It becomes financially advantageous not to marry only if both parties have a high income, particularly if this is derived from investments or if they wish to maintain two homes.

Above all, it is probable that few people consider the legal effects of their personal relationships at the time of entry.[14] Middle-class career women may well realize that they are not committing themselves to be domestic servants when they marry. Working-class 'common law wives' may never have conceived of their relationship with men in any other terms. It may also be insulting to women to project on to them the beliefs of a limited section, especially when those beliefs are so obviously related to a refusal to recognize domestic labour as labour.

Some legislative provisions are capable of recognizing cohabitation as a marriage-like relationship. A member of a deceased tenant's family who is living with him at his death can succeed to his tenancy under the Rent Act 1977 or Housing Act 1980. The concept of 'family' was first extended beyond the group related by blood or marriage for the benefit of cohabiting women who had borne the tenant's children.[15] Even where there were no children, the court seemed more sympathetic to the woman who had lived with a man in a marriage-like relationship[16] than to a man who had lived with a woman in a similar relationship where they had deliberately rejected marriage.[17] Not until *Watson* v. *Lucas*[18] was it agreed that a man could be a member of the female tenant's family. Women are obviously *expected* to join their menfolk's families rather than the other way around.

Similarly, under the Inheritance (Provision for Family and Dependants) Act 1975, an adult dependant can claim reasonable provision for her maintenance from the estate. A dependant is someone who was being maintained by the deceased for other than 'full valuable consideration' as defined by ordinary principles. This causes difficulty enough when the couple have effectively pooled their resources for years;[19] it is worse still where the survivor has given domestic services in return for keep.[20] If the services are worth more than her keep, she cannot claim. If they are worth less, she can. Nothing could be a clearer indication of the confused attitude of the law towards domestic labour.

Clearly, then, while the career woman can look after herself whether married or cohabiting, the dependent homemaker is disadvantaged by both. Family law may be somewhat more reluctant to intervene between husband and wife while the marriage is a going concern, but once it is satisfied that the relationship is at an end it has far more effective mechanisms for redressing the balance between the parties. There is no divorce adjustment available for unmarried couples, where the homemaker's domestic labour may go completely unrewarded.[21]

Hence Clive has argued that marriage is an unnecessary legal concept.[22] The welfare state should be reformed by abolishing private dependency and treating poverty as an individual rather than a family phenomenon. Maintenance obligations between spouses could be abolished if financial provision were awarded on the basis of dependent children and the loss suffered as a result of cohabitation, which could be applicable to relationships of all types. Finally: 'Divorce would also disappear if there were no marriage. Is there anyone, apart from those with a financial interest in it, who would regret its passing?'[23] There is no doubt that the state's attempts to preserve the stability of marriage place far more pressure upon the homemaker than upon the breadwinner, but whether those pressures are any different where the couple are unmarried it is difficult to tell. The law's refusal to intervene is not the neutral stance which it is sometimes taken to be.

The Legal Effects of Divorce

The laws we have just been discussing deal with the effects of marriage or cohabitation upon the parties' ordinary legal rights. Divorce laws deal with the way in which the spouses are expected to behave towards one another. They have traditionally been dominated by two ideas: first, that the principles governing divorce and other matrimonial causes can be used as an instrument for keeping couples together; and, second, that it is both necessary and proper for the law to prescribe norms of marital conduct. Both ideas are rooted in the Christian concept of marriage as a life-long, indissoluble commitment. Matrimonial remedies were originally available only in the ecclesiastical courts. Total release from the bonds of a valid marriage was quite impossible, save for the very few people who could persuade Parliament to legislate for them alone. For the rest the obligation to live together might be enforced, through the decree of restitution of conjugal rights, against a deserter. Partial release, either by way of defence to this suit or by way of a decree of separation, was available only for adultery or serious cruelty.

The law has known for a long time that it cannot coerce people into loving one another[24] or even into living together. Sanctions for disobeying a decree of restitution were abolished in 1884, although the decree itself remained until the Matrimonial Proceedings and Property Act 1970. It last surfaced in the law reports when an Indian wife, who thought that it meant what it said, was actually restrained from forcing herself upon the home which her husband had established with a new cohabitant.[25] But the law has clung for a great deal longer to the belief that it is possible to persuade couples to stay together through the medium of divorce laws based on a strict idea of matrimonial right and wrong.

Jurisdiction in matrimonial causes was transferred to the secular courts in 1857, and they were given the power to grant judicial divorce, originally on grounds more limited than those on which they could allow separation. Any type of matrimonial relief depended upon proof of a matrimonial offence. Divorce was seen as the punishment suffered by the guilty spouse. Put the other way round, the offence was a fundamental breach of the marital contract, which allowed the innocent spouse to repudiate it if he or she so chose. The punishment would deter some potential offenders, but for others it might be a perfectly acceptable price for the release which they earnestly desired. Hence an additional deterrent was required in the right of the innocent party to choose whether or not to petition. Because their mutual commitment was meant to be life-long, however, there was always an inherent moral pressure upon the innocent party to put the stability of the marriage above personal interests and wishes. The stigma of being divorced could thus be applied almost as severely to the innocent as to the guilty. By the same token, divorce by simple consent was unthinkable because it would imply that the supposedly life-long commitment could be abandoned at will.[26] Plausible or not, belief in the deterrent effect of divorce laws remained firmly entrenched in establishment thinking, at least as it is shown by the majority Report of the Royal Commission on Marriage and Divorce as late as 1956.[27]

It is well known that from 1857 to 1923 the grounds for divorce discriminated between men and women to the latter's disadvantage. But even when that form of discrimination was removed, divorce laws based upon marital fault discriminated against the non-breadwinner spouse in other ways. If they operate as any deterrent at all, they must always operate most powerfully against the spouse who has most to fear from separation or divorce. A dependent wife stood to lose both home and support by being found the guilty party. She also stood to lose very considerably by becoming the innocent party, even where her former husband could be obliged to support her in the manner to which she had been accustomed. Such cases became rarer and rarer as divorce crept lower and lower down the social scale. Economic pressure combined with moral pressure to put the stability of marriage first. By definition, the homemaker has adopted a career which depends upon her having a home to make. Her loss of status when she cannot keep her husband there is almost as great as when she leaves him. Innocent or guilty, her only safe way out of one marriage is straight into another, and thus the cycle is perpetuated. The association which Ross and Sawhill have noted between the rising divorce rate and the rising rate of wives at outside work is not surprising.[28] The work gives alternative sources of supply as well as satisfaction. It also liberates men from the responsibility which dependence engenders in all but the most callous.

Aside from deterrence, the old matrimonial offences were clearly designed to set norms of marital behaviour. They may well have reflected popular values which hold good today, but they could still discriminate against the non-breadwinner by the way in which those duties were defined. The prime example lies in the choice of the family home. Early cases such as *Mansey* v. *Mansey*[29] suggested that the husband was entitled to choose the family home simply because of his status as head of the family, so that a wife who refused to join him there was automatically in desertion. Mr Justice Henn Collins indulged in a typical complaint of the period: 'The rights of a husband as they used to be have been considerably circumscribed in favour of the wife without very much, if any, curtailment of his obligations, but we have not yet got to the point where the wife can decide where the matrimonial home is to be. . . .' In *King* v. *King*[30] Lord Merriman did not disagree with that as a general proposition but thought that the husband should have abided by an agreement made before marriage to join his wife at her place of business. Her business, not her marriage, gave her the necessary status to make such a contract with him. By *Dunn* v. *Dunn*[31] Lord Justice Denning was saying that 'each is entitled to an equal voice in the ordering of the affairs which are their common concern.' No one had the casting vote, but a spouse who was behaving unreasonably would still be guilty of desertion. In that case, the wife's deafness and social isolation were a reasonable excuse for refusing to join her husband. But reasonableness usually meant going where the breadwinner's work took him. In *Walter* v. *Walter*[32] neither was in desertion because the demands of dual employment kept them apart. There is nothing to suggest that a non-breadwinner spouse has an equal voice in deciding whether the breadwinner should take a job involving a move which she does not want. Nowadays a similar attitude might be displayed in deciding upon the occupation or sale of the matrimonial home,[33] although the divorce court is now markedly less sympathetic to the argument that he who pays the piper must call the tune.

However, although the discrimination against the role is plain, there is less evidence from the reported cases that the courts used the actual grounds for divorce (as opposed to some of the ancillary consequences) as a means of compelling wives to adopt that role or to penalise those who did it badly. In *Bartholomew* v. *Bartholomew*[34] it was held that a lazy and dirty wife who refused to make any effort about the house was not guilty of constructive desertion. It was therefore unreasonable for her husband to leave. The court's reason was that the necessary element of intention to drive her husband away was lacking. Even after it was decided that a spouse may be *presumed* to intend the natural and probable consequences of her actions, Lord Merriman doubted in *Majoram* v. *Majoram*[35] whether mere 'sluttishness' was sufficiently grave and weighty behaviour to justify the husband's departure.

Similarly, in *Kaslefsky* v. *Kaslefsky*[36] the Court of Appeal decided that certain types of behaviour could amount to cruelty only if they were 'aimed at' the other spouse. The wife's complete disregard of 'wifely duties' in staying up late, getting up late, not doing any work and leaving her husband to get their little boy's breakfast fell into this category. It was 'all very wrong of her', in the words of Lord Justice Denning, but it was not cruelty because she did not mean it against her husband. This case, and the requirement for conduct to be 'aimed at' the other spouse, was overruled by the House of Lords in *Gollins* v. *Gollins*[37] and plays no part in the modern law. Significantly, though, Mr Gollins was a lazy and feckless husband who left his wife to do all the work of earning their living and maintaining their home. It could be that the judges were readier to condemn husbands who were bad providers than they were to condemn wives who were bad housekeepers. The man who fails to work for pay commits a much graver social offence, as we can see from the law of social security, than does the woman who fails to look after her home. Such relative condemnation would reinforce stereotyped sex roles. The modern law gives the court an equal opportunity to condemn both but, by reducing the emphasis upon fault, reduces society's need for it to do so.

The Divorce Law Reform Act 1969 swept away the old quasi-criminal grounds for divorce and replaced them with the single ground that the marriage had irretrievably broken down (now contained in the Matrimonial Causes Act 1973, section 1(1)). On the face of it, such a law involves a complete departure from both of the old ideas. It embodies the value that dead marriages should be set aside, no matter how the death occurred or who was responsible for it.[38] It sets no standards of marital behaviour and makes little attempt to keep married couples together. Restrictive laws are merely an inconvenience to spouses who both want to divorce.[39] Even if only one of them does, it is not the ground for divorce which determines whether they will stay together or separate but whether the spouse who wants to break up the marriage is able to arrange for them to live apart. That, of course, depends upon their respective economic positions or the willingness of the courts to redress any imbalance between them.

There was still a view that the law should make some attempt to deter the over-hasty. Hence irretrievable breakdown can be proved only by reference to any of five 'facts' (set out in the Matrimonial Causes Act 1973, section 1(2)). Only two of these abandon all reference to fault. Most such laws in other countries rely upon a minimum period of separation or reflection to ensure that the breakdown is indeed complete. Here, if both want a divorce, they may have one if they have been able to maintain separate households for a total of two years out of the previous two and a half. If only one wants a divorce, they must have lived separately for five years out of the previous five and a half. A spouse who has been prepared to keep his or her side of the bargain may thus be divorced against his or her will. (It was always, wrongly, assumed that these would be wives.) But the impossibility of divorce has never kept husbands at home and it was thought that wives would usually suffer no more from the divorce than they already had from separation.

The Law Society, among others, has argued that these periods are too long and should not differentiate between joint and sole decisions.[40] The marriage is just as dead in each case. It still believes that breakdown should be proved by reference to separation. Yet this clearly discriminates against the spouse who is unable to arrange alternative accommodation. The court's powers to adjust entitlement to the matrimonial home do not arise until there is a divorce. In the meantime they will be reluctant to use their powers to decide who should occupy the home unless it is unreasonable to expect the couple to stay there together. The House of Lords' recent re-emphasis of the importance of conduct in this context reinforces the difficulty.[41] The local authority's duty to rehouse the homeless depends upon an even more stringent test. Norwegian divorce law solves this problem by retaining its insistence upon a period of separation before divorce gives the right to marry again but allowing all the ancillary questions to be decided at the outset.

However, English law allows an immediate divorce on proof of either of two apparently fault-based facts.[42] It is no coincidence that women use these much more frequently than men, particularly when they have children. The most common allegation is that the respondent has behaved in such a way that the petitioner cannot reasonably be expected to live with him. It is clear that the level of toleration for incompatible personalities and lifestyles need not be high.[43] The Law Society maintains that 'after several years of marriage, virtually any spouse can assemble a list of events which, taken out of context, can be presented as unreasonable (sic) behaviour on which to found a divorce petition.'[44] If the cause is undefended, the usual 'special' procedure for granting decrees without a hearing ensures that only the allegations, as opposed to the evidence for them, are scrutinized by the court. Much the same is true of the other common fact, that the respondent has committed adultery and the petitioner finds it intolerable to live with her or him. The emphasis has again shifted from the infidelity itself to the level of toleration in this particular family. But it has gone further because reasonableness does not come into the matter at all and the standards employed can be wholly subjective. Nor need the intolerability have anything to do with the adultery, which may have been totally irrelevant to the breakdown of the marriage.[45] It may even have been encouraged by the petitioner.

Thus neither fact is necessarily fault-based. Most courts probably share the view of Mr Justice Ormrod in *Wachtel* v. *Wachtel*[46] that the law 'is much too clumsy a tool for dissecting the complex interactions which go on all the time in a family. Shares in responsibility for breakdown cannot be properly assessed without a meticulous examination and understanding of the characters and personalities of the spouses concerned, and the more thorough the investigation the more the shares will, in most cases, approach equality.' Nevertheless, these 'facts' still give some opportunity for the courts to pass judgment upon how married people behave. In *Allen* v. *Allen*[47] Sir John Arnold decided that a wife could not reasonably be expected to live with a husband who expected her to do as she was told, never consulted her wishes, rarely talked to her and kept her extremely short of money on which to provide for them and their six children. Despite this she had stayed with him for twenty-nine years because she felt unable to leave while the children were growing up. Her husband would have been under no such compulsion had he wished to leave. Yet the courts will make such pronouncements only when they are absolutely necessary. Where a no-fault fact is admitted, they will not allow a fault-based petition to proceed.[48] They frequently emphasize that granting a decree to one spouse or the other will have little effect upon the issues relating to the future housing and finance of the parties and their children. Defending a case causes long delays.

This can cut both ways. There are powerful financial disincentives to fighting the divorce itself, particularly where one side is legally aided and the other is not, for the issue must then be transferred to the High Court and the costs can be heavy. This is often cited as evidence of discrimination against the breadwinner/husband.[49] He certainly may be deterred from raising issues of conduct. But if he insists on fighting any issue, the cost to his wife will be as much as, if not more than, the cost to him. Unless all the costs can be recovered, the legal aid fund is entitled to claim the remainder against all the capital she is awarded apart from the first £2,500. The breadwinner will still have his independence, whereas however meritorious was the wife's case, she will still be effectively tied down.[50] The assets so vital to her can so easily be dissipated. The delay while the issue is being resolved will also hurt her much more than him.

Almost three-quarters of all divorces are now initiated by women.[51] They are the majority of petitioners on all five 'facts' and the overwhelming majority where 'behaviour' is alleged. The most popular fact alleged by husbands is adultery. This might indicate that husbands are most often responsible for marital breakdown, or that husbands are typically badly behaved while wives are typically unfaithful. It undoubtedly indicates that women are still reluctant to appear the guilty party to a divorce, except where they have another man to go to. The reasons for this are almost certainly economic. It is far more important for a dependent wife to be able to get a claim for ancillary relief off the ground than it is for a breadwinner husband. This is particularly so when, like the majority, she will need to make some recourse to the state. The state wishes to know who is to care for the children, who is to have the matrimonial home and how much is available to support the family, often before deciding what provision, if any, it can make itself.

In 1966 the Law Commission declared that the object of a good divorce law should be to 'buttress, rather than to undermine, the stability of marriage'.[52] Unfortunately, no one has yet devised a buttress which is capable of being applied equally to both breadwinner and homemaker. In 1981 the Society of Conservative Lawyers called for the state to decide 'whether it should resume responsibility for preserving marriages'.[53] The changes most criticized were those which had gone some way towards reducing the numbers of homemaking women or the deterrent effects of the divorce laws upon them. The reform for which there is currently most enthusiasm, however, is conciliation. This seeks not to reunite the spouses but to enable them to arrange for the consequences of their separation as amicably as possible. It may certainly assist the civilized divorces of the better-off to become even more civilized, but unless carefully handled it may also delay the relief more desperately needed by others in less civilized relationships.

Above all, however, the divorce figures show that women no longer believe that staying married is their greatest protection. They are no longer looking to individual men to protect them from society, although they may be looking to society to protect them from individual men. In this changed climate of opinion a society which wishes to preserve the family might consider ways of making family responsibilities more attractive to both sexes rather than returning to its traditional division and discrimination between them.

The State and Women's Rights

9

The Welfare State:
Social Security and Taxation

Although the law has increasingly recognized men and women as individuals in other areas, the family remains the basic unit for administering social security and taxation systems. The reason is partly historical. The first Poor Laws of 1598 and 1601 were grafted on to, and supplemented, the private law of family obligations, which remained the primary system of financial support. Income tax was introduced in 1799, at the height of women's financial dependence on men, when all property belonging to a married woman automatically transferred to her husband. The specific provision in the 1806 Act that the profits of a married woman 'shall be deemed the profits of the husband' covered unearned income from equitable arrangements, which were the rich women's only independent resource. Even today, when the law allows wives to own property, separate taxation of married couples does not extend to unearned income.

As will be shown, the concept of family and family obligations operating in this area of public law has remained wedded to traditional notions. There has been no development of the concept of husband and wife as equal, co-dependent partners, as has occurred to a limited extent in family law. The model which pertains here is of men as breadwinners and women primarily as dependent homemakers. The reasons for the retention of what at first sight appears to be an outmoded and totally unrealistic model are closely bound up to the development and aims of the welfare state system. The contributory scheme of social security benefits arose out of the voluntary insurance schemes developed by workers in the nineteenth century. There were Friendly Societies which protected women workers. Indeed, some had only women members.[1] However, as the state gradually took over the voluntary schemes in the twentieth century, the terms, conditions and benefits were altered to protect men as workers and women as wives and mothers. As we shall see, the tax system developed on similar lines to offer higher income workers the same incentives and benefits enjoyed under the social security system. A three-tier system was thus established: the taxation system for those in work; the contributory system to protect breadwinners against loss of paid employment; and state support (originally the Poor Law) for all those in need who were not otherwise covered. To be viable the system needed to maximize the number of people in paid work, making contributions to the state, and to minimize the number of claimants. Thus there was built into it a variety of work incentives and a hierarchy of benefits, favouring those in work and disadvantaging non-contributing claimants.

Although the system was rationalized and fully nationalized in 1946, broadly on the lines proposed by the Beveridge Report (1942), these principles remained. The position of women as homemaking wives and mothers has formed an integral part of the work incentive and the means of limiting expenditure under the scheme. Today the majority of married women do undertake paid work and make some financial contribution to the family income. The question of cost has become the dominant reason for refusing to extend benefits to married women and for refusing to accord them equal status with men.

This chapter examines first the position of women in the welfare state as it has developed in the twentieth century. We look at why the new model of equality between the sexes, which was introduced into the law in the 1970s in other areas, was not extended to social security and taxation. We then turn to the changes that have been made recently, the impetus for reform and the form of the law. Welfare law plays an important part in the lives of all women. First, because both the tax system and social security systems operate during marriage and not only at the end of marriage, they effectively define the financial relationships of husbands and wives towards each other in the absence of detailed obligations in private law. Secondly, the rules and regulations surrounding the operation of the social security system — for example, in relation to qualifying employment and unemployment — undermine the position of women as workers and their equal participation in the workforce. Third, the system totally disregards domestic work undertaken by married women in private homes. This leads to a devaluation of such work when undertaken by other members of the community or outside the home. This chapter examines these three issues and asks what changes will result from the recent changes in the law.

The Position of Women in the Welfare State up to 1970

The origins of the welfare state in England are to be found in the latter years of the nineteenth century. The health and environmental improvements undertaken at local authority level began the process. In 1911 direct financial assistance became available under the National Insurance Act, as the state adopted the workers' insurance schemes. Although deemed a national scheme, not all workers were covered. Moreover, it was administered through the private sector, and a variety of schemes remained. This left many workers unprotected and still reliant on the old Poor Law. The limited range of hazards which were covered and the disparity in cover accelerated the change in attitude towards poor law claimants which had already begun.[2] It was realized that many people were in need because of misfortune over which they had no control. The Old Age Pension Act 1908 had already weakened the link between destitution and social condemnation.

Increasingly in the first decades of the twentieth century the non-contributory means-tested benefits came to be perceived as the support system for the contributory system.

The link between paid employment and the welfare state is crucial to the position of women in welfare law. Not only have the risks covered by the contributory scheme reflected the interests of the majority of workers, but also the terms and conditions of the system have been geared to the needs of the economy and employment rates. The years when the pattern of the scheme as we know it today was established were years of recession and depression. From the end of the First World War to the beginning of the Second the aim of Government and trades unions alike was to reduce the number of women in men's jobs. Although in times of job plenty it makes economic sense to recruit as many workers as possible to contributory schemes, in times of unemployment a large number of potential claimants become a hindrance. At such times married women are an obvious target for 'special treatment'. A cut in, or removal of, their benefit does not leave them destitute. Any unacceptable reduction in family income can be alleviated through the finances of husbands, often more cheaply, if only in administrative costs. As the Poor Law Commissioners discovered in 1909, women are much more adept at making do with less and at putting the needs of their families before their own and much more willing to do so. The law has been used both negatively and positively to achieve these ends.

The most obvious method has been to exclude married women from the contributory scheme. Sometimes this aim has been explicit. Women who worked in family businesses were excluded from 1911 National Insurance Act and still do not receive the same protection as do other workers today (for example, in relation to maternity rights under the Employment Protection Consolidation Act 1978, section 146(I)). The Unemployment Insurance No. 3 Act 1931 introduced a break in contributory record for women on marriage, and thus those with insufficient contributions after marriage lost the unemployment benefit which would otherwise have been paid. The National Insurance Act 1946 allowed married women workers to pay a reduced contribution which precluded them from claiming unemployment or sickness benefit in their own right. Indeed, this made economic sense, as married women paying a full contribution received benefits lower than those of other workers. More often the exclusion of married women has been achieved more covertly. The 1931 Unemployment Act excluded seasonal workers and persons working less than two days a week. In the 1920s women who at any time had been domestic servants (and that covered a large number of married women who had moved into other work during the First World War) were held to be suitable for that work. If they refused such work, they lost their unemployment benefit; if they took it, they lost their unemployment protection. Domestic service in a private household became an uninsurable occupation in 1921 (Unemployment Insurance Act, Sched. I, Part II b). Today concern is being expressed that married women who do qualify for unemployment benefit are being denied it where they cannot prove that they will have adequate child-care arrangements to enable them to undertake full-time work.[3]

The testing of a married woman's eligibility for benefits by her domestic labour is not, of course, new. As early as 1913 sickness benefit was being withdrawn from wives caught managing to look after their families. The present Housewives' Non-Contributory Invalidity Pension operates in the same way (see pp. 169-170). Even where married women have not been formally excluded, savings have been made on the amount of benefit payable. Before 1946 the female rate for contributory benefits was four-fifths of the male rate, and this had been further reduced in 1932 in relation to sickness benefit paid to married women. The rates of contributory benefit payable in respect of the claimant remained unequal until 1978 (Social Security Pensions Act 1975). Even today the continuous contribution rules in relation to pensions still discriminate against married women (see p. 168).

The soft approach to achieving the same end has been directed at husbands, buttressing their masculine role as providers. The married man's tax allowance was introduced in 1918 and was increased substantially in 1920 at the expense of the wife's earning allowance. It was followed by extra allowances for wives and children in unemployment benefit (the Unemployment Workers' Dependants Temporary Provisions Act 1921). Maternity benefit, a lump-sum payment, was payable on the husband's contributions, from its introduction in 1911 to its transformation to a universal grant in 1982. Indeed, the 1911 National Insurance Act specifically provided that even where a married woman's contribution also qualified her for the benefit, it should be payable on the husband's record and to him. He was under no duty to hand the money over to her; he was required only to make '*adequate provision to the best of his power* for the maintenance and care of his wife' (section 19).

The inadequacy of some men's wage rates to provide for their families was masked by benefits in kind, such as free milk, school meals (1906) and school medical services (1907). The reason for the introduction of such services was, of course, more complex than support for the male boast, 'My wife doesn't need to work'. The lessons of direct wage supplementation and its effects on wage rates had been well learned.[4] Between the wars many in the labour movement itself fought against the idea of family allowances, although feminists like Eleanor Rathbone believed that they would radically improve maternal and child nutrition and health.[5] The growth of unemployment in the 1930s presented Governments with a financial crisis of unparalleled severity. One way of attempting to alleviate need without raising the cost of unemployment benefit was to give local authorities more permissive powers to provide beneficial services, particularly those which sought to make women better mothers and family managers.[6]

As we shall show, there have been some modifications to the concept of men as breadwinners and women as potential homemakers in both the taxation and the social security system since 1970. But for the most part the principles established in those early years remain. Both the tax and social security systems assumed that after leaving school men would expect to undertake continuous paid employment until retirement age. Single adult women who did not marry were expected to work to support themselves unless prevented by filial obligations to ageing or invalid relatives, particularly parents. Men who married had to work, so far as they were fit to do so, in order to support their wives and, if they had any, their children. The taxation system assumed that all income of a married couple belonged to the husband. He was given a higher personal allowance than a single man because of his family responsibilities. Other allowances, such as mortgage relief (until the recent change to taxation at source), were made against his earnings, regardless of strict legal ownership. A husband contributed to the National Insurance fund to cover periods out of work due to unemployment, sickness or old age. Benefits at such times automatically included extra money for any dependent children and for his wife if she was financially dependent upon him. The rules about the amounts she might earn before she ceased to be so dependent varied from benefit to benefit, but the principle was that a wife would be held to be dependent even though she had some independent earnings. (Until 1983 a woman could claim only for a husband who was incapable of paid employment.) In relation to pensions, a man's contribution automatically provided financial protection for his widow but not vice versa — a situation which still exists today.

It can be seen that under this pattern of welfare provision married women did not need to be treated in the same way as men. They were deemed already to be covered. As Beveridge stated:

> On marriage a woman gains a legal right to maintenance by her husband as a first line of defence against risks which fall directly on the solitary woman; she undertakes at the same time to perform vital unpaid service and becomes exposed to new risks, including the risk that her married life may be ended prematurely by widowhood or separation. [7]

Where the husband was working the taxation system sought to ensure that he had sufficient money to support her unpaid work. When he was not, state benefits were paid to him for her support. If a married woman worked for money outside the home, it was only fair that she should pay tax. Equity (and, as will be shown, the more powerful principle of work incentive) required that she be allowed some personal relief, if only to compensate for payments made to cover substitutes for her work in the home. [8]

Similarly, it was deemed only fair that married women who did take paid employment should make some contribution to the National Insurance fund. The Social Security Act 1975 phased out these reduced contributions and equalized the rates of benefits for all women claimants. Prior to 1978, when that Act came into force, wives could pay full contributions. But contributions for all women were initially at a lower rate on the assumption that if they got married, these contributions would be lost, and if they remained single, they would have only themselves to support. The rates of benefits for married women were lower than for single women, again on equitable grounds. First, their basic wants were already provided for by their husbands.[9] Second, wives who had paid full contributions received a maternity allowance to compensate for loss of earnings and to ensure that they did not jeopardize the health of themselves or their children. In the 1946 Act wives paying reduced contributions qualified for the maternity allowance. This was changed in 1953 when it became payable only on full contributions (National Insurance Act 1953). The amount payable was reduced at the same time, bringing it into line with other short term benefits. Third, except where a husband was permanently incapable of work or could bring in only a very small income indeed, a wife needed no extra allowances for her spouse or her children. Similarly, there was no need for widowers' pensions payable from wives' contributions.

Since the non-contributory system was designed to provide a safety net for those who fell through loopholes or inadequacies in the contributory scheme, they followed the same model. No woman cohabiting with her husband or a man as her husband could claim supplementary benefit except in exceptional circumstances — that is, in '*involuntary* role reversal' situations only.[10] Family allowances, and later the child benefit which replaced it, were paid to the mother. As new forms of non-contributory benefits were introduced in the 1970s (Family Income Supplement 1971, Invalid Care Allowance 1975, Non-Contributory Invalidity Pensions 1975), they too embodied the principle that men were breadwinners and married and cohabiting women homemakers.

The Position of Women, 1970—80

The blanket application of the provisions of Sex Discrimination Act to tax and social security would have had massive financial repercussions. Matters which had monetary implications were deliberately excluded from that Act, in order to reduce opposition to what was felt to be a very contentious matter anyway. Moreover, many other changes were being made in welfare law during this period, and it was necessary to discuss the introduction of sex equality within the terms of reference of the welfare system itself. Successive Governments were criticized for their failure to rid the system of sex discrimination — pressure which escalated over the decade. But the way in which the inequality of women was discussed and the definition of discrimination changed from 1970 to 1980.

In the early 1970s concern focused on the precarious position of wives at a time of rising divorce:

> The main criticisms were that in contemporary economic conditions [a married woman's] earnings had become an essential element in the family's income, no longer the subordinate accessory which Beveridge had assumed, and that full reliance on the husband's insurance record rendered the wife's position vulnerable, not only on termination of marriage but also during its currency — she had no means of ensuring that contributions were paid.[11]

The consequences for separated families were spelled out by the Finer Report on one-parent families in 1974.[12] Finer found that over twice as many single, separated and divorced women relied upon supplementary benefits in 1971 as the combined number of those who relied on maintenance and/or earnings. The low level of women's earnings, the difficulties of combining work and family commitments and the unreliability of maintenance payments made 'many mothers give up the struggle and revert to living on supplementary benefit'.[13] Finer concluded:

> There are of course other disadvantaged groups; but in terms of families with children, which must be the relevant standard of comparison here, there can be no other group of this size who are as poor as fatherless families, of whom so many lack any state benefit, whose financial position is so uncertain and whose hope of improvement in their situation is relatively so remote.[14]

The solution that report proposed, of a non-means tested, non-contributory, guaranteed maintenance allowance, which would be payable to employed and home-based single mothers alike, was never introduced. Instead reliance has been placed on a variety of measures which favour single mothers able to support themselves and their children through paid employment but which fail to accord to the work of child-rearing the symbolic value implicit in the proposed guaranteed maintenance allowance.

Family income supplement is a means-tested benefit payable to a low-income family unit whose breadwinner is in full-time paid employment. Until November 1983 a married woman could not claim as the breadwinner (under the 1970 Family Income Supplements Act) unless she was separated from her husband. As in the case of supplementary benefit, a woman living with a man as his wife was also precluded from claiming the benefit. One-parent families have represented a substantial number of family income supplement recipients since its introduction in 1971. In 1971 they formed 34 per cent of all such claimants, in 1980 55 per cent.[15] In 1980 regulations lowered the definition of full-time work for single parents from thirty hours per week to twenty-four hours.[16] Like the increases in child benefit for one-parent families, this change encourages more single parents to undertake paid employment and goes some way towards recognizing the practical difficulties of combining the two roles of breadwinner and child-rearer.

As the decade progressed, other changes were made which recognized the dual role undertaken by most married women of wage-earner and child-rearer. The married women's reduced National Insurance contribution was phased out from 1978 (Social Security Pensions Act 1975). The rate of contributory benefits payable to married women was equalized. However, although their role as *workers* was recognized, their work as parents was still assumed to be the day-to-day care for children. Their contributions to family income were not recognized as necessary for the financial support of children. Thus married women claiming unemployment or sickness benefit could not claim extra dependency allowances for their children, as could married men, unless they were in fact the sole bread-winners. The only married women who could do so were single parents and women whose husbands were incapable of paid employment. The extension to wives of automatic allowances for dependent children under the Social Security Act 1980 was postponed until November 1984 (one year after the other 'equality' measures were introduced). The Government has announced that they will be abolished for all claimants of short-term benefits by that date.

The shift from a patronizing concern to protect women as mothers to a partial recognition of married women as workers and mothers is reflected in the home responsibilities provision of the new pension scheme also introduced in 1978. The solution devised to compensate married women for the withdrawal of the reduced contribution was to count those years spent in child-rearing (or in looking after severely disabled family members) in calculating the retirement pension.[17] The way in which this was done recognized the function of carer but failed to treat that work in the same way as paid employment. Instead of giving credits for each week of child or relation care (that is, accrediting the contribution record as if that *week* had been spent in paid employment), the *years* for which child benefit or attendance allowance was paid are counted. There are two points to note here. The first is that the law recognizes only a limited range of domestic responsibilities, continuous care of children under 16 and the care of a person so severely disabled that he or she qualifies for an attendance allowance. The scheme gives no recognition to the myriad other domestic responsibilities which may be difficult to combine with paid employment or with work which earns more than the lower earnings limit. Nor does the scheme recognize the problems of 'redundant homemakers', women who have been engaged on such caring work within the home who cannot find suitable paid employment to return to.

The second point is that even the domestic 'responsibilities' (note: not 'work') which are recognized are treated differently when undertaken by married or cohabiting women. Men and single women looking after persons in receipt of an attendance allowance have qualified since 1975 for an invalid care allowance (Social Security Benefits Act, section 7). This is a small weekly sum

> designed to assist those who sacrificed their own work opportunities to care for persons in receipt of attendance allowance. . . . Quite apart from the justice of compensating a group who performed an unattractive and unpaid task, there was the economic consideration that by doing so they relieved the social services of additional burdens.[18]

But married and cohabiting women cannot claim the invalid care allowance. It is assumed that they do not have work opportunities the loss of which needs to be compensated, and that they will not return to paid employment. Every man or single woman claiming invalid care allowance is given contribution credits for each week for which the benefit is paid. Thus the right to unemployment or sickness benefit is preserved should the claimant seek to return to paid employment. A married or cohabiting woman in that situation has no such rights. Nor can she claim supplementary benefit while she continues to live with her husband or with a man as her husband. Yet the statistics show quite clearly that the majority of people doing what Ogus and Barendt call an 'unattractive and unpaid task', which saves the country so much money, are the very women who are excluded from claiming invalid care allowance. Only 8,000 people currently claim the allowance, although there are between 80,000 and 110,000 women who would qualify if the discriminatory bar were lifted.[19] Its payment would not only recognize the sacrifice that married women make in giving up paid employment and give them some financial protection in the future; perhaps more important, it would also give them dignity and the ability to pay for often much needed relief in their care duties.[20]

The other benefit which shares the assumption of women's primary role is the Housewives' Non-Contributory Invalidity Pension (HNCIP). The non-contributory invalidity pension was introduced (by Social Security Benefit Act 1975, section 6) to help disabled people who fell outside the long-term sickness benefit. The Non-Contributory Invalidity Pension (NCIP) is a non-contributory, non-means-tested benefit, guaranteeing a minimum income to those persons incapable of paid employment. Married and cohabiting women were automatically excluded from claiming it. In 1977 the benefit was extended to them if they could show that, in addition to being incapable of paid work, they were also incapable of performing 'normal household duties' without substantial assistance.[21] 'Figures culled from [Department of Health and Social Security] sources revealed that 65 per cent of all women applying for NCIP during one week in 1979 had been in paid employment during the last five years and 75 per cent had given up work for reasons connected with disability.'[22] Thus the law compounds one discrimination with another. Women who worked but paid a reduced contribution, because the system did not make it worthwhile to pay in full, are denied an invalidity pension as of right. They are then further discriminated against because their inability to work is insufficient grounds for a non-contributory pension. They too have to suffer further loss in dignity and integrity by proving themselves substantially incapable of the domestic work which the rest of the social security system defines as their proper function. They have to prove themselves dependent on men not only financially but physically and socially also. The estimated cost given in the House of Lords debate in July 1983 for the lifting of the additional household duties test, £275 million per year on 1983/84 rates, indicates the extent of the discrimination and the numbers of women adversely affected. In November 1983 it was announced that changes in NCIP and HNCIP would be included in the Health and Social Security Bill 1983, which would remove this sex discrimination. As we shall see, the proposed reforms will provide theoretical sex equality. They will not increase the number of potential claimants. Instead it is estimated that fewer people will qualify in future.[23]

In the law on HNCIP we see the transition between the way in which the problem was defined at the beginning and end of the 1970s. Its introduction went some way to give some financial assistance to married women who were not in paid employment — mainly older, disabled homemaker spouses. This idea of protection is very much in line with Lord Denning's ideas on family law (see p. 115). It is also easy to see why married and cohabiting women were dealt with differently. The various new non-means-tested benefits introduced in the 1970s for the disabled resulted from embarrassment at the failure of the contributory system to fulfil its promises to workers. 'The OPCS survey of 1968—9 revealed that 40 per cent of the "very seriously" handicapped, 37 per cent of the "severely handicapped" and 35 per cent of the "appreciably handicapped" were in receipt of supplementary benefit.'[24] But under the social security system before 1975 married women were not thought of as workers. We would argue that the separate taxation of a wife's earnings introduced in 1972 was primarily a measure designed to help to reduce the tax bill of male higher wage-earners rather than a recognition of married women as workers. Moreover, until the changes in the 1980 Social Security Act most married women were unable to claim supplementary benefit, so the embarrassment at having so many disabled 'workers' dependent on a means-tested benefit did not extend to married and cohabiting women.

The legislation of 1975 changed that perception. The Sex Discrimination Act has been enforced primarily in the employment sphere. The Social Security Pensions Act gave recognition to married women workers in eliminating the differences in rates of contribution. Section 16 of that Act also allowed a disabled husband to claim an invalidity pension on his widow's contributions if her insurance record was better than his. The Sex Discrimination Act required employers to give women equal access to occupational pension schemes, though not equal benefits.[25]

The changes to the social security system contained in the 1980 Act that purport to eradicate sex discrimination are the direct result of EEC legislation. European law is based on the notion of women as workers. Indeed, all the anti-discrimination measures of the EEC can be justified only on that assumption. We therefore turn to look at recent developments in the law and the limitations imposed in the social security system by the definition of work as paid employment only.

The 'Equality' Reforms of the 1980s

Directive 79/7 required member states of the European Community to introduce equal treatment into their social security systems by the end of 1984.[26] The Social Security Act 1980 included measures intended to implement the European law in this country. The directive did not prescribe equal treatment for all types of social security benefit. For instance, it was limited to benefits received by the working population, and family benefits were specifically excluded. Although there is today a closer link between national insurance and taxation as such, all aspects of taxation are outside the directive.

The major changes to the English law have concerned unemployment benefit, supplementary benefit, child carers' allowances and family income supplement.[27] The last was outside the scope of the directive but was included in the 1980 Act because of its obvious interplay with supplementary benefit. At its simplest, the 1980 Act lifts the formal restrictions against married and cohabiting women claiming these benefits. However, the Act continues to treat married and cohabiting couples differently from single people. 'Individualized treatment, irrespective of sex *and* marital status, embodying the principle of financial independence, has been firmly rejected.'[28] Either member of a cohabiting couple may choose to be the claimant for social security purposes, so that voluntary role reversal has been accepted. But the law still expects the majority of couples to comprise one breadwinner and one dependent homemaker. The only exception to the one-claimant rule in the new regulations is for very poor families, in which one person may claim supplementary benefit, the other family income supplement.

The regulations made under the Social Security Act 1980 do not give couples a free choice as to which one is to be the claiming partner. An exceedingly complex list of conditions has been laid down to establish who is to be deemed to be the claiming partner, although in certain circumstances couples can apply for a change.[29] These regulations appear on the face of it to be free from sex discrimination. In order to be eligible a claimant must establish a link with paid employment. But part-time work is recognized as sufficient for these purposes. Influenced by the argument that not to recognize part-time workers paying full contributions would constitute indirect discrimination and would thus infringe European law, the 1980 Act allows those working at least eight hours a week to qualify as potential claimants. However, applicants who cannot establish a continuous period of even such part-time work over the preceding six months will not be eligible. Thus married or cohabiting women who have been precluded by domestic commitments from undertaking paid work, but who wish to do so, will not be able to claim even supplementary benefit. According to the Social Security Advisory Committee, in the Government's view, 'to allow women to claim generally in these circumstances would come too close to free choice and its risks of manipulation.'[30] The Committee went on to note: 'where neither partner can satisfy a test of contact with employment, it will be open to a woman wishing to leave her full-time child-care to become the claimant on the basis of her current availability alone.'[31] However, the claiming partner will have to make herself or himself available for work, since the other partner will be presumed to be taking care of the domestic responsibilities. As with claimants who qualify through connection with part-time work, the availability required is likely to be full-time.[32] This may not help couples when the man cannot make himself available for work (if he is a student, for instance) but the woman can fit paid work around school hours.

The choice of claiming partner may make a significant difference to the amount which might be claimed from the social security system, although the majority of couples are unlikely to decide how to divide paid and unpaid work between them with reference to their position under the social security system. It is quite clear that for the majority of couples it will make financial sense for the man to continue in full-time employment and, if they agree for one parent to give up paid work or to take part-time work, for that to be the woman. In 1980 only 8 per cent of women earned as much or more than their working husbands. [33] Many of these will be older women who are towards the top of their job structure. The changes in the law will, presumably, have little effect on their family relationships.

Moreover, the sex bias has not been totally eradicated. The rules in relation to long-term benefits still favour couples where the man is breadwinner and claiming partner, the woman part-time worker and 'dependent' homemaker. A wife is allowed to earn more than a husband before the claimant loses the additional allowance in respect of a spouse. The reason appears to be that Article 7(f) of the directive exempts from its ambit increased benefits for dependent wives of men claiming long-term benefits. Despite the fact that English law now recognizes wives as workers, it appears that part-time or low-paid work still makes them dependent upon men.

As with the implementation of European law in other areas, particular attention has been paid to the exact wording of the directive rather than its spirit. The way in which the 1980 Act has been drafted, in relation to long-term benefits and other matters excluded from the scope of the directive, demonstrate that the formal equality that it purports to enshrine masks the continuation of the status quo. For instance, a claimant of either sex may now claim an additional allowance for a person taking care of his or her child. Before the 1980 Act the child-minder had to be female. After the 1980 Act the child-minder may be a man. However, in the case of long-term benefits more generous rules apply in relation to the earned income from other sources for a resident child-minder if she is a woman. Child-rearing is still first and foremost women's work.

The 1980 Act does not change the law in relation to the housewives' non-contributory pension and the invalid care allowance, both of which, as we have seen, are based on similar notions of female role and dependency. It seems that the Government has now been persuaded that the former was within the European directive. The Health and Social Security Bill 1983 proposes to abolish the present non-contributory invalidity pensions and to replace them with a new 'severe disablement allowance'. Claimants under 20 years of age will continue to be tested on their incapacity for paid employment. Older claimants who had not established claims under the old law will receive the benefit only if they can show an 80 per cent loss of faculty. This is the test applied for industrial injuries, which has been criticized on the ground that it takes no account of the disabling effect of handicap on people's lives. Ogus and Barendt state that 'empirical work has shown that claimants of industrial injury benefit feel the system of compensation to be unjust and incomprehensible' [34] and that current theories on disability feel that for a fairer assessment of disability 'regard should be had not only to such activities as self-care, mobility and performing household duties...but also to establishing and maintaining relationships within and outside the family.'[35] It seems significant that when the male breadwinner test of paid employment was found to be discriminatory, it was proposed to change to an 'objective test' operating totally within the paid employment sphere, which no longer accords with professional definitions of disability, rather than a test which is not linked to paid employment. As we have shown, the social and domestic functions by which the professional would test disability are precisely those which the social security system has deemed to be the province of women in the past.

Until 1981 it could have been argued that invalid care allowance was a family benefit and thus outside the scope of the directive. Until then the allowance was paid only for the care of a disabled relative who was in receipt of one of the attendance allowances. However, since 1981[36] it has been payable in respect of care for non-relatives. Although the definition of family operating within the social security system is wider than that in private law, it seems unlikely that invalid care allowance paid in respect of a non-relative would fall within the 'family benefit' exemption. Its inclusion depends on recognizing the function of caring as a 'family function' — that is, unpaid care carried out primarily by women. But the principle of equal treatment that is the basis of the directive is defined as 'no discrimination whatsoever on the ground of sex either directly or indirectly by reference in particular to marital or family status'. It would appear that the allowance may now fall within the scope of the directive. First, the allowance may be described as social assistance designed to supplement a statutory scheme providing protection against sickness and invalidity (attendance allowances).[37] Second, as we have seen, the invalid care allowance was introduced as a non-means-tested alternative to supplementary benefit for those whose domestic commitments precluded any prospect of paid employment. Married and cohabiting women were excluded from the invalid care allowance because at the time they were unable to claim supplementary benefit. Since the European law has required that that discrimination be removed, it appears that the sex discrimination in the invalid care allowance law must also be removed.

The 1980 Act must be welcomed for introducing some measure of equality into the social security system. However, it can be seen that its underlying philosophy goes little further than the partial recognition of wives as workers already to be found in earlier legislation. Indeed, the proposed reforms of the non-contributory invalidity pension shows how strong is the hold of the male world of paid employment.

The new law gives no recognition to the joint responsibility of both partners for breadwinner and homemaker functions. The European draft parental leave directive currently being proposed[38] may enforce changes in the law. Even then, a law which allows *either* spouse to take parental leave is unlikely to alter the cultural assumptions about the woman's role. In Sweden only fathers at the ends of the wage scales are taking up the sex-neutral parental leave and benefits scheme.[39] In this country a married couple's earnings continue to be aggregated for tax purposes. In taxation law all such earnings notionally belong to the husband. Thus where the wife commands a higher salary than her husband, it may be financially advantageous for him to stay at home with children. However, at present few couples are in this position, and the number is unlikely to increase drastically in the near future. The provisions of the Social Security Act 1980, which enable married and cohabiting women to claim benefits from which they were previously precluded, may change the division of responsibility among some couples, particularly the very poor. But the evidence suggests that cultural customs change to allow families to survive in the prevailing economic structure[40] and that families at the extremes of the financial structure are the most likely to spearhead these changes. We have already mentioned the finding of Moss and Plewis that some working-class mothers would prefer to work part-time rather than full-time if they could afford to do so.[41] If this hypothesis is correct, one may question whether the changes in the social security system giving partial, theoretical equality will alter the cultural assumptions about family relationships. To understand fully the practical choices open to women in determining the financial and domestic aspects of their personal relationships, we must look at how the welfare system undermines the position of women.

Women Workers and Welfare

As we have already seen, only a very small proportion of the female workforce conforms to the male work pattern. The majority of the female workforce is married, and many women work only part-time. Few women workers, be they single, married or divorced, will have a continuous full-time work record. Domestic commitments and care of children, sick or elderly relatives affect most women workers and result in periods away from paid work or a switch, at least temporarily, to part-time work.[43] So long as these women were paying a full National Insurance contribution before such interruptions, the new home responsibilities protection plan is likely to preserve the pension rights of many more women in future. Official recognition of a different work pattern for women does not, however, extend to other contributory benefits. As we have seen, weekly credits are not given to women under the home responsibilities scheme, enabling them to make up their record should unemployment or sickness befall them in the year after they return to work or if they cannot find paid employment when they wish to return. Since credits are given only to working mothers for the duration of the maternity allowance, the majority of women who take advantage of the unpaid maternity leave provisions of the Employment Protection Act are similarly disadvantaged. Whatever the rhetoric, this discrimination by the state gives the lie to sentiments that women workers are to be treated as seriously as men.

Such notions of inferiority are bolstered by discrimination concerning rates of pay. As we have noted, very few women earn as much as, or more than, their husbands. Even in cases where their gross income is the same, the married man's tax allowance ensures that the woman's take-home pay will be lower. Separate taxation, that is the 'wife's earnings election' introduced in 1972, solves this problem but is likely to result in loss of income unless they are high wage-earners. The majority of women workers, however, are segregated at the lower end of the job market, suffering not only lower gross pay but often also less job security. The latter stems not only from the type of work undertaken by women (unskilled workers being very susceptible to redundancy and job contraction) but also from the lack of legal protection for many part-time workers. Part-time workers are easier to lay off in times of recession and cheaper to employ when needed. Even where part-timers receive the same rate of pay as full-timers, an employer's overheads can be lower if part-timers do not have to pay national insurance. The United Kingdom is the only country in the EEC where more women than men have more than one job. Even where men do use two jobs to make up their wages, one of them is more likely to be self employed work than is the case for women. Since National Insurance contributions are calculated on gross earnings per employment, the high distribution of two part-time jobs among women has implications for their unemployment support and for the calculation of female unemployment generally. As long as each job pays below the lower earnings limit, no contributions are made and so no unemployment benefit is payable. Even if the worker does pay the full rate, the second part-time job may affect her availability for work, thus disentitling her from benefit. Official figures show a higher rate of unemployment among men than among women, but they are known to be distorted by the number of married women and part-timers who do not count as registered unemployed. There are problems in assessing the true extent of female unemployment: for instance, it is not easy to assess the number of women looking after dependants who would like to work were there facilities for looking after their children or relatives.

Surveys such as the Census show a higher rate of unemployment among single, widowed and divorced women than among men but a much lower rate among married women. But even where such studies include self-definition sections they cannot be relied upon. It seems that women working in the home do not perceive themselves to be 'economically active' unless actively looking for work which they think they have a realistic chance of getting.[43]

The new ability of married and cohabiting women to claim supplementary benefit if unemployed will not alleviate the position. Few women will be designated the claiming partner under the regulations. If the draft part-time directive proposed by the European Commission were accepted by the Council of Ministers, more women might qualify under the contributory system. It seems that changes would have to be made in the contribution rules and the test of whether a woman is available for work. The Greek presidency of the European Council has expressed a determination to gain a consensus on the part-time directive as soon as possible.[44] The terms of such agreement remain to be seen.

At present European legislation is the most persuasive tool for achieving change in English law in relation to women's rights. The draft directives on part-time work, occupational pensions, parental leave and temporary work are to be welcomed. But the Treaty of Rome concerns only workers, that is, those engaged in work carrying monetary reward. The exclusion of domestic work undertaken without pay by women for their families remains a fundamental flaw in all attempts to legislate against sex discrimination at a European level. As Ann Wickham has so clearly pointed out:

> The directives and programmes are concerned not with 'women' in all aspects of life but only in those areas which are to do with forms of waged work: equal pay, equal access to jobs and training. Social Security provisions for those women who have been employed on the market, even planned provisions for educational change, all are constructed in terms of access to jobs after leaving school, forms of recruitment and advancement and the ability to leave and re-enter the labour force.[45]

Thus Community policy, like that of Scandinavian countries implementing what Nielsen calls 'state feminism', recognizes women's unpaid work only in relation to their paid work. If women do not 'qualify' under the state scheme as workers, European law cannot remedy discrimination perpetuated by the state against them in connection with their unpaid work. Women are thus forced into the world of paid work and into substantial conformity with male patterns if they want to enjoy status equal to that of men. But, as Nielsen concludes:

> The easiest way to enable women to combine family and paid work is probably to sharpen the sexual segregation of the labour market by organizing women's sectors of the labour market with soft working conditions; part-time, flexi-time, wide access to leave for family reasons, low job responsibility, etc.[46]

This is to a large extent what has happened in Scandinavia, where the vast majority of women are in paid employment but in a labour market that is segregated by sex. In England too the majority of women are in paid work which shares the same characteristics as unpaid work inside the home.

The Relationship between Welfare Law and the Undervaluation of Women's Work

Controversy exists within the women's movement as to how society should recognize the value of domestic work within the home, undertaken primarily by women. There are fears that allowances paid for domestic work could be used to justify the restriction of women to domestic work. The scheme suggested by Kent's Social Services Director, paying women a relatively small amount to look after the housebound elderly and infirm as a means of saving public money, goes some way to confirm these fears: 'You pay a neighbour £15 a week and get £50 service.'[47] Women employees would lose their paid work, with all the associated employment protection and social security, to undertake or be replaced by women doing the same work for much lower pay and no security.

The social security system plays an important role in this systematic under-valuation of women's work. As we have seen, invalid care allowances are not paid primarily for the work of caring but in order to compensate workers for giving up paid employment. The Social Security Act 1975 restricts the definition of 'worker' to men and single, non-cohabiting women. The fact that a married woman has undertaken paid work does not alter the situation. The EOC cites the example of one woman who had to give up the struggle to do a paid job and take care of her disabled husband. She complained, 'Whilst I was working I was named the breadwinner by the tax authorities and was given the full tax allowances for a married couple (incidentally it didn't mean anything as I wasn't earning enough to pay tax). If I was regarded as the breadwinner by the tax authority, why not by the DHSS — we have no other monies coming in?'[48]

It can be argued that the zero economic value placed on work inside the home by both the private and the public law affects the way in which value is attached to various component skills of work in paid employment. Doubt is therefore expressed as to the effectiveness of job-evaluation schemes as a means of eradicating sex discrimination in pay. 'Female' elements such as nurturing, which are not as accessible to scientific measurement, are inevitably tinged with the cultural devaluation associated with their location in the home. Helen Remick has pointed out that 'In the United States the systems are based on economic forces as seen from the viewpoint of the private sector; for example, responsibility is assessed in terms of fiscal responsibility only, not the life—death and teaching or counselling responsibilities usually part of public-sector jobs.'[49] The development of the welfare state in Britain exemplifies the link more directly. The development of state social services has meant predominantly an increase in women's jobs in the health service, in the education system and in community support. Those promoting the legislation which introduced such services recognized the need for women workers in such posts, often making them gender-exclusive or requiring female representation for certain aspects of the work. But they also perceived them as necessary to aid women in society to do their work (the unpaid work) more effectively. The professionalization and expansion of nursing, midwifery and home-help services, for instance, was intimately connected with the prolonged campaign between the wars to cut maternal and infant mortality and, in later years, to produce a healthy new work force.[50] The philosophy adopted by the Poor Law Commissioners in 1909 in relation to early social work rehabilitation of single mothers can still be found in relation to reinstatement of battered wives in the family and the rehabilitation of female offenders through domestic skills in our prisons.[51]

It is the areas where local authority services have met needs perceived to be the province of the 'family', rather than those concerned with social control of the family, that have suffered the worst cut-backs: 'When hospital places for the senile, homes for the handicapped, nursing homes for post-operative patients and so on are not available, these people are sent "home" if there is a woman to care for them.'[52] The lifting of mandatory school-meal provision in the Education Act 1980, first introduced for the poor in 1906 and made a universal right in 1940, has resulted in the loss of female staff and has returned to the family the duty of providing children with a balanced diet. The reduction in, or privatization of, ancillary services in the health service in order to save money affects mostly women. In the latter case the abolition of the Fair Wages Resolution (15 September 1983) means that women will have to take work as cooks, cleaners and laundresses at wages much lower than previously. In some cases patients' families are having to provide laundering services themselves.

The low pay associated with female work has implications for women who service female workers. The National Association recommended rate of pay for registered child-minders is £20 for a forty-five-hour week. Rates of pay in the 'informal economy' (the hidden, sometimes irregular types of support work, such as unregistered child-minders) are usually even lower.[53] It seems that the closer a job resembles work traditionally undertaken by women for their families, particularly if it is located in people's homes, the lower the pay. The lower the pay, the less likely it is that men will consider the work suitable for them. As we shall see in the next chapter, this continuous buttressing of notions of which work is suitable for women spills over into public service. The distribution of elected women representatives in local government (unpaid) compared with that in central government (paid) suggests that the notion that women are better suited to supervise services to the community still persists.[54] Throughout the welfare state, from the formulation of policy to its administration and implementation, there exists a demarcation of men's and women's work, the latter being inferior, low-paid or unpaid. The concentration of such segregation in the health service and local authorities (among the largest employers in the country) has implications for the wider valuation of work in the market place.

All matters of tax and social security were exempted from the Sex Discrimination Act 1975 (section 51). Although that Act applies generally to employment in the public sector, the various exclusion sections take out some of the key employments, particularly those of a residential nature (section 7(2)(b) and (c)) or those in hospitals, prisons or similar establishments (section 7(2)(d)). The Act's definition of when sex is a genuine occupational qualification incorporates the very notions of women's work which we have explored in this chapter. For example, it provides that employers can stipulate the gender of job applicants where 'the holder of the job provides individuals with personal services promoting their welfare or education or similar personal services and those services can most effectively be provided by a *man* (sic)' (section 7(2)(e)) and where 'the job is one of two to be held by a married couple' (section 7(2)(h)). There is evidence to suggest that the Act generally has operated in favour more of men than of women.[55] In welfare state employment (for example, in schools and hospitals) this has meant an increase in the trend towards the appointment of men to top jobs. Women are increasingly segregated in the lower service jobs most particularly susceptible to retraction. It seems to be no coincidence that the lifting of restrictions on male midwives [56] comes at a time of almost total hospitalization of confinement and its accompanying technology. Emphasis has shifted from the intimate post-delivery support role of the job to medical concern for 'safe deliveries', from women to babies.

Part of the reason why there was no change in welfare law in the early 1970s similar to that seen in other areas must be the definition of equality generally accepted at the time. Efforts were concentrated on removing barriers to the male world — to jobs, educational opportunities, etc. Women wanted to be treated equally, that is, like men. The maternity leave provisions of the 1975 Employment Act and the home responsibility provisions of the Social Security Act 1975 are the only statutory recognition of the fact that many women could not compete equally in a system designed for men. The latter provisions at least might be regarded by sceptics as the minimum compensation for the imposition in that Act of full contributions for married women who otherwise continued to get an unequal deal.

Pressurized by a very successful campaign through the media, the Government has published a Green Paper on equalizing taxation law, *The Taxation of Husband and Wife* (1980). The contents of that document explain the Government's failure to go any further. It is trapped between an ideology of respect for the individual, for privacy and for equity, and the need to cut administrative costs, to retain both the male work incentive (particularly in relation to unemployment benefits) and women as a reserve labour force. In particular, as repeated in the reforms of the maternity benefits system proposed in the same year, there was great concern that working mothers should not be better off than mothers who stayed at home. [57] As the Green Paper admits, the option of transferable allowance favoured by the Government fails to afford privacy but does support married men in 'traditional' families and discourages women workers: 'Looked at from the point of view of the family as a whole, a fully transferable allowance could well discourage married women from taking up work in the first place. This would be particularly true when she is contemplating part-time work, when *all* her income could bear tax at her husband's marginal rate.' [58] The alternative of increased cash benefits payable to the 'supported' spouse engaged in domestic unpaid work, rather than help for men so that they could pay for their wives' services, was rejected on the ground that 'it would be difficult to defend their provision of full benefit regardless of total income, where one spouse earns full-time and the other part-time.' [59] Yet, as Land among others has shown, the unpaid work remains the same whether combined with paid work or not. [60] It seems clear that such a move is 'difficult to defend' because it would involve a major distribution of resources from men to women in the majority of families and would seriously undermine all notions of female dependence and the concomitant male work incentive.

Our analysis suggests that 'wages for housework' is not the answer. The low valuation of such work in paid employment would simply be transferred to work in the home, as can be seen already from the low rates for benefits like the invalid care allowance. Additionally, the payment of allowances for domestic jobs would increase the occupational segregation and lack of employment protection and opportunities already experienced by many women. Moreover, there seem to be fundamental objections to evaluating all aspects of life by the standard of paid employment. We have seen, in relation to the definition of disability (see p. 172) that some professionals recognize the value of the social and domestic world which has been thought to be the primary concern of women.

The high level of unemployment between the wars forced a reappraisal of social security and particularly the non-contributory system. The present economic situation and the changing employment structure seem likely to lead to a similar reassessment. No longer can men expect to be in continuous employment from the time when they leave school until retirement age. Men are having to find a role for themselves outside paid employment. For the majority the choice will not be the 'either/or' choice offered by the new 'equality' provisions of the Social Security Act 1980. The European draft directives are likely to bring about changes in the law relating to temporary workers, the reduction of working time, removal of the distinction between full-time and part-time work and an extension of parental rights. There is likely to be an increase, among women and men, in combining both paid and unpaid work. This may result in the application of more pressure over the next decade to find a new definition of equality on which to reform the social security system.

10

Women as Citizens

The analysis contained in the preceding chapters raises difficult questions about the influence of women in the legal process. To what extent have women influenced the changes in the law which first allowed them some independence from men and, later, a type of equality? Some feminists clearly expected that granting women the parliamentary vote would significantly alter other legal disabilities then suffered by women. Indeed, male MPs in 1918 feared the effect of a predominantly female electorate so much that they postponed universal female suffrage, which occurred only in 1928.[1] As we have shown, great changes have taken place since 1918, emanating from both Parliament and the courts. But to what extent have women been responsible? Can we expect that more female participation in public life will result in changes in the inequalities that remain? Moreover, should we? Can and should certain issues be raised as women's issues? Should women and men resist attempts by such bodies as the European Commission to do so?[2]

In this chapter we do not aim to provide any definitive answers to such questions. We look instead at the participation allowed women by law, the policies behind the law and how discrimination continues to operate within the law-making processes. Finally, we try to assess the most effective strategies for the future reform of laws which discriminate against women.

The policy of the law in relation to women's citizenship exhibits the same development as that seen in other areas of law already discussed. The Victorian concepts of family and morality and the biologically based notions of gender and competence which shaped the law in relation to family law, work and taxation, for instance, also governed the reintroduction of citizenship rights for women. Prior to the 1830s women were allowed to participate in public life, although it appears that such participation was sporadic and often localized and that its legal foundations were uncertain.[3] As in other fields, increased statutory intervention resulted in a firm exclusion, which was lifted only gradually. The 1832 Reform Act and the 1835 Municipal Corporations Act had deprived women of the vote, putting an end to a judicial uncertainty as to the legal position which had lasted for over two hundred years.[4] Parliament returned to female ratepayers (i.e. unmarried women only) the right to vote in local elections. An 1853 Act gave them a vote in parish elections,[5] and in 1869 they were able to vote for councillors, auditors and assessors in municipal elections. This right was extended in 1870 to the election of school boards.[6] Unmarried women were denied a vote in county elections until 1888.[7] Married women were debarred from any local vote until 1894.[8] Even then, the property qualification effectively disenfranchised all but those who owned their own property or had been registered by their husbands in respect of separate property until the qualification's removal in 1918.[9]

Women's right to hold public office was even more limited. Female ratepayers and property owners had been eligible for election as Poor Law Guardians since 1834,[10] but no woman was actually elected until 1875, when a Miss Merrington became a Poor Law Guardian at Kensington.[11] No women could stand in municipal elections until 1894[12] or for county elections until 1907.[13] No women were eligible to vote for MPs or to stand for Parliament until 1918.[14]

Although few formal restrictions operate today, such factors continue to influence the law. In one area where women are treated differently from men, nationality, the law continues to discriminate against women on the ground of their 'natural' dependence on male breadwinners. Similarly, although women are no longer restricted to local government elections or assigned a special role in relation to children or domestic issues, more women are to be found in local as opposed to central government, in education and social services rather than the Treasury or foreign affairs.[15]

In a country where there is no written constitution stating and guaranteeing precise rights of citizenship it is difficult to perceive such an imbalance as discrimination.[16] Our immediate understanding of discrimination requires the exclusion of a woman from some benefit by a prejudiced individual. Even if we could prove that sort of discrimination among the selection boards of political parties or public offices,[17] it would remain an instance of private discrimination, not discrimination perpetuated by the law itself. There is, in any event, some evidence of a willingness to appoint women to high-level posts,[18] but the structures which determine such appointments inevitably lead to the availability of few suitably qualified women for consideration. A wider definition of discrimination which looks at the law-making structure may begin to reveal systemic rather than individual causes of sex differences.

In the preceding chapters we have shown that women have been consigned to a particular role in society which has limited their opportunities not only in the public sphere but in their private relationships also. The structures by which those opportunities are offered are generally based on a lifestyle very different from that of men, often with conflicting terms and values. This is as true in relation to politics and law as in relation to more obvious areas such as employment. Indeed, there is often a very close connection between the two. For example, 'the kinds of attitudes, skills and experience compatible with holding office at the summit of the contemporary political system presuppose paid employment and indeed employment of a specific kind and this is part of the explanation for the small numbers and only very gradual increase of women in this political arena.'[19] It may not be that sex or gender affects the views or needs of men and women on every issue. As the early women MPs recognized, women's opinions cover a political spectrum as broad as that of men's. What has not been generally recognized is that women have views on a wide range of issues. Until recently women's opinions have been sought only on domestic issues, in which they were thought to have some expertise. Where women have given their views on other topics, these have been considered legitimate only when they accorded with male definitions. At times some of these opinions will be similar to those offered by men, not least because the women share the same background as their male colleagues (for example, as lawyers, doctors, etc.). But at other times women's different experiences may lead to different definitions of problems under debate or to very different solutions. If the way in which society is structured pre-empts women's equal participation in the law-making process and in the distribution of benefits in society, then they are not being accorded equal citizenship.[20]

A fundamental problem arises in relation to tackling this structural discrimination. If the philosophies and practices of the legislature, the administration and the judiciary militate against an appreciation of women's points of view, what would be an appropriate forum in which to advance the necessary arguments? If, as will be suggested, discrimination occurs in the often complex interaction of various state bodies, it is difficult to identify as such, being the result of practices which appear quite justifiable in context. Moreover, who has the power or the political will to order and enforce the necessary changes? There may be good reason for not acknowledging this discrimination even where it is recognized.

However, in recent years the discrimination implicit in the form and the practice of one aspect of citizenship has been widely acknowledged. The law of nationality, now contained in the British Nationality Act 1981, defines who is a citizen. Indeed, nationality, and particularly the right of entry, is today more or less the only aspect of citizenship which commands public attention. It is a fundamental right, determining to a great extent the exercise of other rights, such as the vote and election to public office. Thus the continuing definition of women as second-class citizens in the nationality law has an effect on other citizenship rights which is not entirely symbolic. The subordination of women, by reason first of their marital status and second of their status as workers, affects their participation in all aspects of life.

Who is a Citizen?

The degree of autonomy allowed woman by the nationality law has reflected the family law position. Thus in the nineteenth century a husband's right to determine all questions of importance concerning his family was supported by the nationality laws. In 1844 alien wives were given British nationality automatically upon marrigae to a British subject.[21] In 1870 the Naturalization Act, section 10, deprived female subjects of their British nationality, just as automatically, upon marriage to alien men. The law thus achieved some consistency. Women had a duty to live with their husbands and (although no immigration control was imposed upon aliens until the British Nationality and Status of Aliens Act 1914) in the majority of cases involving foreign husbands that meant in his country. The parliamentary debates on the 1870 Bill show that the deprivation of a woman's citizenship was felt to be of little importance. Citizenship gave rights to hold property, to vote, to take a full part in public affairs and to stand for Parliament. One MP, Roundell Palmer, remarked that since the Bill would allow aliens unrestricted rights to hold property (a right extended in a much more limited form later that year to married women), women would not suffer in any matter of substance: 'it was only political status that was involved.'[22] As we have already shown, women had little political status in 1870.

In terms of citizenship, then, even unmarried women had little to lose on marriage to a foreigner. Matters which most affected all women related to their family status, which was covered not by nationality but by the law of domicile. The test of domicile is residence in a country to which one is, or intends to be, permanently attached. But a married woman automatically assumed her husband's domicile,[23] thus her marital status and family life was governed by the law of his country of domicile. If he deserted her and went to live in another country or jurisdiction, she became domiciled there too, even though she might never leave her own country.[24] If the law of that country was more restrictive in personal matters (for example, divorce), there was nothing she could do. This remained the law until 1974. (Section 1(1) Domicile and Matrimonial Proceedings Act 1973 provides that a married woman retains her domicile on marriage and her independence in changing domicile subsequently.)

Thus in practical terms the loss of nationality was not felt to be of great importance. Only one Member of Parliament expressed any concern in the debate on the Naturalization Act 1870. For most it was simply a tidying-up measure. The automatic assumption of a husband's domicile, and the regulation of the relationship between him and his wife by the law of that jurisdiction, was now to be logically complemented by the automatic assumption of his citizenship.[25]

The long campaign waged by women inside and outside Parliament for the repeal of the law was beset by this problem of making others see a wife's loss of citizenship as a matter of discrimination and injustice. They appeared to have succeeded in the 1920s (for instance, the House of Commons passed a unanimous resolution on the principle of equal citizenship in 1925). But the problems of male unemployment and international relations predominated in any law reform. The Prime Minister's support for Ellen Wilkinson MP's Private Member's Bill in 1929, and a concerted public campaign involving women's organizations, MPs and the Dominion Societies, produced a measure that reached the statute book in 1933. But the British Nationality and Status of Aliens Act 1933 did not return citizenship on the terms hoped for by the campaigners. Rather, it incorporated the concerns of the League of Nations, allowing married women to retain their nationality only when threatened with statelessness. In order to protect women married to foreigners in times of war, the act also introduced procedures by which married women could regain their nationality. The predominant importance of international affairs can be seen in all the nationality legislation from 1870, when the key concern was amicable relations with the USA, an important trading partner,[26] to the Acts of 1981/2, where there are special provisions affecting Gibraltarians, certain important persons in Hong Kong and the Falkland Islanders.[27]

The connection between the number of citizens and male employment has an equally long history. It was estimated that in 1860 there were 2,500,000 British-born subjects in the USA who could legitimately return, flooding the British labour market with children and grandchildren who were all British citizens under British law as it then stood. At the same time emigration to the Colonies, and particularly the USA, was being promoted enthusiastically as a means of reducing unemployment and the 'surplus female population'.[28] The 1870 Act allowed emigrants to renounce British citizenship for the first time and, significantly, ensured that women who married American citizens automatically did so. This fear of swamping by 'surplus' women continued to hold back the extension of civic rights for women until the Second World War,[29] but ironically, and in a way unforeseen by male legislators, the emigration of women was a policy which indirectly promoted female emancipation. Middle-class women, armed for the first time with an education and often professional training equal to men's, took every opportunity to participate fully in public life in their adopted countries.[30] These women were among the first in the world to regain equal voting rights with men; in New Zealand (1893), Australia (1899, 1902 and 1909) and in the States of North America from 1895.[31] Thus in terms of their professional activities and their civic status they served as a model for the women who remained in Britain and have continued to invigorate the British women's movement.

Since 1948, when women gained independent citizenship for themselves (but not equal capacity to transmit citizenship), women's rights have been subordinated to the control of male immigration. In 1969 the rights of female British citizens to live in their own country with their husbands began to be reduced. From January of that year Commonwealth citizens were no longer allowed into England to live with their British wives. The Immigration Act 1971 extended the rule to all non-British husbands. Only if the wife could prove that she would suffer exceptional hardship if she were to live in her husband's country were they allowed to live together in hers (a paternalistic test which recurs in the naturalization provisions of the 1933 Act). The reasons given were clear and have been put forward as reasonable ever since. Women who marry foreigners should live in the man's country. Any attempt to reverse this 'natural' order must be regarded as an attempt by men to gain access to the British labour market.[32] Although the rule in relation to foreign husbands and fiancés was modified three times in the following decade, the principle remained. Since the 1981 British Nationality Act full British citizens (mostly white women) have a right to bring in foreign husbands, but their marriage is still subject to official scrutiny. The husband must gain entry clearance, and if there is any indication that the marriage has been made with the aim of settlement, permission will be refused.[33] Although the test is aimed at 'arranged marriages' (i.e. the Asian community), it can be seen that Immigration officials, acting under administrative regulations, have a wide power to enforce traditional notions of what the private aspects of a marriage relationship should entail. In the past such power has included home visits by police to check sleeping arrangements and the notorious 'virginity testing'.[34] While the primary purpose of the marriage must not be the entry of the husband into the British labour market, he must nevertheless be able to fulfil the traditional role of breadwinner. Moreover, the immigration system operates to enforce the dependence of wives. There is no immigration rule on the subject, but the Home Office does not allow married women living with their husbands to qualify as 'heads of households' under the voucher system introduced in 1968 to control the influx of East African Asians.[35] Since November 1983 married women who have claimed supplementary benefit in their own right have done so at the risk of losing the chance of being reunited with their husbands in this country. A man dependent on his wife may be refused the requisite entry clearance. Women who are less than full British citizens under the 1981 Act or who are settlers, students or work-permit holders cannot bring their husbands into England on their papers.[36] By contrast, the right of all men to bring in their wives, regardless of whether the husbands are citizens, students or work-permit holders, rests only on their ability to provide financial support. As a background paper to the Joint Council for the Welfare of Immigrants Conference 1983 points out, 'Women are seen by the legislators purely in relation to men, not as individual people; either as passive "dependants" coming to this country in order to be with a man who has made the arrangements for them to come as and when he wants or as agents being used by (black) men in order to come to this country to work.'

So, despite an appearance of equality, women are still discriminated against by reason of marriage. The British Nationality Act 1981, on the face of it, appears to treat women equally. Non-British wives of British citizens no longer gain citizenship by registration after marriage. The rules as to entry clearance and length of residence required for naturalization are now the same for men and women.[37] Indeed, this change in the law has necessitated Britain's withdrawal from the United Nations Convention on the Nationality of Married Women 1957. However, British women have a right to retain their citizenship on marriage and, for the first time, can transmit nationality to their legitimate children (although men still cannot transmit their nationality to their illegitimate children).[38] Through the discretionary operation of the immigration rules sex discrimination remains in practice. As we shall see, this makes it much harder to challenge. Three test cases are going to the European Court of Human Rights. In allowing them to go before the Court the European Commission on Human Rights decided on 13 October 1983 that the British Immigration rules did contravene the European Convention by discriminating against women on the grounds of sex and by failing to guarantee the right to family life.[39] The removal of jus soli by the 1981 Act means that the citizenship of children born after 1 January 1983 depends upon the citizenship or settled status of the parent. Thus the decision as to who is a citizen depends increasingly upon right of entry, which in turn depends largely upon a man's status as worker. Even foreign husbands who gain entry to England and apply for naturalization under the special provisions for spouses under the 1981 Act may find their applications turned down because of their work status. Naturalization is discretionary, and there is no right of appeal.[40] A family in that situation may have no alternative but to leave the country, thus effectively denying the wife citizenship in all but name.

Women in Public Life

It is a curious anomaly that while the formal rights of citizenship have been extended to women on proof of their masculine equivalence, the rules assigned to them in public life have been those firmly entrenched in traditional notions of femininity. In the nineteenth century only women who held property, predominantly a male reserve, could vote in local elections. Women's First World War efforts won them the parliamentary vote and access to Parliament, the professions, the Civil Service, jury service and the magistracy.[41] The women under 30 who had contributed most to the war effort were denied a chance to protect their post-war employment opportunities. The 1918 Act rewarded ex-soldiers over 19 with the vote. Women qualified only if they were over 30 and then only if they held property, were married or had otherwise proved their maturity by education at a university.

At a parliamentary level, although women such as Nancy Astor and Mrs Wintringham worked on legislation designed to improve the position of women, early female MPs generally confined their interests to women as wives and mothers, perhaps because their experience of other fields was limited and because several entered Parliament in place of their husbands. Women who were selected on their own merits and were concerned to pursue a political career had to prove themselves on the more serious 'political' topics: 'Women MP's "fight shy of 'women's issues' in order to keep their place in a man's world", because masculine standards are taken as the criterion of success and in this world "women's issues" are at the bottom of the political agenda.'[42]

It is questionable whether the legislation which allowed women to enter public office in the nineteenth century shaped this public perception or was itself influenced by such ideas. Were women allowed to be Poor Law guardians and elementary school board governors because these were public offices deemed inferior by reason of the female qualities required by the job? Or were women recruited because their 'natural' talents made them particularly suitable for these offices? It would seem that while many men and women held the latter view,[43] some feminists clearly felt they were being consigned to second-class citizenship because of their sex: 'Political freedom begins for women, as it began for men, with freedom in local government. It rests with women to pursue the advantage that has been won and to advance from the position that has been conceded to them in local representation to that which is the goal of our efforts — the concession to share in the representation of our common country.'[44]

It was such encroachment into the male sphere that legislators worked hard to check. When the school boards were taken over by county councils in 1902 women could not serve on the education committees but were confined to the non-representative status of co-opted members of education subcommittees.[45] When finally women did gain the right to be county councillors, the Act explicitly prevented women who became chairmen of such councils or mayors of borough councils from also gaining, ex officio, the status of Justice of Peace.[46] Similarly, the 1919 Sex Disqualification Removal Act allowed women some entry into the Civil Service but made specific provision for controlling the terms of entry into the home Civil Service and for the continuation of the foreign Civil Service as a male preserve.

Legal restrictions on women's participation have now all been lifted. But the patterns of the past remain. More women are found in local government than in central government.[47] Even within local government women are better represented in the second-tier authorities than at the higher levels (for example, on Community Health Councils rather than in Regional Health Authorities),[48] although an exception has to be made for county councils, where women's membership is relatively high (between 11 and 20 per cent).[49] Wormald suggests that the larger number of women nominated by the Conservative Party for local elections accounts for their high representation particularly in the southern and shire counties.[50] The question remains: do women prefer local government because it is easier to fit in with their domestic responsibilities and concerns matters of more interest to them, or do they contest local elections because parties support them only at that level?

The evidence of the first elections to the European Parliament in 1979 suggests that, most recently at least, women stand a worse chance at elections for Westminster because of its prestige. That is to say, women are relegated to local and European elections not because of any special suitability they may have but because of the inferior political status of those bodies. In 1979 not only was the proportion of women candidates selected for Europe higher than for the Westminster elections that year but also their success rate was over four times that of women standing for Westminster and higher even than that of male candidates in the European elections.[51] It appears that not only were parties more prepared to select women but that they were willing to place them in 'winnable' seats. Wormald may be right in saying that 'It may be surmised that women were both more willing to put themselves forward as candidates and more likely to be selected where there was not a well-established tradition of male dominance.'[52] But these findings also cast doubt on the idea that women shy away from Westminster on pragmatic grounds and grounds of interest. It cannot be easier to fit in family responsibilities with commitments in Strasbourg than with those in Westminster. Nor can it be said that the matters for debate are less 'technical' or more domestic than those discussed by the national Parliament. A further explanation becomes apparent if one analyses the result in terms of where power lies. Even within the European institutions Parliament has little power, with only one effective veto over the budget. Most power lies with the Council of Ministers, that is, with representatives from national Governments; the ability of the British Government to resist or minimize European influence has been noted earlier. If one extends the analysis to the processes of law-making at a national level, it becomes clear that beneath a veneer of formal equality, women have very little influence indeed.

Stetson has outlined five stages in the process of law reform.[53] First, there must be a demand for change which has to come to the attention of authority. Secondly, the issue has to compete with other issues for official time and consideration. Thirdly, since any demand for change will involve at least two lines of argument, reform versus the status quo, and is likely to involve many options for reform, the issues to be confronted by law-makers have to be defined. Fourthly, an appropriate body must be selected for resolving these conflicting definitions and promoting a policy. Finally, the exact policy and its legal formulation must be decided. Women can and have played an important part at each of these stages, as members of pressure groups, as voters, as elected representatives and as technical experts. Earlier chapters are full of examples of women who have directly and indirectly influenced changes in the law. Throughout most of the nineteenth century men controlled which issues received public attention, the various options and justifications for reform and indeed the precise formulation of the law. Women had to rely upon a handful of male MPs to raise their concerns and to present their case on such matters as the vote, their exclusion from mining, their loss of nationality. As we have shown, the election and appointment of women to public office changed the sources of information and the definition of the issues. Whereas in the early years the debate on working mothers centred upon morality and homely comfort, the work of the women Factory Inspectors (first appointed in 1893) highlighted the necessity of female earnings and led to the introduction of maternity benefit (see p. 16).[54] From the late nineteenth century women were recruited on to Royal Commissions (the first three women in 1895 on the Royal Commission on Secondary Education), Parliamentary Committees and Commissions of Inquiry. This was not simply patriarchal benevolence on the part of men in authority, not just acquiescence in the placating 'statutory woman' syndrome. Through their own efforts in voluntary work, community service and intensive research, women put themselves into a position where they could not be ignored.[55]

The strength of women's position can be seen from their representation on the various investigative and policy-making committees of the post-First World War Government. At a time when there was only one woman MP, the Women's Employment Committee of the Ministry of Reconstruction contained twelve women, including two trade unionists and twelve men. Even though the Atkin Committee on Equal Pay took a very different view on the future of women's employment — a view heavily influenced by the background of its members[56]

— there too, two out of its five members were women. The 1923 Wood Committee on Domestic Service was totally female!

Such participation did not conflict with the prevailing view of women at the time. Women's intellectual abilities and their right to make an independent contribution to public debate were recognized. But for the most part they were expected to confine themselves to matters in which they were thought to have special knowledge and skills: the care of women and children. Edward Heath's support for more women 'in the House of Commons and outside it at all levels, so long as they are providing what women can, and not just duplicating what men can do, which probably would lead to them not making a women's contribution anyway' typifies the approach.[57] Although Vallance's study of women MPs' activity in the House of Commons proves that they do take an interest in a wide range of topics,[58] it seems that they have been most effective when they have pressed demands within their 'special sphere'. The use of Bills by women MPs and peers to force government legislation on matters such as maintenance, sex discrimination and male fiancés do suggest a link between perceptions of competence and the female role.[59]

The last decade has seen some change in attitudes towards women's participation in public life. The new climate of equality demanded that women were to be treated in exactly the same way as men, were to undertake the same jobs as men and were to be allowed to participate along the same broad spectrum as men. At parliamentary level this change was exemplified by Harold Wilson's policy of promoting women to offices outside their 'normal' spheres, (e.g. Barbara Castle to Transport and Employment, Judith Hart to Paymaster General),[60] although even he admitted 'he would never have dared appoint a woman overlord of those strongholds of male chauvinism, the Home Office, the Treasury and the Foreign Office.'[61]

In the long term this new equality may have liberated women able to devote their energies to non-traditional areas. For example, Hills mentions the higher percentage of left-wing female Labour MPs in the 1974—9 Parliament for whom 'areas of policy such as taxation, nationalization and economic planning were of primary importance.'[62] But to a large extent it has contributed to a decline in the numbers of women in public life, particularly in positions of influence. Despite all recent evidence of no significant differences in voting patterns between men and women electors or in favour of male or female candidates,[63] the 1983 Parliament contains fewer women MPs than those after the Second World War.[64] Although one-third more female candidates stood in 1983 than 1979, the twenty-three women MPs constitute only 3.5 per cent of all MPs.[65] The proportion of women MPs has never been higher than 4.6 per cent (1964), and their vulnerability in marginable seats accounts at least in part for their even smaller representation in government office. Outside Parliament women do not appear to do any better:[66] 'The Whitehall lists of well-known and experienced people who are generally called upon to staff government committees, councils and governing bodies (the lists of the so-called 'great and good') are sparse on female representation. On public bodies too, women's representation is often not only limited but nonexistent.'[67] There have been occasions when the 'new equality' has not dislodged the perception that a particularly contentious issue is a 'woman's issue'. It is striking that there has been a tendency to call upon suitably qualified women in such circumstances (for example, the Warnock Committee on Human Fertilization and Embryology). Yet their use may be more an attempt to allay criticism of a male conspiracy than a recognition of their undoubted expertise (for example, the Lane Committee on Abortion, 1971 and the Heilbron Advisory Group on Rape, 1975).

For the most part, however, the need to appoint women to play a particular role or for symbolic reasons has disappeared. As a consequence, women now stand less chance of selection, for a variety of reasons. The most obvious is that women are underrepresented at the levels and in the areas of work from which such appointments are usually made. Underrepresentation is inevitable on bodies where employers' organizations or trade unions have the right of nomination. It is interesting to note in this context that the Government's original proposals for reforming the Supplementary Benefit Appeals Tribunal would have gone some way to improving women's representation as tribunal members. The Health and Social Services and Social Security Adjudications Bill had proposed to abolish the separate trades council category of nominees. There would have been a greater chance that one of the lay members might have been a woman, from such organizations as Gingerbread or Child Poverty Action Group. The Health and Social Security Bill 1983 proposes to introduce a single panel for Social Security Appeals Tribunals. Both statutes are likely to broaden the background of lay, non-union and non-employer organization members. Neither will necessarily result in a tribunal's having one female member. Nor will a tribunal necessarily include a member who represents the interests of the female appellant or shares her experience. Ironically, the chances of this happening will be greater the further up the appeal system one goes. But the increased legalism of these tribunals without the introduction of legal aid means that very few women claimants are likely to benefit.[68] Secondly, women may be unavailable or unwilling to be considered for selection, particularly through political party or trade union affiliation. Women are underrepresented in 'active' positions in these organizations, and many find their time already fully committed in combining paid work, domestic responsibilities and some public activities.[69] Thirdly, as Rendel has pointed out: 'Women join organizations and are active in them...but they are concerned with topics often perceived as being apolitical.'[70]

These three reasons seem to be connected. Studies have shown that while paid employment increases the likelihood of involvement in political organizations, the type of work and the extent of a woman's domestic commitments determine the type of political action. The women found at a national level are more likely to be working full-time, without dependent children or, more recently, to be pursuing a professional career with paid child-care assistance. Women with family commitments are more likely to be combining part-time work with involvement at the lower level of organized politics, or in grass-roots, often ad hoc, politics located within their local communities, or campaigning on a single issue.[71] Few of the latter types of organization, even those which have an institutionalized structure such as National Women's Aid, are likely to be canvassed for representation.[72] In the composition of the EOC the use of normal selection procedures for public bodies appears to have given more weight to the traditional balances between both sides of industry, across party lines and 'professional' areas. The membership rules of the Women's National Commission, which is formally consulted by Governments on issues affecting women, also militate against the involvement of many of the new women's groups or less structured organizations.[73]

This underrepresentation of women occurs at a time when policy is increasingly being made away from Parliament, a forum traditionally susceptible to female participation.[74] Emphasis on the technical aspects of law reform and the need for professional scrutiny has led to the consideration of many matters of particular concern to women by government departments (for example, taxation of married women, equal treatment in social security and equal pay for work of equal value) and/or expert advisory bodies such as the Social Security Advisory Committee and the Law Commission (for example, illegitimacy and maintenance). Although public consultation is sought, there are a number of reasons why women may be less able to participate effectively in the determination of new policy. First, unless the demand for change has emanated from women's organizations or they have been involved in campaigning for reform (as in the case of taxation), they may be unaware that a particular issue is being reviewed. Individual experts in the field will know to write to the appropriate body for a copy of the consultation document. Organizations traditionally consulted will be notified as a matter of course. But even if ordinary women or the less institutionalized organizations do see a news item which relates to the proposed reform, they may not understand its relevance to them, nor the procedure for consultation. Secondly, the language used and the presentation of options for reform outlined in such preliminary papers may confine the debate and obscure other viable interpretations. In the Law Commission's Working Paper, *Illegitimacy*, for example, the different treatment accorded to father and children was clearly described as direct discrimination; that accorded single mothers was outlined under the heading 'Procedural Discrimination'.[75] Women in organizations that are unused to responding to such documents may lack the expertise to contribute in any but a reactive way, if at all.[76] Although the limits of the review drawn up by the Treasury prevented discussion of the sex discrimination which runs throughout the taxation system, or fuller consideration of the weak economic position of women more generally, the response to the Chancellor's proposals on the taxation of husband and wife, adduced by a media campaign, shows what might occur if women were informed and encouraged.

There are signs that such a lesson has been learned by the voluntary organizations. The past few years have seen an increase in the use of educational workshops on proposed law reforms to inform women about topics of particular importance to them and to co-ordinate their efforts. There has also been a strengthening of the alliance that began in the mid-1970s between the radical or separatist elements of the women's movement, the more established women's organizations and women in the labour and trade union movement.[77] Not only do such strategies have the potential to overcome the structural discrimination outlined above but they have proved to be quite successful — for example, over abortion (1977—9), child benefit (1975) and, most recently, equal pay and Housewives' Non-Contributory Invalidity Benefit.[78] The input of a wider range of women's views may not always be able to alter the original definition of a problem or the eventual translation of a solution into policy, since legal, political and economic reasons also operate to determine what is feasible. But as the Law Commission's report on illegitimacy shows, the submission of evidence and opinion from ordinary women and men with practical experience can provide an important perspective that might otherwise fail to be appreciated fully. In rejecting their original proposal for the automatic conferral of parental rights on all fathers, the Law Commission was swayed by the 'profound division of opinion amongst both legal and non-legal commentators'. It concluded, 'We do not think it would be right for us to ignore such anxieties where we cannot show them to be without foundation and where the countervailing advantages of the reform are not clearly demonstrable.'[79] The more a reform is perceived to be a technical matter for expert comment, the less likely it is that lay participation will meet with such a response. For instance, legislation may be presented to reform the law to accord with judicial practice, — for example, the Sexual Offences (Amendment) Act 1976. Even though the judicial practice may be subject to criticism within and outside Parliament, the professionalization of such proposed reforms gives them an apolitical aura and some degree of immunity from criticism. This phenomenon is apparent even in relation to the Matrimonial and Family Proceedings Bill 1983, which was called for by outside lay bodies. Opening the Bill's Second Reading in the House of Lords, the Lord Chancellor began by defending the measure precisely in these terms. Seeking to answer vociferous public criticism of his personal support for a most contentious reform he said, 'Lest anyone should think that I have introduced this measure out of my own ideas let me reassure them. Apart from Part V and the miscellaneous Part VI, there is nothing in this Bill which has not been proposed by the Law Commission. . . . This is not — if I may contradict a religious programme — Lord Hailsham's Bill; it is a Law Commission Bill backed by the Government.'[80] On the reintroduction of conduct into questions of maintenance he declared that the Bill simply 'made plain beyond doubt' what was current judicial practice.[81]

The 'technical' nature of a proposed reform may dictate the procedure by which it is introduced. Statutory instruments determine the substance of the law reform in relation to social security (see p. 171, e.g.). As we have shown, both the equality regulations made under the Social Security Act 1980 and the introduction of equal pay for work of equal value have far-reaching implications which make them more than the technical adjustments that the use of such procedure would imply. If, as seems likely, the EEC institutions are to play an increasing role in the instigation of law reform in relation to women, this is a factor which may increase in importance, since section 2(2) of the European Communities Act 1972 allows statutes to be amended by statutory instrument.[82] Even though this procedure does provide an opportunity for parliamentary debate, there is less chance for public input in these final stages than at the outset of the policy formulation. A statutory instrument may be stopped in Parliament but cannot be amended on the floor of the House. Any such amendment will take place within the sponsoring department, consequently with a less public consultation process. The problem is not limited to EEC-induced legislation. The Sex Discrimination Act itself allows amendment of its provisions by statutory instrument (section 80). Although the EOC has to be consulted under section 80(2) of the Act before the Secretary of State can lay such an order before Parliament, the Commission has no legal power to determine the content of such revision. Indeed, the position of the Commission in relation to law reform generally is limited to consultation. Although the Act imposes a duty to review legislation (section 55(1)(a) and section 53(2)(c)) and to submit proposals for reform if required to do so by the Secretary of State, it has no independent channel to the parliamentary process. This is a problem which is shared by many other quangos. Were the EOC answerable directly to a parliamentary select committee, as is the parliamentary ombudsman, for instance, its access to the law-making process would be greatly strengthened. The Law Commission has no such direct approach to Parliament, but the fact that it annexes Bills of Parliament to its reports ensures parliamentary attention. One way to increase the power of the EOC would be to attach parliamentary draftsmen to its staff. They would give status and authority to proposals which at present may too easily be ignored. Ultimately the Commission is as dependent upon executive discretion or the support of Members of Parliament as is any voluntary organization presenting a case for reform.

Even where women have been able to influence the legislature,[83] the intentions of Parliament can be stymied or less than fulfilled by the judiciary's interpretation of statutes, as we have shown throughout. There is some evidence from the United States, where feminist organizations have campaigned to secure the election of more female judges, that an increase of women lawyers could affect the interpretation of the law.[84] Such findings could be attributable to considerations other than sex, such as party affiliation. In England the scarcity of female judges makes an assessment even harder.[85] There have been instances however, when a female member of an adjudicating bench does seem to have taken a significantly different, though no less technical, approach to a case.[86] In other cases it is clear that an identification by male and female judges with traditionally 'male' values and male interpretations of situations have affected the perception of the issues involved.[87] In most cases, however, no such personal influence is apparent. Yet the use of accepted legal doctrines to solve new problems posed by new legislation may result in decisions contrary to Parliament's intentions (see pp. 33, 142-3). In family matters the judiciary has been allowed great autonomy in determining rules of procedure which have significantly altered the intended use of the law — for example, in the cases of the introduction of administrative divorce and the short-time limits on 'domestic violence' orders (see pp. 155, 143). Even more generally, because of the doctrine of precedent the approach of the higher courts affects the approach of the legal profession as a whole: it affects advice given by solicitors on the validity and outcome of any particular case, which in turn influences the types of cases brought in the future. Few individuals have the resources or the interest to break through such self-fulfilling prophecies. Those who do persevere may find their bona fides doubted because of it.[88] The EOC has both the resources and the 'legitimate' interest. The cases it has sponsored to the European Court have shown how effective such a policy can be.

The Use of Law in the Quest for Equal Citizenship

As in the nineteenth century women brought cases to test the law on the important citizenship rights of the day,[89] so have they in the twentieth century. In recent years individuals have attempted to use the Sex Discrimination Act 1975 to challenge discrimination in relation to civic rights, including discrimination by the Home Office in relation to immigration. The courts have decided that neither the refusal to consider married women 'heads of household' within the special voucher scheme, nor the discriminatory treatment of husbands of students is unlawful within the meaning of that Act.[90] The reasoning of the House of Lords and Court of Appeal seems to extend beyond the operation of the immigration rules to government departments generally. It would appear that where the discrimination complained of results from the exercise of administrative discretion as opposed to the performance of an administrative duty, the Sex Discrimination Act does not apply.

Similar reasoning has been used in the interpretation of the sections of the Act which apply specifically to the actions of government departments. Section 85, which appears to bring government service within the Act, has been construed to exclude relationships which do not approximate to the employee—employer relationship. In *Department of Environment* v. *Fox*[91] the position of rent officer was held to be outside the scope of the Act. The job was a creation of statute, the number of officers and the terms and conditions laid down by the Secretary of State, with the appointments administered by local authorities. The crucial factor in the case appears to have been the fact that rent officers' duties are self-contained. The EAT held that they could not be said to 'work for' anyone, with the result that anyone working under them is covered by the Act but not the rent officers themselves. The same interpretation of section 85(2) was used in a case involving a prospective Justice of the Peace.[92] The EAT in that case also considered section 86, which appears to cover non-employment appointments by Ministers or government departments. The Tribunal took a rather technical approach to that section as well, expressing some doubt as to whether magistrates were appointed by a Minister. They suggested that instead such appointments were made by the Crown, an interpretation which, if right, could limit the scope of the Act still further. The point was not decided because the Tribunal held that it had no jurisdiction to hear the case. Even if magistrates were covered, it decided, no *individual* had a right to bring a case to tribunal or court under the Act, since the section prohibiting it was not within those parts of the Act upon which an individual could take action. This means that despite an obvious underrepresentation of women on all public bodies,[93] no individual can bring a case, even where she knows she has been discriminated against or wishes to test the lawfulness of a condition which she feels to be indirectly discriminatory. Only the EOC has any jurisdiction. As Mr Justice Woolf pointed out in *Home Office* v. *CRE*,[94] the ability to gather the information necessary to conduct a formal investigation in the end depends upon the Secretary of State at the Home Office,[95] the appointing and controlling department not only for the Commission itself but also for many other public bodies. We have seen that in the employment field, action by the EOC is likely to be more effective than an individual case. Here the reverse is true. For all sorts of practical and political reasons, the EOC may find it much more difficult to take legal action than would an individual.

The judgment of Mr Justice Woolf in *Home Office* v. *CRE* suggests that the powers of the EOC to mount a formal investigation may be more limited than those of the Commission for Racial Equality. Thus it would not have any powers in relation to matters exempted from the Act — for example, the appointment of MPs to government office (including those of the Attorney-General and Solicitor-General),[96] the armed services, the cadet corps or any civilians attached to the armed services.[97] Even if a court held that the duty to 'promote equality of opportunity generally' did enable the EOC to go further than to investigate only discrimination made unlawful under the provisions of the Act itself, any such formal investigation could result only in a recommendation as to change. The EOC would have no power to enforce change. In such sensitive areas the policy of consultation, research and education appears to be more advisable and effective.

However, the Commission has been criticized for adopting such a low-profile consultative strategy in relation to industry as well as government departments, to areas of discrimination clearly within the Act as well as those excluded from its purview. In 1978 Byrne and Lovenduski commented: 'It may seem odd that consultation should virtually always be preferred to confrontation when one considers that the Labour Government which created the Equal Opportunities Commission explicitly rejected the Conservative notion of an advisory agency, arguing that if the new law was to work properly, an agency with real enforcement powers was necessary.'[98] Yet the paradox is easily explained by the Commission's weak political position. First, funded through the Home Office, it is dependent upon government departments in the last resort in the exercise of its strategic powers. Secondly, because it is a quango it lacks the supportive constituency required for any confrontationist approach. Most of its influence in relation to government departments can be expected to be exercised through informal contacts. Of necessity that means that the public will be largely unaware of what is being done and leaves the EOC open to criticism. Additionally, it leaves the EOC dependent upon the government department concerned. If it decides not to seek the EOC's advice on an issue or does not take the EOC into its confidence, there is little the Commission can do to force the issue. It is reliant upon good relations with the departments.[99] There may be much to be said for the replacement of the EOC by an independent campaigning organization like MIND or CPAG[100] because, should the Commission try to force its influence, it might suffer the same fate as the CRE. The Commission for Racial Equality attempted to create such a constituency among ethnic minority groups and to represent their interests. It was severely criticized and redirected towards a stricter law-enforcement role.[101] As we have seen, that means enforcement of the law against private persons rather than the actions of the executive. Unlike its American counterpart, the EOC has not enjoyed the personal support of heads of Government nor any similar strengthening of its legal powers by executive action and judicial interpretation. Unlike Sweden and Norway, where there are specific ministerial departments whose brief is to co-ordinate on matters of equality and where the public-service sector has set the example in relation to equality of opportunity and positive action,[102] the English Civil Service has been the respondent in a number of sex and race discrimination cases.[103] The latest statistics show that while nearly half of all white-collar civil servants are female, women occupy three-quarters of the most junior posts and less than 5 per cent of posts at senior grades.[104] Thus the lack of any institutional or structured commitment to combating sex discrimination within the administration is complemented by a perpetuation of tradition within the professional Civil Service. Although there have been some reforms in relation to female staff (for example, changes in age limits after the *Price* case and a women-only management training course at the Civil Service College),[105] the situation in relation to sex discrimination compares unfavourably with the appointment of a Minister with special responsibility for race relations and other race-sensitive measures introduced into the public administration after the House of Commons Home Affairs Committee's review.[106] The combined responsibility of the American EEOC for both sex and race discrimination has undoubtedly strengthened the position of that body in relation to various Governments and the executive.

There are signs that increased interaction with EEC institutions is providing the EOC with the political support it otherwise lacks. Both the European Commission and the European Parliament have set up an institutional framework to co-ordinate and inform on sex discrimination issues within Europe. A representative from the English EOC sits on the Permanent Advisory Committee on Equality Opportunities for women and men. This committee supports the Commission in the formulation of Community policy and the implementation of the new action plan.[107] The European Parliament's Committee of Inquiry on the Situation of Women in Europe also exists to monitor the present law and to campaign for the implementation of the wider parliamentary resolution on women passed in 1982. As well as these formal and informal networks with the European administrative and legislative bodies, the EOC has gained political support from the cases it has sponsored in the European Court. The cases have had an effect on the judiciary, the legislature and the public at large. Appeals to the European Court of Justice have provided an added dimension to the discussion of discrimination by the judiciary in subsequent cases. They have focused attention on the loopholes and inadequacies of present legislation.[108] The case of *Jenkins* v. *Kingsgate (Clothing Productions) Ltd*[109] concerning part-time workers in the national and European courts has led to the inclusion of a provision related to part-timers in Jo Richardson's Sex Equality Bill 1983. Similarly, the retirement exclusion cases[110] may be seen as having played a part in the introduction of a Private Member's Bill on the Equalization of Pension Age[111] and to the serious consideration of this issue by the House of Commons Select Committee on Social Services and a new Committee of Inquiry into Pensions set up by the Government in response.[112] Action on the unequal rights of women in relation to nationality and immigration is likely to occur should the European Court of Human Rights agree with the findings of the European Commission on Human Rights that these laws contravene the European Convention, which is binding upon the UK Government. Although it had been thought that the discrimination against women in the nationality law would contravene Community Law,[113] a recent decision of the European Court has held that the Treaty of Rome does not cover non-EEC spouses of workers who remain in their own country.[114] Thus a woman who has *never left* the UK to work in an EEC country cannot look to European law to support the entry of her husband into this country. However, it would seem, despite *R.* v. *Secretary of State for Home Department, ex parte Ayub*,[115] that an Englishwoman who had worked in an EEC country, or even one who had seriously looked for work there, would be able to use the Treaty of Rome.[116]

Nevertheless, action through the international courts is not without difficulty. In cases where an individual has a right of application the process may be expensive, longwinded and of limited direct effect. Judgments of the European Court are technically binding only to the parties to the case, although the English courts seem prepared to incorporate them in the common law doctrine of precedent. Judgments of that court in relation to Article 169 proceedings, the two failures to implement the directives cases (see pp. 47, 58), concern only the Government which has some latitude in the exact form of implementation. Judgments of the European Court of Human Rights are directed also at Governments requiring changes in the law. Although in the last two instances individuals have no right to enforce the judgments, they may use the authority of the European courts in support of lobbying efforts in the parliamentary process. For example, despite the low profile and lessened opportunity for public debate afforded by the procedure adopted for implementing Article 169 judgments, the EOC, the TUC, women's organizations and others have been successful in mobilizing public discussion of the equal value regulations. The potential defeat of the statutory instrument in the Houe of Lords, the consequence of the effective campaigning of Baroness Seear and, it is reported, the opposition of the law lord Lord Scarman, caused the Government to postpone the debate and to withdraw the draft regulations for reconsideration.[117] Indeed, it is suggested that the mobilization around cases taken to court may be a very effective strategy in pursuing demands for change in the law through Parliament. Since the discrimination suffered by women is privatized and individualized and is not perceived to present the public order threat feared from racial discrimination, such demands must of necessity be made piecemeal around contentious issues. In this respect the increasing amount of research on women in society, including the research published by the EOC and its general education and information programme, seems to be playing a significant part in preventing each issue from being dealt with in isolation from the structural framework of discrimination. This educative process can be seen to have affected legal perceptions and definitions of problems not only in the courts[118] but also among policy-making bodies.[119]

All the evidence suggests that whereas Stetson's analysis of women's participation in the law-making process was true for much of the previous decade,[120] it does not hold for the future. Women are able to put forward their views either directly through their own organizations or indirectly through a changed awareness in other organizations that participate in the process, even when the policy formulation takes place at a technical or professional level. Moreover, issues which have previously been given low political priority because they have been labelled 'women's issues' are increasingly being perceived as important to men and women generally, either as private individuals or, more often, in the public and professional spheres. This happened with abortion; with the concerted campaign against the Corrie Bill in 1980, joined by the TUC and the British Medical Association; more recently, with sexual harassment,[121] equal value and the women's peace movement. What Gloria Steinem, editor of the American feminist magazine *Ms*, has said of her own country applies equally to Britain and at the European level: 'Feminism has brought America closer to the democracy it ought to be, and has found words like sexual harassment for events that "ten years ago were called life".'[122] Such a trend indicates a new awareness of what citizenship means to women. It indicates that the concern is not just for more female representation in public life: no longer, it seems, is there a belief that more women *per se* would change the substance of the debate. It also suggests that the presentation of the one female viewpoint or a singular, consensual feminism is too simplistic. Ultimately, the extension of the debate, to encompass a variety of viewpoints about how an issue is perceived by women, must affect the substance and the application of the law.

Notes and References

Introduction

1 H. Land, 'Who Cares for the Family?', *Journal of Social Policy*, vol. 7, 1978, p. 284.
2 C. Ungerson, 'Why Do Women Care?', in J. Finch and D. Groves (eds.), *A Labour of Love: Women, Work and Caring*, London, Routledge & Kegan Paul, 1983, p. 45.
3 Sir W. Blackstone, *Commentaries on the Laws of England*, Oxford, Clarendon Press, 1765, p. 445.
4 Blackstone, *Commentaries on the Laws of England*, 15th edn, with notes and additions by Edward Christian, London, Cadell & Davies, 1809; see note 23 on p. 445, which ends: 'Thus female honour, which is dearer to the sex than their lives, is left by the common law to be the sport of an abandoned calumniator.'
5 A. Macfarlane, *The Origins of English Individualism*, Oxford, Blackwell, 1978.
6 R. Deem, *Women and Schooling*, London, Routledge & Kegan Paul, 1978, p. 141.

1 The Historical Legacy

1 J. W. Scott and L. A. Tilley, 'Women's Work and the Family in 19th-Century Europe', in A. M. Amsden (ed.), *Economics of Women and Work*, Harmondsworth, Penguin, 1980, p. 91.
2 S. Lewenhak, *Women and Trade Unions*, London, Benn, 1977.
3 D. Stenton, *The English Woman in History*, London, Allen & Unwin, 1957.
4 S. E. Thorne, *Bracton on the Laws and Customs of England*, Cambridge, Mass., Harvard University Press, 1968—77, vol. 2, p. 31.
5 Indeed, one important provision of the Equal Pay Act 1970 was to raise the skilled woman's rate to the level of the lowest unskilled male rate.
6 Ministry of Labour, *Report of the Committee on the Supply of Female Domestic Servants* (the Wood Committee), London, HMSO, 1923.
7 I. Pinchbeck, *Women Workers and the Industrial Revolution 1750—1850*, London, Virago, 1981.
8 Lewenhak, *Women and Trade Unions*, p. 6.
9 A. Plummer, *The London Weavers' Company 1600—1970*, London, Routledge & Kegan Paul, 1972.
10 Pinchbeck, *Women Workers and the Industrial Revolution 1750—1850*.
11 W. R. Wood, Sub-Commissioner for Bradford and Leeds, *Report of the Royal Commission on Children's Employment (Mines)*, Cmnd 380, 1842, p. 33. Throughout the century both male and female workers felt it necessary to give evidence to rebut such

such assertions of immorality. Yet it seems to have persisted in the public imagination. In the Report of the Royal Commission on Labour in 1893 the Lady Commissioners were still discussing the employment of married women in these terms.

12 M. Bondfield, *A Life's Work*, London, Hutchinson, 1948.
13 Home Office, *Women in Industry*, Cmnd 3508, London, HMSO, 1929—30.
14 A. Sachs and J. Hoff Wilson, *Sexism and the Law*, Oxford, Martin Robertson, 1978.
15 A. Myrdal and V. Klein, *Women's Two Roles*, London, Routledge & Kegan Paul, 1956.
16 Central Statistical Office, *Social Trends*, 12, London, HMSO, 1982, p. 42.
17 T. Blackstone, 'The Limits of Legislating for Equality for Women', *New Community*, vol. 5, nos. 1—2, 1976, p. 22.
18 R. Deem, *Women and Schooling*, London, Routledge & Kegan Paul, 1978.
19 *Differentiation of the Curricula between the Sexes in Secondary Education*, Report of the Consultative Committee to the Board of Education (the Hadow Report), London, HMSO, 1923, pp. 1—2.
20 *Curriculum and Examinations in Secondary Schools*, Report of the Committee of the Secondary Schools Examination Council (the Norwood Report), London, HMSO, 1943; *15—18*, Report of the Central Advisory Council for Education (the Crowther Report), London, HMSO, 1959; *Half our future*, Report of the Central Advisory Council for Education (the Newsom Report), London, HMSO, 1963.
21 *Half Our Future*, p. 37; see also P. Byrne and J. Lovenduski, 'Sex Equality and the Law', *British Journal of Law and Society*, vol. 5, no. 2, 1978, p. 148.
22 *15—18*, p. 34.
23 M. Hewitt, *Wives and Mothers in Victorian Industry*, London, Rockliff, 1958.
24 The Registrar-General, in his introduction to the 1851 Census.
25 Hewitt, *Wives and Mothers in Victorian Industry*.
26 Ibid.
27 *Beatrice Webb's Diaries*, ed. M. Cole, London, Longman, 1952; *Report of the Royal Commission on Equal Pay* (the Asquith Commission), 1944, Cmnd 6937, London, HMSO, 1944.
28 *Report of the Women's Employment Committee of the Ministry of Reconstruction*, Cmnd 9239, London, HMSO, 1918.
29 *Reports of Commissioners*, Cmnd 6650, London, HMSO, 1944.
30 Lewenhak, *Women and Trade Unions*.
31 Ibid.
32 Ibid., p. 169.
33 Equal Opportunities Commission, *Health and Safety Legislation: Should We Distinguish between Men and Women?*, Manchester, Equal Opportunities Commission, 1979; O. Banks, *Faces of Feminism*, Oxford, Martin Robertson, 1981.
34 *Report of the Board of Trade on the Increased Employment of Women during the War*, Cmnd 9164, London, HMSO, 1918.
35 J. B. Priestley, *British Women Go to War*, London, Collins, 1943; R. Adam, *A Woman's Place*, London, Chatto & Windus, 1975.
36 Unemployment Insurance Act 1935.
37 Ministry of Labour and National Service, *Report on the Years 1939/46*, Cmnd 7225, London, HMSO, 1947.
38 Central Statistical Office, *Social Trends*, 5, London, HMSO, 1974, table 20.
39 Central Policy Review Staff, *Services for Young Children with Working Mothers*,

London, HMSO, 1978; B. Jackson and S. Jackson, *Childminder*, London, Routledge & Kegan Paul, 1979.

40 *Sixth Report of the Expenditure Committee*, Department of Health and Social Security, Cmnd 5186, London, HMSO, 1972—3.

41 *Census*, London, HMSO, 1981.

42 Central Statistical Office, *Social Trends*, 13, London, HMSO, 1983, p. 27; see also P. Elias and B. Main, 'Women's Working Lives', evidence from the National Training Survey, Institute for Employment Research, University of Warwick, 1982, for a full analysis.

43 Lewenhak, *Women and Trade Unions*.

44 Ibid.

45 See *Report of the Royal Commission on Equal Pay*, 1944.

46 W. B. Creighton, *Working Women and the Law*, London, Mansell, 1979, p. 152.

47 Research now suggests that in the majority of occupations in which women are most likely to continue to work after the birth of children, the change in employers' policy pre-dated the introduction of the law; see W. W. Daniel, 'Employers' Experience of Maternity Rights Legislation', *Employment Gazette*, 1981, p. 296.

48 Equal Opportunities Commission, 'Gender and the Secondary School Curriculum', *Research Bulletin* No. 6, Spring 1982; S. Delamont, *Sex Roles and the School*, London, Methuen, 1980; G. Lobban, 'The Influence of the School on Sex-Role Stereotyping', in J. Chetwynd and O. Hartnett (eds.), *The Sex Role System*, London, Routledge & Kegan Paul, 1978; J. Whyte, *Beyond the Wendy House: Sex Role Stereotyping in Primary Schools*, London, Longman (for the Schools Council), 1983; D. Spender and E. Sarah (eds.), *Learning to Lose*, London, Women's Press, 1981; T. Bedeman and H. Harvey, 'Young People on YOP', *Employment Gazette*, 1981, p.362. A. Sawdon, P. Matthews and D. Warnock, 'Unemployment and YOP in the Inner City', Youthaid, November 1982.

49 Her Majesty's Inspectors, *Girls and Science*, Matters for Discussion: 13, DES, London, HMSO, 1980; *Report of the Commission of Inquiry into the Teaching of Mathematics in Schools* (the Cockcroft Report), London, HMSO, 1982.

50 Equal Opportunities Commission, *Seventh Annual Report*, Manchester, Equal Opportunities Commission, 1982.

2 Equality at Work

1 See also *O'Brien* v. *Sim Chem Ltd* [1980] 1 WLR 1011.

2 [1979] 1 WLR 1189.

3 For example, in *Capper Pass Ltd* v. *Lawton* [1977] QB 852 the work of a female cook in the small directors' dining-room was equated with that of a male chef in the works canteen.

4 See *Electrolux Ltd* v. *Hutchinson* [1977] ICR 252 and *Shield* v. *E. Coomes (Holdings) Ltd* [1978] 1 WLR 1408.

5 [1978] IRLR 462.

6 See also *National Vulcan Engineering Insurance Group Ltd* v. *Wade* [1979] QB 132.

7 *National Coal Board* v. *Sherwin and Spruce* [1978] ICR 700.

8 *Clay Cross (Quarry Services) Ltd* v. *Fletcher* [1978] 1 WLR 1429.

9 *Shield* v. *E. Coomes (Holdings) Ltd* [1978] 1 WLR 1408.

10 *Steel* v. *UPOW* [1978] 1 WLR 64 (see p. 30).

11 See *Methven* v. *Cow Industrial Polymers Ltd* [1980] ICR 463.

12 [1980] ICR 194.

13 C. Hakim, 'Occupational Segregation', Research Paper No. 9, Department of Employment, 1979; C. Craig, E. Garnsey and J. Rubery, 'Women's Pay in Informal Payment Systems', *Employment Gazette*, 1983, p. 139.

14 M. W. Snell, P. Glucklich and M. Povall, 'Equal Pay and Opportunities', Research Paper No. 20, Department of Employment, 1981.

15 *Jenkins* v. *Kingsgate (Clothing Productions) Ltd* [1981] ICR 592.

16 [1977] ICR 252.

17 *Steel* v. *UPOW and the Post Office* [1978] 1 WLR 64; *British Airways Engine Overhaul Ltd* v. *Francis* [1981] ICR 279.

18 Snell, Glucklich and Povall, 'Equal Pay and Opportunities'; Craig, Garnsey and Rubery, 'Women's Pay in Informal Payment Systems'.

19 Snell, Glucklich and Povall, 'Equal Pay and Opportunities'.

20 *Clay Cross (Quarry Services) Ltd* v. *Fletcher* [1977] IRLR 259; *Eaton Ltd* v. *Nuttall* [1977] IRLR 71.

21 A. Lester and G. Bindman, *Race and Law*, Harmondsworth, Penguin, 1972.

22 Barbara Castle: Hansard, vol. 795, col. 918, 1970.

23 *Employment Gazette*, 1983, p. 165.

24 Ibid.

25 *Owen and Briggs* v. *James* [1981] IRLR 133.

26 *Nasse* v. *SRC* [1980] AC 1028.

27 Snell, Glucklich and Povall, 'Equal Pay and Opportunities'.

28 [1979] QB 144; Lord Denning at p. 173.

29 [1980] AC 1089.

30 Snell, Glucklich and Povall, 'Equal Pay and Opportunities', p. 95.

31 *Employment Gazette*, 1983, p. 168.

32 W. B. Creighton, *Working Women and the Law*, London, Mansell, 1979; L. Lustgarten, *Legal Control of Racial Discrimination*, London, Macmillan, 1980.

33 [1978] 1 WLR 64.

34 C. McCrudden, 'Institutional Discrimination', *Oxford Journal of Legal Studies*, 1983, p. 353.

35 Lord Justice Lawton in the *Clay Cross* case.

36 [1983] ICR 165.

37 *Price* v. *Civil Service Commisioners* [1978] IRLR 3; *Steel* v. *UPOW* [1978] 1 WLR 64.

38 *Mandla* v. *Dowell Lee* [1983] 2 AC 548.

39 *Ojutiku* v. *MSC* [1982] ICR 661.

40 At p. 668.

41 *Seide* v. *Gillette* [1980] IRLR 427.

42 Lustgarten, *Legal Control of Racial Discrimination*, p. 1058.

43 As in *Steel* v. *UPOW* [1978] 1 WLR 64 and *Clarke and Powell* v. *Eley (IMI) Kynoch Ltd* [1983] ICR 165.

44 For example, *Worringham* v. *Lloyds Bank* [1982] ICR 299.

45 For example, *Price* v. *Civil Service Commissioners* [1978] IRLR 3 and *NCB* v. *Sherwin* [1978] ICR 700.

46 *Clay Cross (Quarry Services) Ltd* v. *Fletcher* [1978] 1 WLR 1429.

47 For example, Lord Justice Shaw in *Skyrail Oceanic Ltd* v. *Coleman* 1981 ICR 864.

48 *National Vulcan Engineering Insurance Group* v. *Wade* [1979] QB 132, at p. 139.

49 *Shield* v. *E. Coomes (Holdings) Ltd* [1978] 1 WLR 1408; *Clay Cross (Quarry Services) Ltd* v. *Fletcher* [1978] 1 WLR 1429; *Gill* v. *El Vino Co. Ltd* [1983] 2 WLR 155.

50 [1980] AC 1028, p. 1043.

51 Lester and Bindman, *Race and Law.*

52 Roy Jenkins in the debate on the Sex Discrimination Bill 1975, Hansard, 1975, vol. 889, col. 514; *CRE* v. *Amari Plastics Ltd* [1982] QB 1194.

53 *Shield* v. *E. Coomes (Holdings) Ltd* [1978] 1 WLR 1408; *Macarthys Ltd* v. *Smith* [1979] 1 WLR 1189.

54 See p. 25 and *Albion Shipping Agency* v. *Arnold* [1982] ICR 22.

55 *CRE* v. *Genture Restaurants Ltd and Edwards* [1981] IDS Brief 211, p. 14.

56 [1978] QB 233.

57 [1979] QB 132.

58 *Gill* v. *El Vino Co. Ltd* [1983] 2 WLR 155.

59 [1983] ICR 422.

60 [1977] IRLR 10.

61 Hansard, vol. 889, col. 523.

62 *Associated Newspapers* v. *Dingle* [1964] AC 371.

63 *Rook* v. *Fairrie* [1941] 1 KB 507.

64 *Associated Newspapers Ltd* v. *Dingle* [1964] AC 371.

65 See *Methven* v. *Cow Industrial Polymers Ltd* [1980] ICR 463.

66 [1981] ICR 872.

67 *Employment Gazette*, 1983, p. 169.

68 Ibid., p. 443.

69 See Craig, Garnsey and Rubery, 'Women's Pay in Informal Payment Systems'.

70 *Virdee* v. *EEC Quarries* [1978] IRLR 295; *Roadburg* v. *Lothian Regional Council* [1976] IRLR 283.

71 [1981] ICR 777.

72 [1979] IRLR 46.

73 *R.* v. *CRE ex parte Hillingdon LBC* [1982] AC 779; see also *CRE* v. *Genture Restaurants Ltd and Edwards* [1981] IDS Brief 211, p. 14.

74 Lord Justice Oliver, *Mandla* v. *Lee* [1983] QB 1, at p. 18.

75 [1982] QB 1194.

76 Lord Denning, MR, at p. 1202.

77 Lord Justice Griffiths, at p. 1206.

78 [1983] 2 AC 548.

79 C. Peck, 'The Equal Employment Opportunity Commission: Developments in the Administrative Process', *Washington Law Review*, vol. 51, 1976, p. 831.

80 S. Robarts, 'Positive Action for Women', National Campaign for Civil Liberties, London, 1981.

81 *Home Office* v. *CRE* [1981] 2 WLR 703.

82 Peck, 'The Equal Employment Opportunity Commission'.

83 *Macarthys Ltd* v. *Smith* [1981] QB 180.

84 *Macarthys Ltd* v. *Smith* [1981] QB 180; *Worringham* v. *Lloyds Bank* [1981] 1 WLR 950; *Jenkins* v. *Kingsgate (Clothing Productions) Ltd* [1981] 1 WLR 972; *Garland* v. *British Rail Engineering Ltd* [1982] 2 WLR 918.

85 [1982] ICR 578; [1984] ICR 192.

86 *Clay Cross (Quarry Services) Ltd* v. *Fletcher* [1978] 1 WLR 1429; *Shield* v. *E. Coomes (Holdings) Ltd* [1978] 1 WLR 1408; *MOD* v. *Jeremiah* [1980] QB 87.

87 *Macarthys Ltd* v. *Smith* [1981] 1 QB 180.

88 *Worringham* v. *Lloyds Bank* [1981] 1 WLR 950.

89 *Garland* v. *British Rail Engineering Ltd* [1982] 2 WLR 918.
90 *Jenkins* v. *Kingsgate (Clothing Productions) Ltd* [1981] 1 WLR 972.
91 Lord Justice Cumming Bruce, in *Macarthys Ltd* v. *Smith* [1981] QB 180.
92 [1983] IRLR 237.
93 [1983] ICR 521.
94 Department of Employment, 'Women and Work', Manpower Paper No. 11, 1975; Hakim, 'Occupational Segregation'; A. McIntosh, 'Women at Work: a Survey of Employers', *Employment Gazette*, 1980, p. 1144.
95 [1983] 2 WLR 155.
96 *MOD* v. *Jeremiah* [1980] QB 87.
97 [1980] ICR 66.
98 Section 60, Employment Protection (Consolidation) Act 1978.
99 [1981] IRLR 51.
100 SI 1979, No. 959.
101 Section 8, Employment Act 1980.
102 S.Yeandle, 'Variation and Flexibility: Key Characteristics of Female Labour', *Sociology* vol. 16, no. 3, 1982, p. 422; P. Elias and B. Main, 'Women's Working Lives', evidence from the National Training Survey, Institute for Employment Research, University of Warwick, 1982.
103 *Hurley* v. *Mustoe* [1981] ICR 490.
104 [1977] IRLR 360.
105 But see M. Rubinstein, 'The Law of Sexual Harassment at Work', *Industrial Law Journal*, 1983, p. 1; D. Pannick, 'Sex Discrimination and Pregnancy: Anatomy is not Destiny', *Oxford Journal of Legal Studies*, 1983, p. 1.
106 [1982] ICR 755.
107 *Lavery* v. *Plessey* [1983] ICR 534; section 11 Employment Act 1980.
108 *Elegbede* v. *The Wellcome Foundation Ltd* [1977] IRLR 383.
109 *Turley* v. *Allders Department Stores Ltd* [1980] ICR 66; *Reaney* v. *Kanda Jeans Ltd* [1978] IRLR 427; *Page* v. *Freight Hire Ltd* [1981] ICR 299.
110 W. W. Daniel, 'Employers' Experience of Maternity Rights Legislation', *Employment Gazette*, 1981, p. 296.
111 See *The Commission of the European Communities* v. *United Kingdom* (Case 165/82) [1984] ICR 192.
112 Elias and Main, 'Women's Working Lives'.
113 This approach is cogently summed up by Betty Friedan in *The Second Stage*, London, Michael Joseph, 1982.

3 Beyond Equality of Opportunity

1 *The Commission of the European Communities* v. *United Kingdom (Case 61/81)* [1982] ICR 578.
2 House of Lords Debates, 5 December 1983, col. 924.
3 [1977] ICR 272.
4 Cf. *Gill* v. *El Vino Co. Ltd* [1983] 2 WLR 155.
5 A. Lester, 'Unequal Pay — Unequal Justice', *New Law Journal*, 1983.
6 *Jenkins* v. *Kingsgate (Clothing Productions) Ltd* [1981] 1 WLR 972.
7 House of Lords Debates, 5 December 1983, col. 884.

8 Ibid., col. 889.

9 *Defrenne* v. *Sabena* [1976] ICR 547.

10 Lord Denning, House of Lords Debates, 5 December 1983; D. Pannick, 'When the party of the first part should be intelligible', *Guardian*, 21 November 1983; J. Morris, 'No More Peanuts: An Evaluation of Women's Work', NCCL, 1983.

11 Netherlands Stb 1975 No. 129 and *AFSCME* v. *State of Washington* (1983), reported *New York Times*, 18 September 1983.

12 101 S. Ct. 2242 (1981).

13 C. Hakim, 'Occupational Segregation', Research Paper No. 9, Department of Employment, 1979; A. McIntosh, 'Women at Work: A Survey of Employers', *Employment Gazette*, 1980.

14 Morris, 'No More Peanuts'.

15 *Webber* v. *Kaiser Aluminum and Chemical Corporation* 99 S. Ct. 2721 (1979).

16 R. Nielsen, *Equality Legislation in a Comparative Perspective: Towards State Feminism?*, Copenhagen, Kvindevidenskabeligt Forlag, 1983; R. Liljestrom, 'Integration of Family Policy and Labour Market Policy in Sweden', in R. S. Ratner (ed.), *Equal Employment Policy for Women*, Philadelphia, Temple University Press, 1980.

17 See S. Robarts, *Positive Action for Women*, London, NCCL, 1981, for a fuller account of American law and its effect in practice.

18 U. Huws, 'New Technology and Women's Employment: Case Studies from West Yorkshire', Leeds Trade Union and Community Resource and Information Centre and EOC, December 1982.

19 A. Wickham, 'The State and Training Programmes for Women', in E. Whitelegg *et al.* (eds.), *The Changing Experience of Women*, Oxford, Martin Robertson/Milton Keynes, Open University, 1982; Centre for Research on European Women (CREW), *Reports*, Brussels, December 1983.

20 CRE, 'The Race Relations Act 1976 — Time for a Change?', July 1983.

21 B. Rollen, 'Equality between Men and Women in the Labour Market: the Swedish National Labour Market Board', in R. S. Ratner (ed.), *Equal Employment Policy for Women*, Philadelphia, Temple University Press, 1980.

22 Nielsen, *Equality Legislation in a Comparative Perspective*.

23 A. Cook, 'Collective Bargaining in Sweden and West Germany', in R. S. Ratner (ed.), *Equal Employment Policy for Women*, Philadelphia, Temple University Press, 1980.

24 Robarts, 'Positive Action for Women'.

25 CRE, 'The Race Relations Act 1976 — Time for a Change?'.

26 *The Commission of the European Communities* v. *United Kingdom (Case 165/82)* [1984] ICR 192.

27 See D. Pannick, 'Sex Discrimination and Pregnancy: Anatomy is not Destiny', *Oxford Journal of Legal Studies*, 1983; CRE, 'The Race Relations Act 1976 — Time for a Change?'; Robarts, 'Positive Action for Women'.

28 R. Widdison, 'Class Actions: A Survey', *New Law Journal*, 1983, p. 778.

29 See V. Ellis, 'The Role of Trade Unions in the Promotion of Equal Opportunities', EOC, 1981; Robarts, 'Positive Action for Women'.

30 See Wages Council Act 1979; P. Davies and M. Freedland, *Labour Law*, London, Weidenfeld & Nicolson, 1979.

31 M. W. Snell, P. Glucklich and M. Povall, 'Equal Pay and Opportunities', Research Paper No. 20, Department of Employment, 1981; see also A. Cook, 'Collective Bargaining as a Strategy for Achieving Equal Opportunity and Equal Pay: Sweden

and West Germany', and M. Greenberger, 'The Effectiveness of Federal Laws Prohibiting Sex Discrimination in Employment in the United States', both in R. S. Ratner (ed.), *Equal Employment Policy for Women*, Philadelphia, Temple University Press, 1980.

32 *R. v. Central Arbitration Committee ex parte Hy-Mac Ltd* [1979] IRLR 46.

33 CRE, 'The Race Relations Act 1976 — Time for a Change?'.

34 EOC, 'Gender and the Secondary School Curriculum', Research Bulletin No. 6, Spring 1982.

35 CREW, *Reports*, vol. 3, no. 7, 1983.

36 Ibid., no. 8.

37 *Southampton and South-West Hampshire Health Authority (Teaching)* v. *Marshall* [1983] IRLR 237.

38 Equal Opportunities Commission, *Women and Under-Achievement at Work*, Research Bulletin No. 5, Manchester, Equal Opportunities Commission, 1981; CRE, 'The Race Relations Act 1976 — Time for a Change?'.

39 *Streamlining the Cities*, Cmnd 9063, London, HMSO, 1983.

40 H. Land, *Parity Begins at Home: Women's and Men's Work in the Home and its Effects on their Paid Employment*, EOC, 1981.

4 Sexuality

1 *Report of the Committee on Homosexual Offences and Prostitution* (the Wolfenden Report), Cmnd 247, London, HMSO, 1957, para. 13.

2 Criminal Law Revision Committee Working Paper, *Sexual Offences*, London, HMSO, 1980.

3 Criminal Law Revision Committee, 15th Report, *Sexual Offences*, Cmnd 9213, London, HMSO, 1984.

4 Ibid., para. 3.7.

5 Ibid., para. 10.26.

6 Policy Advisory Committee on Sexual Offences, *Report on the Age of Consent in relation to Sexual Offences*, Cmnd 8216, London, HMSO, 1981.

7 Criminal Law Revision Committee, *Sexual Offences* (1980), para. 58.

8 Criminal Law Revision Committee, *Sexual Offences* (1984), paras. 4.8 and 4.24.

9 Criminal Law Revision Committee, *Sexual Offences* (1980), para. 50.

10 Ibid., para. 47.

11 See, for example, S. Edwards, 'Contributory Negligence in Compensation Claims by Victims of Sexual Assault', *New Law Journal*, vol. 132, 1982, pp. 1140—2.

12 Criminal Law Revision Committee, *Sexual Offences* (1984), para. 2.6.

13 [1982] 1 WLR 133.

14 R. Walmsley and K. White, *Sexual Offences, Consent and Sentencing*, Home Office Research Study No. 54, London, HMSO, 1979.

15 Sexual Offences (Amendment) Act 1976, section 1(1)(a).

16 [1982] QB 320.

17 Criminal Law Revision Committee, *Sexual Offences* (1980), p. 58.

18 Criminal Law Revision Committee, *Sexual Offences* (1984), para. 2.29.

19 [1976] AC 132.

20 Quoting Lord Diplock in *Sweet* v. *Parsley* [1970] AC 132.

21 G. Chambers and A. Millar, *Investigating Sexual Assault*, Scottish Office Social Research Study, Edinburgh, HMSO, 1983, p. 92.

22 Ibid., p. 93.

23 K. L. Soothill, C. Way and T. C. N. Gibbens, 'Rape Acquittals', *Modern Law Review*, vol. 43, 1980, pp. 159—72.

24 *R.* v. *Caldwell* [1982] AC 341; *R.* v. *Lawrence* [1982] AC 510.

25 *Lawrence* at p. 526.

26 See *Elliott* v. *C.* [1983] 2 All ER 1005.

27 [1982] 1 WLR 762.

28 *Pleading, Evidence and Practice in Criminal Cases*, 41st edn, ed. S. Mitchell, London, Sweet & Maxwell, 1982, para. 17—25.

29 J. Temkin, 'The Limits of Reckless Rape', *Criminal Law Review*, 1983, pp. 5—16.

30 *R.* v. *Satnam: R.* v. *Kewal* [1984] 78 Cr. Att. R. 149.

31 Criminal Law Revision Committee, *Sexual Offences* (1984), para. 2.41.

32 *R.* v. *Miller* [1954] 2 QB 282.

33 See *R.* v. *Clarence* (1888) 22 QBD 23, in which the husband infected the wife with the venereal disease from which he knew that he was suffering.

34 *R.* v. *Clarke* [1949] 2 All ER 448.

35 *R.* v. *O'Brien* [1974] 3 All ER 663.

36 *R.* v. *Steele* (1976) 65 Cr. App. R. 22.

37 See M. D. A. Freeman, '"But if You Can't Rape Your Wife, Whom Can You Rape?"': the Marital Rape Exemption Re-examined', *Family Law Quarterly*, vol. 15, 1981, pp. 1—29.

38 Criminal Law Revision Committee, *Sexual Offences* (1984), para. 2.79.

39 Ibid., para. 9.3.

40 Criminal Law Revision Committee, *Sexual Offences* (1980), para. 33.

41 See Criminal Law Revision Committee, *Sexual Offences* (1984), para. 2.64.

42 [1924] AC 349.

43 See also N. Morris and A. L. Turner, 'Two Problems in the Law of Rape', *University of Queensland Law Journal*, vol. 2, 1952—5, pp. 247—63, quoted with apparent approval by J. C. Smith and B. Hogan, *Criminal Law*, 4th edn, London, Butterworth, 1978, p. 403.

44 Criminal Law Revision Committee, *Sexual Offences* (1980), para. 42.

45 See *R.* v. *Cullinane* (1984), *The Times*, 1 March.

46 (1969) 53 Cr. App. R. 150.

47 *Pleading, Evidence and Practice in Criminal Cases*, para. 16—21.

48 See, for example, Criminal Law Revision Committee, *Sexual Offences* (1984), para. 2.7.

49 *R.* v. *Trigg* [1963] 1 WLR 305; *R.* v. *Midwinter* [1971] 55 Cr. App. R. 523.

50 Law Commission, *Illegitimacy*, Working Paper No. 74, London, HMSO, 1979, para. 9.47; Law Commission, *Illegitimacy*, Law Com. No. 118, London, HMSO, 1982, paras. 6.21, 6.22.

51 Lord Diplock in *DPP* v. *Hester* [1973] AC 296.

52 S. Edwards, *Female Sexuality and the Law*, Oxford, Martin Robertson, 1981, ch. 4.

53 See e.g. C. E. Legrand, 'Rape and Rape Laws: Sexism in Society and Law', *California Law Review*, vol. 61, 1973, pp. 919—41.

54 Chambers and Millar, *Investigating Sexual Assault*.

55 Mrs Justice Heilbron, *Report of the Advisory Group on the Law of Rape*, Cmnd 6352, London, HMSO, 1975, paras. 93—109.

56 (1973) 57 Cr. App. R. 466.
57 Lord Coleridge, Chief Justice, in *R.* v. *Riley* (1887) 18 QBD 481, 483.
58 *R.* v. *Lawrence* [1977] Crim. L. R. 492.
59 *R.* v. *Turner* [1944] KB 463, approved in *Selvey* v. *DPP* [1970] AC 304.
60 Heilbron, *Report of the Advisory Group on the Law of Rape*, para. 127.
61 (1973) 57 Cr. App. R. 466.
62 [1982] 1 WLR 1138.
63 See *R.* v. *Mills* [1979] 69 Cr. App. R. 327, approving *R.* v. *Lawrence* [1977] Crim. L. R. 492.
64 Z. Adler, 'Rape — the Intention of Parliament and the Practice of the Courts', *Modern Law Review*, vol. 45, 1982, pp. 664—75.
65 See Chambers and Millar, *Investigating Sexual Assault*, for the Scottish evidence.
66 Walmsley and White, *Sexual Offences, Consent and Sentencing*, p. 23, cf. C. Roberts, 'Rape Counselling and Research Project', *Bethlem and Maudsley Gazette*, 1976.
67 *Crook* v. *Edmondson* [1966] 2 QB 81; *R.* v. *Dodd* (1977) 66 Cr. App. R. 87.
68 Criminal Law Revision Committee Working Paper, *Offences Relating to Prostitution and Allied Offences*, London, HMSO, 1982, paras. 3.44-3.46.
69 Ibid., para. 3.35.
70 Child Care Act 1980, section 3(1)(*b*)(*v*).
71 E. McLeod, *Women Working: Prostitution Now*, London, Croom Helm, 1982, p. 96.
72 *Shaw* v. *DPP* [1962] AC 220.
73 R. Leng and A. Sanders, 'The CLRC Working Paper on Prostitution', *Criminal Law Review*, 1983, pp. 644—55.
74 McLeod, *Women Working: Prostitution Now*, p. 10.
75 Cited in Sir M. Finer and O. R. McGregor, 'The History of the Obligation to Maintain', Appendix 5, *Report of the Committee on One-Parent Families*, Cmnd 5629—I, London, HMSO, 1974, p. 95.
76 See *Gardner* v. *Gardner* [1947] 1 All ER 630; *Spicer* v. *Spicer* [1954] 1 WLR 1051; *Coffer* v. *Coffer* (1964), *The Times*, 16 May.
77 *Butterworth* v. *Butterworth and Englefield* [1920] P 126.
78 *Holborn* v. *Holborn* [1947] 1 All ER 32.
79 *Beevor* v. *Beevor* [1945] 2 All ER 200.
80 Which combination of circumstances occurred in the leading case of *Synge* v. *Synge* [1900] P. 180.
81 *Clark* v. *Clark* (1958), *The Times*, 25 June.
82 *Hayes* v. *Hayes* (1958), unreported, 6 March.
83 *Evans* v. *Evans* [1965] 2 All ER 789.
84 *P. (D.)* v. *P. (J.)* [1965] 1 WLR 963.
85 *Sheldon* v. *Sheldon* [1966] P. 62.
86 *B. (L.)* v. *B. (R.)* [1965] 1 WLR 1413; see also *P.* v. *P.* [1964] 3 All ER 263.
87 *Potter* v. *Potter* (1975) 5 Family Law 161.
88 See *Dowden* v. *Dowden* (1977) 8 Family Law 66.
89 P. M. Bromley, *Family Law*, 6th edn, London, Butterworths, 1981, p. 203.

5 Motherhood

1 A. Oakley, *Subject Women*, Oxford, Martin Robertson, 1981, p. 206.

2 G. Petrie, 'A Legal Anomaly', review of L. Holcombe, *Wives and Property, New Society*, vol. 66, no. 1091, 1983, p. 66.

3 DHSS, *Report on Confidential Enquiries into Maternal Deaths 1973—5*, No. 14, London, HMSO, 1979; see Oakley, *Subject Women*, p. 188.

4 *Re Agar-Ellis, Agar-Ellis* v. *Lascelles* (1883) 24 Ch. D. 317.

5 *Cowen* v. *Cowen* [1946] P. 36; *J.* v. *J.* [1947] P. 15.

6 [1948] AC 274.

7 *White* v. *White* [1948] P. 330; *Walsham* v. *Walsham* [1949] P. 350; *Cackett* v. *Cackett* [1950] P. 253; *Knott* v. *Knott* [1955] P. 249.

8 *Lawrence* v. *Lawrence* [1950] P. 84.

9 [1954] 3 All ER 59, where, however, the wife's petition failed on the facts.

10 [1952] TLR 143.

11 [1956] P. 16.

12 (1972), *The Times*, 19 April.

13 See *R.* v. *Lord Audley* (1631) 3 State Tr. 401.

14 [1979] 1 QB 276.

15 See *Forster* v. *Forster* (1970) 1 Hag. Con. 144.

16 428 US 52 (1976).

17 410 US 113 (1973).

18 In an emergency, however, a single doctor may perform a termination outside a hospital (Aborton Act 1967, section 1).

19 Oakley, *Subject Women*, p. 192.

20 G. L. Williams, *Textbook on Criminal Law*, 2nd edn, London, Stevens, 1983, p. 297.

21 S. Baldwin and C. Glendinning, 'Employment, Women and their Disabled Children', in J. Finch and D. Groves (eds.), *A Labour of Love: Women, Work and Caring*, London, Routledge & Kegan Paul, 1983.

22 J. J. Thomson, 'A Defence of Abortion', in R. M. Dworkin, *The Philosophy of Law*, Oxford, Oxford University Press, 1977.

23 See J. Finch 'Paternalism and Professionalism in Childbirth', *New Law Journal*, vol. 132, pp. 995—6, 1011—12.

24 Ibid.

25 T. Chard and M. Richards (eds.), *Benefits and Hazards of the New Obstetrics*, London, Heinemann, 1977; S. Kitzinger and J. A. Davis (eds.), *The Place of Birth*, Oxford, Oxford University Press, 1978; A. Oakley, *Becoming a Mother*, Oxford, Martin Robertson, 1979; A. Oakley, *Women Confined: Towards a Sociology of Childbirth*, Oxford, Martin Robertson, 1980.

26 *Whitehouse* v. *Jordan* [1981] 1 WLR 246; *Bolam* v. *Friern Hospital Management Committee* [1957] 2 All ER 118.

27 J. M. Eekelaar and R. Dingwall, 'Some Legal Issues in Obstetric Practice', *Journal of Social Welfare Law*, forthcoming.

28 *Whitehouse* v. *Jordan* [1981] 1 WLR 246.

29 Except for injuries caused by her careless driving.

30 Law Commission, *Injuries to Unborn Children*, Law Com. No. 60, London, HMSO, 1974, paras. 53—64.

31 (1983), *The Times*, 3 January.

32 [1980] CA Transcript 597.

33 [1983] 1 WLR 1098.

34 D. Brahams, 'Damages for Unplanned Babies: A Trend to be Discouraged?', *New Law Journal*, vol. 133, 1983, pp. 643—5.

35 *Thake* v. *Maurice* (1984), *The Times*, 10 April.

36 Lord Simon of Glaisdale in *The Ampthill Peerage Case* [1977] AC 547.

37 *Re J. S. (A Minor)* [1981] Fam. 22.

38 F. Engels, *The Origins of the Family, Private Property and the State*, New York, Lawrence & Wishart, 1884, especially ch. II, section 4 on monogamy.

39 Sir W. Blackstone, *Commentaries on the Laws of England*, Oxford, Clarendon Press, 1765.

40 See *R.* v. *Howes* (1860) 3 E. & E. 332; *Thomasset* v. *Thomasset* [1894] P. 295.

41 See P. H. Pettitt, 'Parental Control and Guardianship', in R. H. Graveson and F. R. Crane (eds.), *A Century of Family Law 1857—1957*, London, Sweet & Maxwell, 1957.

42 (1827) 2 Sim. 35.

43 Lord Justice Sachs in *Hewer* v. *Bryant* [1970] 1 QB 357.

44 *Re Agar-Ellis, Agar-Ellis* v. *Lascelles* (1883) 24 Ch. D. 317.

45 *Clout* v. *Clout* (1861) 2 Sw. & Tr. 391.

46 *Re Besant* (1879) 11 Ch. D. 508.

47 [1897] 1 Ch. D. 716.

48 [1910] P. 190.

49 The same principle is now embodied in section 1 of the Guardianship of Minors Act 1981.

50 *Allen* v. *Allen* [1948] 2 All ER 413; *Willoughby* v. *Willoughby* [1951] P. 14.

51 [1954] 1 All ER 434.

52 *Dipper* v. *Dipper* [1981] Fam. 31.

53 [1962] 3 All ER 1.

54 *S. (B. D.)* v. *S. (D. J.) (Infants: Care and Consent)* [1977] Fam. 109.

55 [1977] Fam. 179.

56 [1970] AC 668.

57 M. Dodds, 'A Study of the Practice of the Divorce Courts in relation to Children', LL.M. thesis, University of Manchester, 1981.

58 *Re D. (An Infant)* [1977] AC 602.

59 (1978) 1 FLR 143.

60 S. Maidment, *Child Custody: What Chance for Fathers?*, Forward from Finer No. 7, London, One Parent Families, 1981.

61 J. M. Eekelaar and E. Clive, *Custody after Divorce: The Disposition of Custody in Divorce Cases in Great Britain*, Oxford, Centre for Socio-Legal Studies, 1977; S. Maidment, 'A Study in Child Custody', *Family Law*, vol. 6, 1976, pp. 195—200, 236—41; J. M. Eekelaar, 'Children in Divorce: Some Further Data', *Oxford Journal of Legal Studies*, vol. 2, 1982, pp. 62—85.

62 Eekelaar and Clive, *Custody after Divorce*, para. 5.3; and only six of these were as a result of court orders, two of them in contested cases.

63 Eekelaar, 'Children in Divorce'.

64 Maidment, *Child Custody: What Chance for Fathers?*

65 Ibid., pp. 15—16; but c.f. Eekelaar, *Children in Divorce*, at p. 79.

66 A good example is *Re W. (A Minor)* (1982) 13 Family Law 47.

67 (1983) 14 Family Law 17.

68 (1983) 13 Family Law 150.

69 Mr Justice Latey in *M.* v. *M. (Child: Access)* [1973] 2 All ER 81.

70 M. Richards, 'Post-Divorce Arrangements for Children: A Psychological Perspective', *Journal of Social Welfare Law*, 1982, pp. 133—51.

71 M. Dodds, 'Children and Divorce', *Journal of Social Welfare Law*, 1983, pp. 228—37.

72 Eekelaar and Clive, *Custody after Divorce*, paras. 5.6, 6.6, 13.16.

73 See, for example, *Re B.* (1983) 13 Family Law 176.

74 Law Commission, *Illegitimacy*, Working Paper No. 74, London, HMSO, 1979, para. 3.17.

75 *An Accident of Birth: A Response to the Law Commission's Working Paper on Illegitimacy*, London, One Parent Families, 1980.

76 Law Commission, *Illegitimacy*, Law Com. No. 118, London, HMSO, 1982, paras. 4.26, 4.37—4.40.

77 Law Commission, *Illegitimacy* (1979), para. 2.12.

78 Eekelaar and Clive, *Custody after Divorce*, para. 3.6.

79 Central Statistical Office, *Social Trends* 14 (1984 edn), London, HMSO, 1983, table 2.10.

80 J. Masson, D. Norbury and S. G. Chatterton, *Mine, Yours or Ours? A Study of Step-Parent Adoption*, London, HMSO, 1983.

81 Lord Justice Stamp in *R. (B. M.)* v. *R. (D. N.)* [1977] 1 WLR 1256.

82 *W.* v. *A. (Child: Surname)* [1981] Fam. 14.

83 *D.* v. *B. (otherwise D.)* [1979] Fam. 38.

84 J. Burgoyne and D. Clark, 'Reconstituted Families', in R. N. Rapoport, M. P. Fogarty and R. Rapoport (eds.), *Families in Britain*, London, Routledge & Kegan Paul, 1982, p. 299.

85 Children and Young Persons Act 1969, section 1; *F.* v. *Suffolk County Council* (1981) 79 LGR 554.

86 Child Care Act 1980, section 3(1).

87 Children Act 1975, section 12(2); *Re W. (An Infant)* [1971] AC 682.

88 1975 Act, sections 14—16.

89 *Re C. B. (A Minor)* [1981] WLR 379.

90 *A.* v. *Liverpool City Council* [1982] AC 363; but see also *Re E. (S. A.)* [1984] 1 All ER 289.

91 Children Act 1975, section 28.

92 Now see the Foster Children Act 1980.

93 Nurseries and Childminders Regulation Act 1948.

94 Central Policy Review Staff, *Services for Young Children with Working Mothers*, London, HMSO, 1978; B. Jackson and S. Jackson, *Childminder: A Study in Action Research*, London, Routledge & Kegan Paul, 1979.

95 C. Bell, L. McKee and K. Priestley, *Fathers, Childbirth and Work*, Manchester, EOC, 1983.

6 Breadwinners and Homemakers: Partners or Dependants?

1 M. McIntosh, 'The Welfare State and the Needs of the Dependent Family', in S. Burman (ed.), *Fit Work for Women*, London, Croom Helm, 1979, p. 154.

2 M. Spring Rice, *Working Class Wives*, 2nd edn, London, Virago, 1981.

3 J. M. Krauskopf, 'Partnership Marriage: Legal Reforms Needed', in J. R. Chapman and M. Gates (eds.), *Women into Wives: The Legal and Economic Impact of Marriage*, London, Sage Publications, 1977, p. 93.

4 A. Oakley, *The Sociology of Housework*, London, Martin Robertson, 1974; see discussion in C. Ungerson, 'Why Do Women Care?', in J. Finch and D. Groves (eds.), *A Labour of Love: Women, Work and Caring*, London, Routledge & Kegan Paul, 1983.

5 R. N. Rapoport and R. Rapoport, 'The Impact of Work on the Family', in P. Moss

and N. Fonda (eds.), *Work and the Family*, London, Temple Smith, 1980; see particularly H. Gavron, *The Captive Wife*, London, Routledge & Kegan Paul, 1966; J. Bernard, *The Future of Marriage*, London, Souvenir Press, 1973; A. Oakley, 'Conventional Families', in R. N. Rapoport, M. Fogarty and R. Rapoport (eds.), *Families in Britain*, London, Routledge & Kegan Paul, 1982; Oakley, *The Sociology of Housework*; M. Young and P. Willmott, *The Symmetrical Family*, London, Routledge & Kegan Paul, 1973; R. Rapoport, R. Rapoport and Z. Strelitz, *Fathers, Mothers and Others*, London, Routlede & Kegan Paul, 1977.

6 J. Pahl and R. E. Pahl, *Managers and their Wives*, London, Allen Lane, 1971; S. Edgell, *Middle Class Couples: A Study of Segregation, Domination and Inequality in Marriage*, London, Allen & Unwin, 1983.

7 R. Layard *et al.*, *The Causes of Poverty*, Royal Commission on the Distribution of Income and Wealth, Background Paper No. 5, London, HMSO, 1978.

8 Central Statistical Office, *Social Trends* 13 (1983 edn), London, HMSO, 1982, tables 4.3 and 2.9.

9 Inland Revenue, *The Taxation of Husband and Wife*, Cmnd 8093, London, HMSO, 1980.

10 Central Statistical Office, *Social Trends* 14 (1984 edn), London, HMSO, 1983, table 4.3.

11 P. Moss and I. Plewis, 'Young Children in the Inner City', T. Coram Research Unit Pre-School Project, unpublished report to the DHSS, 1979.

12 E. Boulding, 'Familial Constraints on Women's Work Roles', in M. Blaxall and B. Reagan, *Women and the Workplace*, Chicago, University of Chicago Press, 1976, quoted in H. Land, *Parity Begins at Home: Women's and Men's Work in the Home and its Effect on Paid Employment*, Manchester, EOC, 1981; see also A. Hunt, *Women and Work*, London, HMSO, 1965.

13 Rapoport and Rapoport, 'The Impact of Work on the Family', p. 175.

14 Young and Willmott, *The Symmetrical Family*; Oakley, *The Sociology of Housework*.

15 Bernard, *The Future of Marriage*.

16 R. Liljestrom, *Roles in Transition*, reports of an investigation made for the Advisory Council on Equality between Men and Women, Sweden, 1978, quoted in Land, *Parity Begins at Home*.

17 H. Land, 'Who Cares for the Family?', *Journal of Social Policy*, vol. 7, 1978, pp. 257—84; J. Finch and D. Groves (eds.), *A Labour of Love: Women, Work and Caring*, London, Routledge & Kegan Paul, 1983.

18 K. O'Donovan, 'The Male Appendage — Legal Definitions of Women', in S. Burman (ed.), *Fit Work for Women*, London, Croom Helm, 1979, pp. 132—52, at p. 135.

19 *Cunningham* v. *Harrison* [1973] QB 942; *Connelly* v. *Joyce* [1974] QB 454.

20 D. A. McI. Kemp and S. Kemp, *The Quantum of Damages*, vol. 1, London, Sweet & Maxwell, 1975, p. 115.

21 [1952] AC 716.

22 Kemp and Kemp, *The Quantum of Damages*, vol. 1, p. 305. Similar claims are now allowed where a cohabiting couple have been together for two years.

23 *Moriarty* v. *Moriarty* [1978] 1 WLR 155.

24 See *Hoddinot* v. *Hoddinot* [1949] 2 KB 406.

25 [1973] Fam. 120.

26 I. Pinchbeck, *Women Workers and the Industrial Revolution 1750—1850*, 2nd edn, London, Cass, 1969, p. 33.

27 L. Tilly and J. W. Scott, *Women, Work and Family*, New York, Holt, Rinehart and Winston, 1979, p. 124.

28 *Balfour* v. *Balfour* [1919] 2 KB 571.
29 Law Commission, *The Financial Consequences of Divorce: The Basic Policy*, Discussion Paper, Cmnd 8041, London, HMSO, 1980, paras. 9—13, 24.
30 Sir M. Finer and O. R. McGregor, 'The History of the Obligation to Maintain', Appendix 5, *Report of the Committee on One-Parent Families*, Cmnd 5629-I, London, HMSO, 1974, p. 104.
31 [1891] P. 272.
32 *Iverson* v. *Iverson* [1968] P. 134.
33 *Porter* v. *Porter* [1969] 1 WLR 1155.
34 Law Commission, *The Financial Consequences of Divorce* (1980), para. 12.
35 See *Ackerman* v. *Ackerman* [1972] Fam. 225.
36 *Attwood* v. *Attwood* [1968] P. 591.
37 O. Kahn-Freund, 'England', in W. Friedman (ed.), *Matrimonial Property Law*, London, Stevens, 1955.
38 Sir J. Simon, 'With All My Worldly Goods', Presidential Address, Holdsworth Club, University of Birmingham, 1964.
39 Pahl and Pahl, *Managers and their Wives*.
40 J. Finch, *Married to the Job: Wives' Incorporation in Men's Work*, London, Allen & Unwin, 1983.
41 M. S. McDougall, H. D. Lasswell and L.-c. Chen, 'Human Rights for Women and World Public Order: The Outlawing of Sex-Based Discrimination', *American Journal of International Law*, vol. 69, 1975, p. 509, quoted in K. J. Gray, *Reallocation of Property on Divorce*, Abingdon, Professional Books, 1977.
42 Gray, *Reallocation of Property on Divorce*, p. 29.
43 E. Clive, 'Marriage: an Unnecessary Legal Concept', in J. M. Eekelaar and S. N. Katz (eds.), *Marriage and Cohabitation in Contemporary Societies: Areas of Legal, Social and Ethical Change*, Toronto, Butterworths, 1980, p. 76.
44 See J. Todd and L. Jones, *Matrimonial Property*, London, HMSO, 1972, and A. J. Manners and I. Rauta, *Family Property in Scotland*, OPCS, 1981.
45 See, for example, Gray, *Reallocation of Property on Divorce*; R. Deech, 'The Principles of Maintenance', *Family Law*, vol. 7, 1977, pp. 229—33; R. Deech, 'Financial Relief: the Retreat from Precedent and Principle', *Law Quarterly Review*, vol. 98, 1982, pp. 621—55.
46 [1973] Fam. 72.
47 *Re Rogers' Question* [1948] 1 All ER 328.
48 *Rimmer* v. *Rimmer* [1953] 1 QB 63.
49 *Allen* v. *Allen* [1961] 1 WLR 1186.
50 *Fribance* v. *Fribance* [1957] 1 WLR 384.
51 Such as Lord Evershed in *Allen*.
52 Todd and Jones, *Matrimonial Property*, para. 4.1.
53 Ibid.
54 A. Hunt, *Families and Their Needs*, London, HMSO, 1973.
55 [1971] AC 886.
56 As in fact happened in *Hazell* v. *Hazell* [1972] 1 WLR 301.
57 P. Jephcott, N. Seear and J. H. Smith, *Married Women Working*, London, Allen & Unwin, 1962.
58 *Appleton* v. *Appleton* [1965] 1 WLR 25.
59 *Jansen* v. *Jansen* [1965] P. 478.

60 *Pettitt* v. *Pettitt* [1970] AC 777.
61 *Nixon* v. *Nixon* [1969] 1 WLR 1676.
62 *Button* v. *Button* [1968] 1 WLR 457.
63 [1971] AC 886.
64 *Cooke* v. *Head* [1972] 1 WLR 51; *Eves* v. *Eves* [1975] 1 WLR 1338.
65 *Walker* v. *Hall* (1983) 14 Family Law 21.
66 *Pettitt* v. *Pettitt* [1970] AC 777.
67 *Bernard* v. *Josephs* [1982] Ch. 391.
68 *Burns* v. *Burns* [1984] 1 All ER 244.
69 See *Bedson* v. *Bedson* [1965] 2 QB 666.
70 *Cracknell* v. *Cracknell* [1971] P. 356.
71 For example, *Re Holliday* [1981] Ch. 405.
72 *Suttill* v. *Graham* [1977] 1 WLR 819.
73 Law Commission, *Family Property Law*, Working Paper No. 42, London, Law Commission, 1971.
74 Law Commission, *First Report on Family Property: A New Approach*, Law Com. No. 52, London, HMSO, 1973; Law Commission, *Third Report on Family Property: The Matrimonial Home (Co-ownership and Occupation Rights) and Household Goods*, Law Com. No. 86, London, HMSO, 1978.
75 *Williams and Glyn's Bank* v. *Boland* [1981] AC 487.
76 Recommended again in 1982: Law Commission, *The Implications of* Williams and Glyn's Bank Ltd *v.* Boland, Law Com. No. 115, London, HMSO, 1982; however, legislation is now planned to retain the effect of *Boland* for wives but reverse it for others, including cohabitants.
77 Scottish Law Commission, *Report on Matrimonial Property* (Scots. Law Com. No. 86), Edinburgh, HMSO, 1984.
78 Matrimonial Causes Act 1973, sections 23, 24 and 24A.
79 1973 Act, section 25(1)(f).
80 [1973] Fam. 72.
81 1973 Act, section 25(1).
82 [1973] Fam. 72.
83 See particularly *Stockford* v. *Stockford* (1981) 12 Family Law 30; *Page* v. *Page* (1981) 11 Family Law 149.
84 *Ashley* v. *Ashley* [1968] P. 582; *Barnes* v. *Barnes* [1972] 1 WLR 1381.
85 *Shallow* v. *Shallow* [1979] Fam. 1; cf. *Smethurst* v. *Smethurst* [1978] Fam. 52. See M. Hayes, 'Supplementary Benefit and Financial Provision Orders', *Journal of Social Welfare Law*, 1978—9, pp. 216—25.
86 Sir M. Finer, *Report of the Committee on One-Parent Families*, Cmnd 5629, London, HMSO, 1974, esp. pt. 5.
87 G. Davis, M. Macleod and M. Murch, 'Divorce: Who Supports the Family?', *Family Law*, vol. 13, 1983, pp. 217—24.
88 See also Central Statistical Office, *Social Trends* 14, table 2.10.
89 M. Maclean and J. M. Eekelaar, *Children and Divorce: Economic Factors*, Oxford, Centre for Socio-Legal Studies, 1983.
90 Davis, Macleod and Murch, 'Divorce: Who Supports the Family?'.
91 Finer, *Report of the Committee on One-Parent Families*; Davis, Macleod and Murch, 'Divorce: Who Supports the Family?'; and see Family Policy Studies Centre, *Divorce: 1983 Matrimonial and Family Proceedings Bill*, Briefing Paper,

London, Family Policy Studies Centre, 1983.

92 Davis, Macleod and Murch, 'Divorce: Who Supports the Family?', p. 223.

93 J. M. Eekelaar and M. Maclean, 'Financial Provision on Divorce: A Reappraisal', paper presented at the W. G. Hart Workshop, Institute of Advanced Legal Studies, 1983.

94 *Browne* v. *Pritchard* [1975] 1 WLR 1366; *H.* v. *H.* [1975] Fam. 9.

95 *Mesher* v. *Mesher* (1973) 1 All ER 126; *Chamberlain* v. *Chamberlain* [1973] 1 WLR 1557; *Scott* v. *Scott* [1978] 3 All ER 65.

96 *Harvey* v. *Harvey* [1982] Fam. 83.

97 *Hanlon* v. *Hanlon* [1978] 1 WLR 592. Nominal maintenance should be paid for the children; if the husband continues to pay the mortgage instalments while the family lives on supplementary benefit, the maximum advantage is obtained for all parties.

98 Eekelaar and Maclean, 'Financial Provision on Divorce'.

99 [1979] AC 593.

100 *Camm* v. *Camm* (1982) 13 Family Law 112.

101 *Tommey* v. *Tommey* [1983] Fam. 15.

102 *Dipper* v. *Dipper* [1981] Fam. 31.

103 *Jessel* v. *Jessel* [1979] 3 All ER 645.

104 *Moore* v. *Moore* (1980), *The Times*, 10 May.

105 (1981) 2 FLR 392.

106 Law Commission, *The Financial Consequences of Divorce*, (1980), para. 63.

107 *Graves* v. *Graves* (1974) 4 Family Law 124; *Frisby* v. *Frisby* (1983) 14 Family Law 19.

108 (1980) 11 Family Law 179.

109 [1982] 1 WLR 1255.

110 *O'D.* v. *O'D.* [1976] Fam. 83; *Preston* v. *Preston* [1982] Fam. 17.

111 For example, *Calderbank* v. *Calderbank* [1976] Fam. 93; *P.* v. *P. (Financial Provision: Lump Sum)* [1978] 3 All ER 70.

112 *Barnes* v. *Barnes* [1972] 1 WLR 1381.

113 *Wilkinson* v. *Wilkinson* (1979) 10 Family Law 48; *Brown* v. *Brown* (1981) 11 Family Law 247; *Macey* v. *Macey* (1981) 11 Family Law 248.

114 *S.* v. *S.* [1977] Fam. 109; *Warder* v. *Warder* (1978) 122 SJ 713.

115 *Martin* v. *Martin* [1978] Fam. 12.

116 *Porter* v. *Porter* [1969] 1 WLR 1155.

117 Campaign for Justice in Divorce, *The Financial Anatomy of Post-Divorce Man*, Aylesbury, Campaign for Justice in Divorce, 1980; D. Allan, *One Step from the Quagmire*, Aylesbury, Campaign for Justice in Divorce, 1982.

118 Maclean and Eekelaar, *Children and Divorce*.

119 Law Commission, *The Financial Consequences of Divorce* (1980); Law Commission, *The Financial Consequences of Divorce: The Response to the Law Commission's Discussion Paper and Recommendations on the Policy of the Law*, Law Com. No. 112, London, HMSO, 1981.

120 Law Commission, *The Financial Consequences of Divorce* (1980), paras. 45—57.

121 Scottish Law Commission, *Report on Aliment and Financial Provision*, Scots Law Com. No. 67, Edinburgh, HMSO, 1981.

122 J. Dewar, 'Reforming Financial Provision: The Alternatives', *Journal of Social Welfare Law*, 1984, pp. 1—13.

123 K. O'Donovan, 'The Principles of Maintenance: An Alternative View', *Family Law*, vol. 8, 1978, pp. 180—4; K. O'Donovan, 'Should all Maintenance of Spouses be Abolished?', *Modern Law Review*, vol. 45, 1982, pp. 424—33.

124 See, for example, *Robinson* v. *Robinson* [1983] 1 All ER 391.

7 Power and Violence in the Home

1 R. Chester and J. Streather, 'Cruelty in English Divorce: Some Empirical Findings', *Journal of Marriage and the Family*, vol. 34, 1972, pp. 706—12.

2 G. Davis and M. Macleod, cited in M. Borkowski, M. Murch and V. Walker, *Marital Violence: The Community Response*, London, Tavistock, 1983, p. 26.

3 J. Haskey, 'The Proportion of Marriages Ending in Divorce', *Population Trends*, no. 27, 1982, pp. 4—7.

4 R. Dobash and R. Dobash, *Violence against Wives: A Case against the Patriarchy*, London, Open Books, 1980, p. 124.

5 Borkowski, Murch and Walker, *Marital Violence*.

6 M. Strauss and R. J. Gelles, *Behind Closed Doors: Violence in the American Family*, New York, Doubleday, 1980.

7 R. J. Gelles, *Family Violence*, London, Sage, 1979, p. 141.

8 E. Pleck, J. Pleck, M. Grossman and P. Bart, 'The Battered Data Syndrome: A Comment on Steinmetz's Article', *Victimology*, vol. 2, 1977, pp. 680—3.

9 E. Wilson, *The Existing Research into Battered Women*, London, National Women's Aid Federation, 1976, pp. 5—6.

10 See J. J. Gayford, 'Wife Battering: A Preliminary Survey of 100 Cases', *British Medical Journal*, vol. 1, 1975, pp. 194—7; R. Gelles, *The Violent Home*, Beverly Hills, Sage, 1972.

11 The view popularized by Erin Pizzey in *Scream Quietly or the Neighbours will Hear*, Harmondsworth, Penguuin, 1974.

12 The most common explanation favoured by the professionals studied by Borkowski, Murch and Walker, *Marital Violence*.

13 The explanation favoured by the British Association of Social Workers, 'Working Party on Home Violence: Discussion Document', *Social Work Today*, vol. 6, 1975, p. 409.

14 M. E. Wolfgang and F. Ferracuti, *The Subculture of Violence: Towards an Integrated Theory in Criminology*, London, Tavistock, 1967; W. A. Westley, *Violence and the Police: A Sociological Study of Law, Custom and Morality*, Cambridge, Mass., MIT Press, 1970.

15 A. Storr, *Human Aggression*, Harmondsworth, Penguin, 1974; M. Jobling, 'Battered Wives: a Survey', *Social Service Quarterly*, vol. 47, 1974, pp. 142—6; E. Pizzey and J. Shapiro, *Prone to Violence*, Feltham, Middx, Hamlyn Paperbacks, 1982.

16 J. E. O'Brien, 'Violence in Divorce-Prone Families', *Journal of Marriage and the Family*, vol. 33, 1971, pp. 692—8.

17 M. Pagelow, *Battered Women: A New Perspective*, Dublin, International Sociological Association, 1977.

18 R. Whitehurst, 'Violence in Husband—Wife Interaction', in S. Steinmetz and M. Strauss (eds.), *Violence in the Family*, New York, Dodd Mead, 1974.

19 W. J. Goode, 'Force and Violence in the Family', *Journal of Marriage and the Family*, vol. 33, 1971, pp. 624—36.

20 J. S. Mill, *The Subjection of Women*, 1869; reprinted in Everyman's Library edn, London, Dent, 1929, p. 251.

21 Dobash and Dobash, *Violence against Wives*, e.g. pp. 98—106.

22 M. D. A. Freeman, 'Violence against Women: Does the Legal System Provide Solutions or Itself Constitute the Problem?', *British Journal of Law and Society*, vol. 7, 1980, pp. 215—41.

23 *Lord Leigh's Case* (1674) 3 Keb. 433.
24 *R.* v. *Lister* (1723) 1 Strange 478.
25 Sir W. Blackstone, *Commentaries on the Laws of England*, Oxford, Clarendon Press, 1765, p. 445.
26 M. May, 'Violence in the Family: an Historical Perspective', in J. P. Martin (ed.), *Violence and the Family*, Chichester, Wiley, 1978.
27 (1840) 8 Dowl. PC 630.
28 *R.* v. *Mead* (1758) 1 Burr. 542.
29 *R.* v. *A. Brooke and Thomas Fladgate* (1766) 4 Burr. 1991.
30 (1852) 18 QB 781.
31 [1891] 1 QB 671.
32 *R.* v. *Reid* [1973] QB 299.
33 Dobash and Dobash, *Violence against Wives*. p. 245.
34 Mill, *The Subjection of Women*, p. 251.
35 [1946] P. 216.
36 P. M. Bromley, *Family Law*, 5th edn, London, Butterworths, 1976, p. 193.
37 Blackstone, *Commentaries on the Laws of England*, pp. 444—5.
38 L. Rosen, *Matrimonial Offences with Particular Reference to the Magistrates' Courts*, 3rd edn, London, Oyez Publishing, 1975, p. 173.
39 Ibid., p. 213.
40 [1983] 1 WLR 279.
41 *Taylor* v. *Taylor* (1755) 2 Lee 172.
42 *Wallscourt* v. *Wallscourt* [1847] 5 NC 121.
43 (1813) 2 Hagg. Con. 153.
44 [1946] P. 216.
45 Dobash and Dobash, *Violence against Wives*, p. 137.
46 (1959), *The Times*, 5 June.
47 [1971] P. 24.
48 [1967] 1 All ER 323.
49 *Horton* v. *Horton* [1940] P. 187; *Atkins* v. *Atkins* [1942] 2 All ER 637; see also *Stevens* v. *Stevens* [1979] 1 WLR 885.
50 (1958), *The Times*, 20 November.
51 [1972] Fam. 135.
52 *Kelly* v. *Kelly* (1870) LR 2 P. & D. 58.
53 For example, *Lauder* v. *Lauder* [1949] P. 277; *Jamieson* v. *Jamieson* [1952] AC 525; *Sleightholme* v. *Sleightholme* (1956), *The Times*, 15 February.
54 Dobash and Dobash, *Violence against Wives*, p. 94.
55 Ibid. throughout, especially chs. 6 and 7.
56 Law Commission, *Reform of the Grounds of Divorce: The Field of Choice*, Cmnd 3123, London, HMSO, 1966, paras. 29—32.
57 Sir M. Finer, *Report of the Committee on One-Parent Families*, Cmnd 5629, London, HMSO, 1974, para. 4.298 *et seq.*
58 Matrimonial Causes Act 1973, section 6(2); Domestic Proceedings and Magistrates' Courts Act 1978, section 26(1).
59 Mrs Justice Booth, *Matrimonial Causes Procedure: Consultative Paper*, London, Lord Chancellor's Department, 1983, p. 38.
60 Lord Evershed, Foreword to R. H. Graveson and F. R. Crane (eds.), *A Century of Family Law 1857—1957*, London, Sweet and Maxwell, 1957, p. xv.

61 Law Reform Committee, *Liability in Tort between Husband and Wife*, 9th Report, Cmnd 1268, London, HMSO, 1961.

62 Law Reform (Husband and Wife) Act 1962, section 1(1)(a).

63 See M. Wasik, 'Criminal Injuries Compensation and Family Violence', *Journal of Social Welfare Law*, 1983, pp. 100—8.

64 Association of Chief Police Officers of England, Wales and Northern Ireland, Memorandum submitted to House of Commons Select Committee on Violence in Marriage; see *Report from the Select Committee on Violence in Marriage*, vol. 2, Minutes of Evidence and Proceedings, HC 553 II, London, HMSO, 1975, pp. 366.

65 J. Pahl, 'Police Response to Battered Women', *Journal of Social Welfare Law*, 1982, pp. 337—43.

66 M. Dow, 'Police Involvement', in M. Borland (ed.), *Violence in the Family*, Manchester, Manchester University Press, 1976, p. 133.

67 [1979] AC 474.

68 Pahl, 'Police Response to Battered Women'.

69 (1980) 72 Cr. App. R. 302.

70 Dobash and Dobash, *Violence against Wives*, p. 222.

71 F. Wasoff, 'Legal Protection from Wife Beating: The Processing of Domestic Assaults by Scottish Prosecutors and Criminal Courts', *International Journal of the Sociology of Law*, vol. 10, 1982, pp. 187—204.

72 A recent example is *R.* v. *Dobbs* (1983), *The Times*, 8 November.

73 *R.* v. *Buchanan* (1980) 2 Cr. App. R. (S.) 13.

74 A. J. Ashworth, 'The Doctrine of Provocation', *Cambridge Law Journal*, 1976, pp. 292—320.

75 D. Thomas, *Principles of Sentencing*, 2nd edn, London, Heinemann, 1979, pp. 76—9, 94—5.

76 See the examples of *Allen*, 1972; *Lawrence*, 1975; and *Bullman*, 1971.

77 [1949] 1 All ER 932.

78 M. Wasik, 'Cumulative Provocation and Domestic Killing', *Criminal Law Review*, 1982, pp. 29—37.

79 [1972] Crim. LR 324.

80 1973; cited by Thomas, *Principles of Sentencing*, at p. 78.

81 S. Maidment, 'The Relevance of the Criminal Law to Domestic Violence', *Journal of Social Welfare Law*, 1980, pp. 26—32.

82 See *Horner* v. *Horner* [1982] Fam. 90.

83 *Montgomery* v. *Montgomery* [1965] P. 46.

84 *O'Malley* v. *O'Malley* [1982] 1 WLR 244.

85 [1970] P. 11.

86 See *Beasley* v. *Beasley* [1969] 1 WLR 226.

87 [1979] AC 264.

88 [1979] Fam. 52.

89 *Bassett* v. *Bassett* [1975] Fam. 76.

90 *Walker* v. *Walker* [1978] 1 WLR 533.

91 *Rennick* v. *Rennick* [1977] 1 WLR 1455.

92 *Samson* v. *Samson* [1982] 1 WLR 252.

93 *Elsworth* v. *Elsworth* [1978] 1 FLR 245.

94 [1982] 1 WLR 247.

95 [1984] AC 174.

96 *Tarr* v. *Tarr* [1973] AC 254.

97 *Davis* v. *Johnson* [1979] AC 264; *Hopper* v. *Hopper* [1978] 1 WLR 1342.

98 *Practice Note* [1978] 1 WLR 1123.

99 *Horner* v. *Horner* [1982] Fam. 90.

100 [1981] 1 WLR 27.

101 V. Binney, G. Harkell and J. Nixon, *Leaving Violent Men: A Study of Refuges for Battered Women*, London, Women's Aid Federation, 1981.

102 [1977] Fam. 138.

103 *O'Malley* v. *O'Malley* [1982] 1 WLR 244.

104 See, for example, the criteria laid down in *Practice Note* [1978] 1 WLR 925, which makes an interesting comparison with the criteria for the grant of ex parte 'Mareva' injunctions prohibiting the disposal of assets which may be required to satisfy judgment in pending financial claims.

105 Home Office, *Statistical Bulletin*, Issue 1/84, London, Home Office, 1984.

106 Binney, Harkell and Nixon, *Leaving Violent Men*.

107 *R.* v. *Ealing Borough Council, ex parte Sidhu* (1982) 80 LGR 534.

108 (1983), *The Times*, 13 July; 14 Family Law 117.

109 See *Wootton* v. *Wootton* (1983), *The Times*, 27 May; *Warwick* v. *Warwick* (1982) 12 Family Law 60.

110 See M. Bryan, 'Domestic Violence: A Question of Housing", *Journal of Social Welfare Laws*, 1984, pp. 195—207.

111 P. W. Robson and P. Watchman, 'The Homeless Persons' Obstacle Race', *Journal of Social Welfare Law*, 1981, pp. 1—20, 65—82; Binney, Harkell and Nixon, *Leaving Violent Men*.

8 The Case against Marriage?

1 L. Weitzman, 'Legal Regulation of Marriage: Tradition and Change', *California Law Review*, vol. 62, 1974, pp. 1169—1288; L. Weitzman, *The Marriage Contract: Spouses, Lovers and the Law*, London, Collier Macmillan, 1981.

2 M. D. A. Freeman, 'Violence against Women: Does the Legal System Provide the Solutions or Itself Constitute the Problem?', *British Journal of Law and Society*, vol. 7, 1980, pp. 215—41, at pp. 225—6.

3 M. A. Glendon, 'Power and Authority in the Family: New Legal Patterns as Reflections of Changing Ideologies', *American Journal of Comparative Law*, vol. 23, 1975, p. 4.

4 *R.* v. *St Faith's, Newton (Inhabitants)* (1823) 3 Dowl. & Ry. 34.

5 D. Leonard, *Sex and Generation: A Study of Courtship and Weddings*, London, Tavistock, 1980, p. 265.

6 See particularly R. Deech, 'The Case against Legal Recognition of Cohabitation', in J. M. Eekelaar and S. N. Katz (eds), *Marriage and Cohabitation in Contemporary Societies: Areas of Legal, Social and Ethical Change*, Toronto, Butterworths, 1980; M. D. A. Freeman and C. M. Lyon, *Cohabitation without Marriage*, Aldershot, Gower, 1983.

7 T. Honoré, *Sex Law*, London, Duckworth, 1978.

8 *Ward* v. *Byham* [1956] 2 All ER 318.

9 P. M. Bromley, *Family Law*, 6th edn, London, Butterworths, 1981, p. 602.

10 [1975] 1 WLR 1346.

11 [1976] 1 WLR 230.

12 J. Burgoyne and D. Clark, *Making a Go of It: A Study of Step-Parents in Sheffield*, London, Routlege & Kegan Paul, 1984.

13 See, for example, A. Whitehead, 'Sex Antagonism in Herefordshire', in D. L. Barker and S. Allen (eds.), *Dependence and Exploitation in Work and Marriage*, Harlow, Longman, 1976.

14 D. Oliver, 'Why do People Live Together?', *Journal of Social Welfare Law*, 1982, pp. 209—22. Weitzman agrees that this must be true of marriage.

15 *Hawes* v. *Evendon* [1953] 1 WLR 1119; cf. *Gammans* v. *Ekins* [1950] 2 KB 32.

16 *Dyson Holdings* v. *Fox* [1976] 1 QB 503.

17 *Helby* v. *Rafferty* [1979] 1 WLR 13.

18 [1980] 1 WLR 1493.

19 See *Jelley* v. *Iliffe* [1981] Fam. 128.

20 *Re Wilkinson* [1978] Fam. 22.

21 *Burns* v. *Burns* [1984] 1 All ER 244.

22 E. Clive, 'Marriage: An Unnecessary Legal Concept?', in Eekelaar and Katz, *Marriage and Cohabitation in Contemporary Societies*.

23 Ibid., p. 78.

24 *Forster* v. *Forster* (1790) 1 Hag. Con. 144.

25 *Nanda* v. *Nanda* [1968] P. 351.

26 It is no accident that the one no-fault ground introduced before 1971 was against a spouse who had been kept in an institution for at least five years because of incurable mental illness. The maximum hardship for an innocent petitioner was thus combined with the minimum understanding by the equally innocent respondent of the gross breach of principle involved.

27 Lord Morton of Henryton, *Report of the Royal Commission on Marriage and Divorce*, Cmd 9678, London, HMSO, 1956.

28 H. Ross and I. Sawhill, *Time of Transition: The Growth of Families Headed by Women*, Washington DC, Urban Institute, 1975.

29 [1940] P. 139.

30 [1942] P. 1.

31 [1949] P. 98.

32 (1949) 65 TLR 680.

33 See *Wroth* v. *Tyler* [1974] Ch. 30.

34 [1952] 2 All ER 1035.

35 [1955] 1 WLR 520.

36 [1951] P. 38.

37 [1964] AC 644.

38 Law Commission, *Reform of the Grounds of Divorce: The Field of Choice*, Cmnd 3123, London, HMSO, 1966.

39 M. Rheinstein, *Marriage Stability, Divorce and the Law*, Chicago, Chicago University Press, 1972.

40 Law Society, Family Law Sub-Committee, *A Better Way Out*, London, Law Society, 1979; Law Society, Standing Committee on Family Law, *A Better Way Out Reviewed*, London, Law Society, 1982.

41 *Richards* v. *Richards* [1984] AC 174; see earlier p. 142.

42 The fifth fact is two years' desertion.

43 *Livingstone-Stallard* v. *Livingstone-Stallard* [1974] Fam. 47.

44 Law Society, *A Better Way Out*, p. 23.
45 *Cleary* v. *Cleary* [1974] 1 WLR 73.
46 [1973] Fam. 72.
47 (1973), *The Times*, 14 October.
48 *Grenfell* v. *Grenfell* [1978] Fam. 128.
49 Campaign for Justice in Divorce, *Unequal Before the Law: Legal Aid in Divorce*, Hereford, Campaign for Justice in Divorce, 1983.
50 See *Hanlon* v. *Law Society* [1981] AC 124.
51 Lord Chancellor's Department, *Judicial Statistics 1982*, Cmnd 9065, London, HMSO, 1983.
52 Law Commission, *Reform of the Grounds of Divorce*, p. 10.
53 Society of Conservative Lawyers, *The Future of Marriage: A Report by a Research Sub-Committee*, London, Conservative Political Centre, 1981, p. 28.

9 The Welfare State: Social Security and Taxation

1 S. Lewenhak, *Women and Trade Unions*, London, Benn, 1977.
2 *Report of the Royal Commissioners on the Poor Laws and Relief of Distress*, Cmnd 4499, London, HMSO, 1909.
3 See Question WQ No. 1040/82 raised by Rogers, MEP, CREW, *Reports*, vol. 2, no. 11, 1982, p. 8; Social Security Advisory Committee, *Report of the Social Security Advisory Committee to Consider New Rules Introducing Equal Treatment for Men and Women into Certain Areas of the Social Security Scheme*, Cmnd 8993, London, HMSO, 1983, para. 19, and Minister's response, para. 7.
4 J. C. Brown, *Family Income Support*, Part 1: *Family Income Supplement*, London, Policy Studies Institute, 1983.
5 H. Land, 'The Mantle of Manhood', *New Statesman*, December 1981, pp. 16—18; J. Lewis, 'In Search of a Real Equality: Women between the Wars', in F. Gloversmith (ed.), *Class Culture and Social Change: A New View of the 1930s*, Brighton, Harvester, 1980; E. Wilson, *Women and the Welfare State*, London, Tavistock, 1977.
6 M. Bondfield, *A Life's Work*, London, Hutchinson, 1948; Lewis, 'In Search of a Real Equality'.
7 W. H. Beveridge, *Social Insurance and Allied Services*, Cmnd 6404, London, HMSO, 1942, para. 108.
8 See M. Hewitt, *Wives and Mothers in Victorian Industry*, London, Rockliff, 1958, on attitudes obtaining when the first wife's earnings rules were introduced in 1894. See also H. Land, 'Sex-Role Stereotyping in the Social Security and Income Tax Systems', in J. Chetwynd and O. Hartnett (eds.), *The Sex Role System*, London, Routlege & Kegan Paul, 1978.
9 Beveridge, *Social Insurance and Allied Services*, paras. 108—13.
10 Brian O'Malley, Minister of State, to DHSS, 1975, quoted in Land, 'Sex-Role Stereotyping in the Social Security and Income Tax Systems', in J. Chetwynd and O. Hartnett (eds.), *The Sex Role System*, London, Routledge & Kegan Paul, 1978, pp. 138—9.
11 A. I. Ogus and E. M. Barendt, *The Law of Social Security*, 2nd edn, London, Butterworths, 1982, p. 62.
12 Sir M. Finer, *Report of the Committee on One-Parent Families*, Cmnd 5629, London, HMSO, 1974.

13 Ibid., p. 268.

14 Ibid., p. 269.

15 Brown, *Family Income Support*, Part 1, *Family Income Supplement*, p. 93.

16 SI 1980/1437, reg. 5(3).

17 S. Atkins, 'Social Security Act 1980 and the EEC Directive on Equal Treatment in Social Security Benefits', *Journal of Social Welfare Law*, 1981, p. 16.

18 Ogus and Barendt, *The Law of Social Security*, p. 141.

19 House of Lords Debates, 12 July 1983, cols. 754—71.

20 Equal Opportunities Commission, *Behind Closed Doors*, Manchester, Equal Opportunities Commission, 1981.

21 Social Security Act 1975, section 36(2), and SI 1975/1058, reg. 12 A(2), inserted by SI 1978/1340. See M. Richards, 'A Study of the Non-Contributory Invalidity Pension for Married Women', *Journal of Social Welfare Law*, 1978—9, p. 66, for full details.

22 Ogus and Barendt, *The Law of Social Security*, p. 166.

23 Hansard, 1 December 1983, col. 612.

24 Ogus and Barendt, *The Law of Social Security*, p. 166.

25 Equal Pay Act 1970, section 6 (1A); Sex Discrimination Act 1975, Sched. 1.

26 See S. Atkins, 'The EEC Directive on Equal Treatment in Social Security Benefits', *Journal of Social Welfare Law*, 1978—9, p. 244, for full details.

27 Atkins, 'Social Security Act 1980 and the EEC Directive on Equal Treatment in Social Security Benefits'; L. Luckhaus, 'Social Security: the Equal Treatment Reforms', *Journal of Social Welfare Law*, 1983, p. 325.

28 Luckhaus, 'Social Security: the Equal Treatment Reforms', p. 326.

29 For full details, see ibid.

30 Social Security Advisory Committee, *Report of the Social Security Advisory Committee to Consider New Rules Introducing Equal Treatment...*, p. 13.

31 Ibid.

32 Ibid., p. 4.

33 Equal Opportunities Commission, *The Fact about Women is...*, Manchester, Equal Opportunities Commission, 1983.

34 Ogus and Barendt, *The Law of Social Security*, p. 303.

35 Ibid., p. 144.

36 SI 1981/655.

37 Directive 79/7, Art. 3.

38 CREW, *Reports*, vol. 3, nos. 9 and 10, 1983.

39 H. Land, *Parity Begins at Home: Women's and Men's Work in the Home and its Effects on Their Paid Employment*, Manchester, Equal Opportunities Commission, 1981.

40 M. Anderson, *Approaches to the History of the Western Family 1500—1914*, London, Macmillan, 1980.

41 P. Moss and I. Plewis, 'Young Children in the Inner City', T. Coram Research Unit, unpublished report to the DHSS, 1979.

42 *Employment Gazette*, 1982, p. 48; Office of Population Censuses and Surveys, *General Household Survey*, London, HMSO, 1979.

43 In the 1979 *General Household Survey* 40 per cent of married women registered as unemployed described themselves as 'economically inactive', compared with 18 per cent of registered unemployed non-married women and 12 per cent of registered unemployed men.

44 CREW, *Reports*, vol. 3, no. 10, 1983.

45 A. Wickham, 'Engendering Social Policy in the EEC', *M/F*, no. 4, 1980, p. 15.

46 R. Nielsen, *Equality Legislation in a Comparative Perspective — Towards State Feminism?*, Copenhagen, Kvindevidenskabeligt Forlag, 1983, p. 304.

47 Trades Union Congress, *Working Women*, London, Trades Union Congress, 1983, p. 20.

48 Equal Opportunities Commission, *Behind Closed Doors*, p. 20.

49 H. Remick, 'Beyond Equal Pay for Equal Work: Comparable Worth in the State of Washington', in R. S. Ratner (ed.), *Equal Employment Policy for Women*, Philadelphia, Temple University Press, 1980, p. 405.

50 Lewis, 'In Search of a Real Equality'.

51 P. Carlen, *Women's Imprisonment: A Study in Social Control*, London, Routledge & Kegan Paul, 1983; Home Office, *Prisons and the Prisoner*, London, HMSO, 1977.

52 M. McIntosh, 'The Welfare State and the Needs of the Dependent Family', in S. Burman (ed.), *Fit Work for Women*, London, Croom Helm, 1979, p. 170.

53 A. Coulter, 'Who Minds about the Minders?', Low Pay Unit pamphlet No. 17, 1981; A. Leira, 'The Organization of Care-Giving Work in the Welfare State: an Illustration of Non-Market Work', Women and the Labour Market Research Newsletter No. 6, February 1983.

54 E. Vallance, *Women in the House*, London, Athlone Press, 1979, p. 22; P. Hollis, *Women in Public 1850—1900*, London, Allen & Unwin, 1979, pp. 268—78.

55 M. W. Snell, P. Glucklich and M. Povall, 'Equal Pay and Opportunities', Research Paper No. 20, Department of Employment, 1981.

56 SI 1983/No. 1202.

57 *The Taxation of Husband and Wife*, Cmnd 8093, London, HMSO, 1980; DHSS, *A Fresh Look at Maternity Benefits*, London, DHSS, 1980; Equal Opportunities Commission, *Response to the DHSS Consultative Document 'A Fresh Look at Maternity Benefits'*, Manchester, Equal Opportunities Commission, 1980.

58 *The Taxation of Husband and Wife*, p. 27.

59 Ibid., p. 29.

60 H. Land, *Parity Begins at Home: Women's and Men's Work in the Home and its Effects on Their Paid Employment*, Manchester, Equal Opportunities Commission, 1981.

10 Women as Citizens

1 R. Adam, *A Woman's Place*, London, Chatto & Windus, 1975; R. Strachey, *The Cause*, London, Virago, 1978; J. Hills, 'Britain', in J. Lovenduski and J. Hills (eds.), *The Politics of the Second Electorate*, London, Routledge & Kegan Paul, 1981.

2 A. Wickham, 'Engendering Social Policy in the EEC', *M/F*, no. 4, 1980, p. 15.

3 A. B. Wallis Chapman and M. Wallis Chapman, *The Status of Women under the English Law*, London, Routledge & Sons, 1909; A Sachs and J. Hoff Wilson, *Sexism and the Law*, Oxford, Martin Robertson, 1978.

4 Wallis Chapman and Wallis Chapman, *The Status of Women under the English Law*, pp. 32—8; *Chorlton* v. *Lings* (1869) 4 LRCP 374; Sachs and Hoff Wilson, *Sexism and the Law*, p. 24.

5 Municipal Franchise Act 1869, section 9.

6 Elementary Education Act 1870, section 29.

7 County Electors Act 1888, section 2.

8 Local Government Act 1894, section 43.
9 Representation of the People Act 1918, section 4(3).
10 Poor Law Act 1834, sections 38 and 109.
11 Wallis Chapman and Wallis Chapman, *The Status of Women under the English Law*, p. 61.
12 Local Government Act 1894, section 43.
13 Qualification of Women (County and Borough Councils) Act 1907, section 1.
14 Representation of the People Act 1918, section 4, and Parliament (Qualification of Women) Act 1918, section 1.
15 Hills, 'Britain'; E. Wormald, 'Political Participation', in I. Reid and E. Wormald (eds.), *Sex Differences in Britain*, London, Grant McIntyre, 1982; E. Vallance, *Women in the House*, London, Athlone Press, 1979; M. Stacey and M. Price, *Women, Power and Politics*, London, Tavistock, 1981.
16 Sachs and Hoff Wilson, *Sexism and the Law*.
17 J. S. Rasmussen, 'Women Candidates in British By-Elections', *Political Studies*, vol. 29, 1981, p. 265; V. Randall, *Women and Politics*, London, Macmillan, 1982.
18 Equal Opportunities Commission, *Women and Public Bodies*, Joint Working Party Report, Manchester, Equal Opportunities Commission, 1982.
19 Randall, *Women and Politics*, p. 89.
20 A. Ware, 'The Concept of Political Equality: a post-Dahl Analysis', *Political Studies*, vol. 29, 1981, p. 393.
21 7 and 8 Victoria c. 66, section 16.
22 Hansard, 1870, vol. 200, col. 1740.
23 *Harvey* v. *Farnie* [1882] 8 App. Cas. 43.
24 *Dolphin* v. *Robins* [1859] 7 HL Cas. 390.
25 Hansard, 1870, vol. 199, col. 1124.
26 Ibid.
27 British Nationalty Act 1981, sections 5 and 4(5); British Nationality (Falkland Islands) Act 1983.
28 Hansard, 1870, vol. 199, col. 1128; P. Hollis, *Women in Public*, London, Allen & Unwin, 1979, pp. 33—41.
29 Hollis, *Women in Public*; Adam, *A Woman's Place*.
30 J. Trollope, *Britannia's Daughters*, London, Hutchinson, 1983.
31 A. Whittick, *Woman into Citizen*, London, Athenaeum/Frederick Muller, 1979.
32 Parliamentary debates discussed in National Association for Asian Youth, 'Which Half Decides? A Contribution to the Debate on Sex Discrimination, British Nationality and Immigration Laws', Southall, 1979; S. Taylor, Immigration Rules, Citizenship and Nationality', *New Community*, 1980, pp. 140—3.
33 Immigration Rules 1980, para. 50.
34 National Association for Asian Youth, 'Which Half Decides?'.
35 *R.* v. *Entry Clearance Officer, Bombay, ex parte Amin* [1983] 2 AC 818.
36 *R.* v. *Immigration Appeal Tribunal, ex parte Kassam* [1980] 1 WLR 1037.
37 British Nationality Act 1981, Sched. 1; *R.* v. *Secretary of State for Home Department, ex parte Brahmbatt* (1983), *The Times*, 17 October.
38 British Nationality Act 1981, section 50(9).
39 Articles, 14, 8, 12 and 3; S. Cook, 'European Court to Rule on Foreign Husbands', *Guardian*, 14 October 1983; S. Cook, 'Foreign Husbands Clear Another Hurdle', *Guardian*, 17 October 1983.

40 British Nationality Act 1981, section 44.

41 Representation of the People Act 1918; Parliament (Qualification of Women) Act 1918; Sex Disqualification (Removal) Act 1919; D. Morgan, *Suffragists and Liberals*, Oxford, Blackwell, 1975; Strachey, *The Cause*.

42 Stacey and Price, *Women, Power and Politics*, p. 168, quoting J. Mitchell, *Women's Estate*, Harmondsworth, Penguin, 1971, p. 32; see also Vallance, *Women in the House*.

43 Hollis, *Women in Public*; M. Llewellyn Davies (ed.), *Life as We Have Known It*, London, Virago, 1977; Strachey, *The Cause*; C. Rowan, '"Mothers Vote Labour": the State, the Labour Movement and Working-Class Mothers, 1900—1918', in R. Brunt and C. Rowan (eds.), *Feminism, Culture and Politics*, London, Lawrence & Wishart, 1982.

44 Lydia Becker (1879), cited in Hollis, *Women in Public*, p. 268.

45 Education Act 1902, Sched. 1A.

46 Qualification of Women (County and Borough Councils) Act 1907, section 1.

47 Wormald, 'Political Participation'; Stacey and Price, *Women, Power and Politics*; Randall, *Women and Politics*.

48 Stacey and Price, *Women, Power and Politics*, p. 149.

49 S. L. Bristow, 'Women Councillors', *County Councils Gazette*, 1978, pp. 38, 229 and 272; Wormald, 'Political Participation'; J. Hills, 'Women Local Councillors: a Reply to Bristow', *Local Government Studies*, vol. 8, no. 1, 1982, p. 61.

50 Wormald, 'Political Participation'.

51 Ibid.

52 Ibid., p. 186.

53 D. M. Stetson, *A Woman's Issue: The Politics of Family Law Reform in England*, Westport, Conn., Greenwood Press, 1982.

54 See P. Tydeman, 'Working in Safety: 150 Years of the Factory Inspectorate', *Employment Gazette*, 1983, p. 400.

55 See *Beatrice Webb's Diaries*, eds. N. and J. MacKenzie, London, Virago in association with LSE, 1982; M. Bondfield, *A Life's Work*, London, Hutchinson, 1948; Llewellyn Davies, *Life as We Have Known It*; O. Banks, *Faces of Feminism*, Oxford, Martin Robertson, 1981.

56 *Beatrice Webb's Diaries*, ed. M. Cole, London, Longman, 1952.

57 P. Brookes, *Women at Westminster*, London, Davies, 1967, p. 267.

58 E. Vallance, 'Women in the House of Commons', *Political Studies*, vol. 29, 1981.

59 M. E. Currell, *Political Woman*, London, Croom Helm 1974; National Association for Asian Youth, 'Which Half Decides?'; W. B. Creighton, *Working Women and the Law*, London, Mansell, 1979.

60 Currell, *Political Woman*, p. 70; Vallance, *Women in the House*, pp. 99—107; Hills, 'Britain', p. 26; Wormald, 'Political Participation'.

61 Randall, *Women and Politics*, p. 98.

62 Hills, 'Britain', p. 26.

63 Ibid.; see also Rasmussen, 'Women Candidates in British By-Elections'.

64 Vallance, *Women in the House*, App. 2.

65 The number of women MPs increased to twenty-five after the by-elections of 3 May 1984.

66 Hills, 'Britain'; Wormald, 'Political Participation'; Equal Opportunities Commission, *Research Bulletin No. 1*, Manchester, Equal Opportunities Commission, 1978—9; Equal Opportunities Commission, *Investigation into the Number of Women Appointed to Public Bodies*, Manchester, Equal Opportunities Commission, 1982; Equal Opportunities Commission, *Women and Public Bodies*.

67 Vallance, *Women in the House,* p. 106.
68 R. Lister, 'Justice for the Claimant', referred to in N. Harris, 'The Reform of the Supplementary Benefit System', *Journal of Social Welfare Law,* 1983, p. 212.
69 Hills, 'Britain'; V. Ellis, *The Role of Trade Unions in the Promotion of Equal Opportunities,* Manchester, Equal Opportunities Commission, 1981.
70 M. Rendel, *Women, Power and Political Systems,* London, Croom Helm, 1981, p. 32. See also Randall, *Women and Politics.*
71 Randall, *Women and Politics; Gillick* v. *West Norfolk and Wisbech Area Health Authority* [1983] 3 WLR 859.
72 J. Evans, 'Women in Politics: a Reappraisal', *Political Studies,* vol. 28, no. 2, 1980, p. 210.
73 Rights of Women Europe, *Women's Rights and the EEC,* London, Rights of Women Europe, 1983.
74 Stetson, *A Woman's Issue.*
75 Law Commission, *Illegitimacy,* Working Paper No. 74, London, HMSO, 1979, pp. 13—18.
76 S. Atkins, 'Law and the Challenge to Patriarchy', in J. Thompson *et al., Women, Class and Adult Education,* Department of Adult Education, University of Southampton, 1980.
77 D. Bouchier, *Idealism and Revolution: New Ideologies of Liberation in Britain and the United States,* London, Edward Arnold, 1978; Banks, *Faces of Feminism.*
78 Randall, *Women and Politics;* Banks, *Faces of Feminism.*
79 Law Commission, *Illegitimacy,* Law Com. No. 118, London, HMSO, 1982, pp. 42—3.
80 House of Lords Debates, 21 November 1983, col. 29.
81 Ibid., col. 36.
82 S. Atkins, 'Equal Pay for Work of Equal Value', *European Law Review,* vol. 8, no. 1, 1983, p. 48.
83 Stetson, *A Woman's Issue;* Wormald, 'Political Participation'; Stacey and Price, *Women, Power and Politics.*
84 B. B. Cook, 'Will Women Judges Make a Difference in Women's Legal Rights? A Prediction from Attitudes and Simulated Behaviour', in Rendel, *Women, Power and Political Systems;* but see H. M. Kritzer and T. M. Uhlman, 'Sisterhood in the Courtroom: Sex of Judge and Defandant in Criminal Case Deposition', in K. O'Connor Blumhagen and W. D. Johnson (eds.), *Women's Studies,* Westport, Conn., Greenwood Press, 1978.
85 Equal Opportunities Commission, *Women in the Legal Services,* Manchester, Equal Opportunities Commission, 1978.
86 For example, Mrs Justice Heilbron in *Bergin* v. *Bergin* [1983] 1 WLR 279, and Ms Smith in *Turley* v. *Allders Department Stores Ltd* [1980] ICR 66.
87 For example, Lord Justice Shaw in *Skyrail Oceanic Ltd* v. *Coleman* [1981] ICR 864; Lord Justice Denning in *Peake* v. *Automotive Products Ltd* [1978] QB 233; Mrs Justice Lane in *D.* v. *B.* [1977] 2 WLR 155; Lords Justice Griffiths and Eveleigh in *Gill* v. *El Vino Co. Ltd* [1983] 2 WLR 155.
88 See *Gill* v. *El Vino Co. Ltd* [1983] 2 WLR 155 in lower court; *Hurley* v. *Mustoe No. 2* [1983] ICR 422.
89 Sachs and Hoff Wilson, *Sexism and the Law.*
90 *R.* v. *Entry Clearance Officer, Bombay, ex parte Amin* [1983] 2 AC 818; *R.* v. *Immigration Appeal Tribunal, ex parte Kassam* [1980] 1 WLR 1037.
91 [1979] ICR 736.
92 *Knight* v. *Attorney-General* [1979] ICR 194.
93 Randall, *Women and Politics;* Hills, 'Britain'.

94 [1981] 2 WLR 703.

95 Sex Discrimination Act 1975, section 59(2).

96 House of Commons Disqualification Act 1975, Sched. 11.

97 Sex Discrimination Act 1975, section 85.

98 P. Byrne and J. Lovenduski, 'Sex Equality and the Law', *British Journal of Law and Society*, vol. 5, no. 2, 1978, p. 148.

99 E. Meeham, 'The Priorities of the Equal Opportunities Commission', *Political Quarterly*, vol. 54, 1983, p. 69.

100 A. Coote, 'Equality and the Curse of the Quango', *New Statesman*, 1 December 1978, p. 734; F. Cairncross, 'Is the EOC Worth £3 Million of Public Money?', *Guardian*, 7 December 1983.

101 House of Commons Home Affairs Committee on the Commission for Racial Equality, First Report, London, HMSO, 1981—2.

102 R. Nielsen, *Equality Legislation in a Comparative Perspective: Towards State Feminism*, Copenhagen, Kvindevidenskabeligt Forlag, 1983.

103 *Price* v. *Civil Service Commission* [1977] 1 WLR 1417; *Khanna* v. *MOD* [1981] ICR 653; *Oxford* v. *DHSS* [1977] ICR 884; *MOD* v. *Jeremiah* [1980] QB 87; *Steel* v. *Post Office* [1978] 1 WLR 64; *Perera* v. *Civil Service Commission* [1982] ICR 350; *Coyne* v. *Export Credit Guarantee Department* [1981] IRLR 51.

104 HM Treasury, *Civil Service Statistics*, London, HMSO, 1983.

105 *Price* v. *Civil Service Commission No. 2* [1978] IRLR 3; S. Robarts, *Positive Action for Women*, London, NCCL, 1981; M. Webb, 'Equal Opportunities for Women in Employment', *Employment Gazette*, 1983, p. 335.

106 House of Commons Home Affairs Committee, *Fifth Report on Racial Disadvantage*, London, HMSO, 1980—1; *The Government's Response*, Cmnd 8476, London, HMSO, 1981—2.

107 Equal Opportunities Commission, *Research Bulletin*, vol. 1, no. 3, 1980; Rights of Women Europe, *Women's Rights and the EEC*; Nielsen, *Equality Legislation in a Comparative Perspective*.

108 Equal Opportunities Commission, *Women and Under-Achievement at Work*, Research Bulletin No. 5, Manchester, Equal Opportunities Commission, 1981; C. Scorer and A. Sedley, *Amending the Equality Laws*, London, NCCL, 1983; Rights of Women Europe, *Women's Rights and the EEC*.

109 [1981] 1 WLR 972.

110 *Garland* v. *British Rail Engineering Ltd* [1982] 2 WLR 918; *Burton* v. *British Railways Board* [1982] QB 1080; *Southampton and South-West Hants Health Authority (Teaching)* v. *Marshall* [1983] IRLR 236.

111 Hansard, 25 November 1983, col. 346.

112 Hansard, 24 November 1983, col. 360.

113 Rights of Women Europe, *Women's Rights and the EEC*.

114 *Morson and Jhanjan* v. *Netherlands* [1983] 2 CMLR 221.

115 (1983), *The Times*, 29 March.

116 C. Greenwood, 'Free Movement of Workers under EEC Law and English Law II', *New Law Journal*, 1983.

117 J. Langdon, 'Equal Pay Orders Withdrawn by Tories', *Guardian*, 27 October 1983; J. Tweedie, 'We End Up with the Worst of Both Worlds: Some Carrots, No Sticks', *Guardian*, 15 November 1983; 'The Vanishing Equal Value Regulations', IDS Brief No. 265, 1983, p. 1.

118 *Skyrail Oceanic Ltd* v. *Coleman,* Lord Justice Lawton in Court of Appeal 1981 ICR 372.

119 Law Commission, *The Financial Consequences of Divorce: The Basic Policy,* Law Com. No. 103, Cmnd 8041, London, HMSO, 1980; Law Commission, *The Financial Consequences of Divorce,* Law Com. No. 112, London, HMSO, 1981.

120 Stetson, *A Woman's Issue.*

121 See *Procter* v. *Provident Personal Credit Ltd* (1983) IDS Brief No. 255; TUC, *Sexual Harassment at Work: Guidelines for Unions,* London, TUC, 1983.

122 Elizabeth Bumiller, 'Twenty Years a Rebel', *Guardian,* 31 October 1983.

Index